Journey
through the
BIBLE

All citations of Bible verses are from the Holy Bible,
New International Version, © 1973,1978,1984, 2011, International Bible Society

Cover design and layout by Megan Colussy
Editing by Margo Kessler, Brittany Leuenberger, Sandy Hafner, Lori Moore and
Heather Tyo

THE JOURNEY is a registered trademark of
The Journey Ministry, Inc., McMurray, PA 15317

Journey Through the Bible
Copyright © 2013 by Ronald D. Moore
McMurray, PA 15317
ronmoore.org

ISBN 978-1-4675-7648-2

Printed in the United States of America.

Introduction

In this book are daily devotionals that will take you on a journey through the Bible. These devotionals have been written in different places . . . from my office at home to hotel rooms across the country. With my iPad I have written many of these devotionals while traveling on planes and on an overnight train in Asia. I have written them in many frames of mind. Some have been penned before and after the funerals of good friends. I wrote several before and after my son's wedding. All that is to say, some of these emotions and even locations will come across the pages as you make your way through the daily readings.

My prayer is that you will use these to meet with God. I pray God uses these straightforward thoughts based on his Word to bring you into a relationship with him or to bring you a step farther in your relationship with him. My desire is that these writings are used by God as a tool to develop you as a follower of Jesus Christ.

As well, I'd love to hear from you as you journey through a year with this guide. E-mail me at rmoore@biblechapel.org. Give me your thoughts on a particular passage. Share a story that illustrates a point. Let me know how God is working in your life.

I hope that you are as encouraged in reading these as I have been in writing them. May God bless you on your journey.

Ron Moore
October 2012

Our Creator and Protector

January 1

Genesis 1:1-3

In the beginning God created the heavens and the earth. Now the earth was formless and empty, darkness was over the surface of the deep, and the Spirit of God was hovering over the waters. And God said, "Let there be light," and there was light.

In the first three verses of the Bible we are introduced to the Triune God - One God in Three Persons - God the Father, Son and Holy Spirit. Each Person is distinct, yet one in being and equal in power.

God the Father is introduced with the Hebrew word "Elohim." It is a plural form of the name of God and is used to emphasize his majesty and sovereign power. We first find the Spirit "hovering over the waters." The word "hover" is used in Scripture to describe an eagle stirring up the nest and hovering over its young. The Spirit's action from the beginning has been one of protection and nurture. In verse three we are introduced to God the Son with the words "and [God] said." The Word of God is the agent or means of creation. In the New Testament we know that the Word is Jesus himself (John 1:1-4).

God the Father: The All-Powerful Creator. God the Son: The Agent of Creation, Re-Creation and Resurrection. God the Spirit: The Protector and Nurturer. How can we respond to such a powerful, gracious and loving God? Only one way - bow down and worship him. Why don't you do that right now? Start the new year on your knees before the Triune God.

Lord, you are God and there is none other. We bow to worship you and you alone. We begin a new year committed to serve you in all areas of our lives. You are our God and we love you. In Jesus' name. Amen.

reflection

RG

further suggested reading:

Genesis 1

One Flesh

January 2

Genesis 2:23-24

The man said, "This is now bone of my bones and flesh of my flesh; she shall be called 'woman,' for she was taken out of man." That is why a man leaves his father and mother and is united to his wife, and they become one flesh.

God saw His creation and proclaimed, "It is good!" Except for one thing - seeing the man standing by himself, God said, "It is not good for the man to be alone." Why? Because the essence of community is found in the Person of the Triune God, and Adam's need for community could not be met in and of himself. Allen Ross says it this way, "The man was thus created in such a way that he needs the help of a partner. Or we may say that human beings cannot fulfill their destiny except in mutual assistance" (*Creation and Blessing*, Baker, 1996, p. 126).

Adam was formed out of the dust, but his partner was formed from the already created man. Today's passage begins with Adam's first words after he woke up to see his partner. When you read the passage, don't miss Adam's sheer excitement. He is beside himself!

Added to Adam's statement of excitement is the foundational instruction for the relationship of a man and woman in marriage. The man and woman are to leave the primary influence of their parents. They are to be united to each other in a life-long commitment. And they are to become one flesh. The one flesh relationship involves physical oneness (exclusive intimacy), emotional oneness (exclusive feelings), spiritual oneness (a common love for God and desire to follow him) and oneness of mission (going the same direction at the same time for the same reasons).

Father, thank you for creating us in your image and passing to us the need for community. Thank you for providing that community in the intimate partnership of marriage. May our marriages be an example of what it looks like when a husband and wife are in love with you and each other. In Jesus' name. Amen.

R.G.

reflection

further suggested reading:

Genesis 2

7

Satan, Sin, Disease, and Death

January 3

Genesis 3:6

When the woman saw that the fruit of the tree was good for food and pleasing to the eye, and also desirable for gaining wisdom, she took some and ate it. She also gave some to her husband, who was with her, and he ate it.

Adam and Eve had everything they could have ever dreamed of - an open relationship with God, living in a literal paradise and no in-laws (just a little humor). Life could not get any better! But then Satan came to convince them there was something they wanted but couldn't have.

Satan is the master of twisting God's Word and intentions. He convinced Eve that the prohibited fruit from the tree in the middle of the garden would not bring death, as God had said, but rather God-likeness. Eve took the fruit, ate it and gave it to Adam. At that moment, sin entered into the world and along with it disease, abuse, murder, war . . . and death.

Just as poison at the beginning of a stream contaminates the entire stream, so sin at the beginning of the human race contaminates us all. "All have sinned," and that sin separates us from God. Actually God did for us what we could not do for ourselves. He sent his Son to pay sin's penalty by his death on the cross. By God's grace, what was destroyed in Genesis 3 was repaired forever at the cross.

Father, thank you for sending Jesus to die on the cross for our sins. He who knew no sin became sin for us so that we might stand before you, righteous and whole. Our desire is to show our deep love and gratitude by letting our light so shine before men that they will see our actions and give praise to you. In Jesus' name. Amen.

RB

reflection

further suggested reading:

Genesis 3-5

Faith in Action

Genesis 6:9

> This is the account of Noah and his family. Noah was a righteous man, blameless among the people of his time, and he walked faithfully with God.

The power of sin, introduced in Genesis 3, continued its march through the human race. By Genesis 6, God saw that "every inclination of the thoughts of [man's] heart was only evil all the time" and he was "grieved that he had made man." God decided to start over with one man and his family. The man's name was Noah.

Noah lived right in the middle of "wickedness on earth," but Noah stood out. He did what was right in the eyes of the Lord. Noah was far from perfect, but his life is described as "blameless" in contrast to the people of his time. Importantly, Noah "walked faithfully with God." He desired to hear God's voice, follow God's leading and obey God's instruction, even the incredible instruction of building an ark before it had ever rained! Noah is honored throughout Scripture for his faith in action (see Hebrews 11:7).

We live in the middle of "wickedness on earth" as well. People all around us are following the evil inclinations of their hearts and ignoring God. But here's the question: Is there a contrast between us and the people of our time? A follow-up question to ponder: Had you lived in Genesis 6, would God have chosen you to build the ark? And one more question: If you are walking faithfully with God, is he asking you to do anything extraordinarily "ark-like"?

Father, we pray that we can be described as a person who walks faithfully with you. If you are calling us to do something "ark-like," please give us the courage to do it. In Jesus' name. Amen.

RG

reflection

further suggested reading:

Genesis 6-9

God Never Backs Down

January 5

Genesis 11:4

Then they said, "Come, let us build ourselves a city, with a tower that reaches to the heavens, so that we may make a name for ourselves; otherwise we will be scattered over the face of the whole earth."

God's plan was for the people to "be fruitful and increase in number and fill the earth" (Genesis 9:1). But the people had a better idea. Their egotistical plan included a tower that reached to the heavens. They thought the demonstration of their tower-power would cause God to back down and allow them to stay in one spot.

Just for the record . . . God never backs down. He dealt with the issue by supernaturally confusing their language. Picture the scene. One minute the parents were bragging about their super-gifted children, and the next minute it all sounded like babbling. Then God gave the rebellious innovators exactly what they didn't want. He "scattered them over the face of the whole earth."

By the way . . . are you building any titanic towers in your life? Are you using bricks of rebellion to show God just how "powerful" you really are? Are you trying to show him that your plan is better? Are you trying to tell him that regardless of what he wants, you'll do what you darn well please? Just for the record . . . God never backs down. If you're a tower builder, get ready for some confusing times.

Father, pride is so deceptive and debilitating. It lives right on the border of a healthy sense of self-worth and sinful self-absorption. Give us discernment. Help us build our lives according to your instructions. Help us build lives that honor you. In Jesus' name. Amen.

RG

reflection

further suggested reading:

Genesis 10-11

10

Begin the Journey

 January 6

Genesis 12:1

The LORD had said to Abram, "Leave your country, your people and your father's household and go to the land I will show you."

What would you do if you got this message from God "Okay, here's the deal. Tomorrow morning, I want you to pack up everything you own and leave everything you have ever known." You ask, "But God, where do you want me to go?" He answers, "Don't worry about that now. I will reveal your destination along the way. Just begin the journey."

That was God's message to Abram (later Abraham). And Abram obeyed. "By faith Abraham, when called to go to a place he would later receive as his inheritance, obeyed and went, even though he did not know where he was going" (Hebrews 11:8).

How about you? Are you willing to step out on faith even when you're not sure where the journey may take you? Are you willing to obey even when it doesn't add up on your spreadsheet? Are you willing to follow God even when the destination is not showing up on your Google map? Sometimes God calls us to a place that we can't quite see from our present vantage point. That's why it's called "faith" - without which it is impossible to please God (Hebrews 11:6).

Father, our prayer is simply this - whatever you call us to do, give us the courageous faith to do it. In Jesus' name. Amen.

RG

reflection

further suggested reading:

Genesis 12-14

God's Promises Always Come True

Genesis 17:1-2

When Abram was ninety-nine years old, the LORD appeared to him and said, "I am God Almighty; walk before me and be blameless. Then I will make my covenant between me and you and will greatly increase your numbers."

Abram was seventy-five years old when God told him to leave his family and "go to the land that I will show you." That instruction came with the promise that one day Abram would be the father of a great nation. Twenty-four years later, Abram was wondering if he had misunderstood God. His wife, Sarai, was barren, and he had only one son by her handmaiden. Most men, even in Abram's day, were not starting their families one year shy of the century mark. But then most men in Abram's day did not walk with God Almighty (El Shaddai).

God Almighty works over and above our circumstance. His power is not limited by nature or norms. What he promises will always come true. God loves to work in what seems to be impossible situations. When something "can't" happen, God's power is proven when it does.

I don't know what your situation is today. Maybe like Abram, you are beginning to feel that God has forgotten you and his promise. You have slidden into that "can't happen" mindset. Let me remind you that his name is still God Almighty. I can't promise that he'll give you everything you want, but I can assure you that he'll give you everything he promised.

God Almighty, thank you for not giving us everything we want. Thank you for giving us everything you have promised. In Jesus' name. Amen.

RG

reflection

further suggested reading:

Genesis 15-17

12

The Cost of Compromise

January 8

Genesis 19:4-8

Before they had gone to bed, all the men from every part of the city of Sodom-both young and old-surrounded the house. They called to Lot, "Where are the men who came to you tonight? Bring them out to us so that we can have sex with them." Lot went outside to meet them and shut the door behind him and said, "No, my friends. Don't do this wicked thing. Look, I have two daughters who have never slept with a man. Let me bring them out to you, and you can do what you like with them. But don't do anything to these men, for they have come under the protection of my roof."

The events of this passage are disconcerting, aren't they? Persistent on their perversion, the men of Sodom (young and old - perversion is not age dependent) demand that Lot share his friends. In an unimaginable response, Lot offers his daughters instead! Many commentators suggest Lot's proposal was due to the high regard for hospitality in his day. Note Lot's comment regarding his guests, " . . . for they have come under the protection of my roof." But even with this explanation, the offer is still despicable! The problem was not Lot in the midst of Sodom's culture, but rather Sodom's culture in the midst of Lot.

Years earlier, Lot had traveled with Abraham, his uncle. When their flocks grew large they decided to split up. Abraham graciously gave Lot the first choice of the land on which to settle. Lot chose the well watered fertile ground where his livestock would thrive. He "pitched his tents near Sodom." There was, however, one major problem. The men of Sodom "were wicked and were sinning greatly against the Lord" (Genesis 13:12-13). Lot was willing to place himself and his family in an ungodly and unhealthy environment in order to prosper.

How about you? Where are your tents pitched? What are you willing to concede for your "flocks to thrive"? Many are willing to compromise their reputation, marriage and family for the sake of power and possessions. Sad, isn't it, how the culture can get into a person and harden his heart? Sad, isn't it, how the hardened heart can rationalize ungodly stuff? Sad, isn't it, the price of compromise?

Father, a life of compromise blinds us from the imminent dangers. Please open our eyes and let us see exactly where we have pitched our tent. Give us the courage to pull up stakes, if need be, and move to a place that is close to you. In Jesus' name. Amen.

further suggested reading:

Genesis 18-20

Where Is Your Allegiance?

Genesis 22:13-14

Abraham looked up and there in a thicket he saw a ram caught by its horns. He went over and took the ram and sacrificed it as a burnt offering instead of his son. So Abraham called that place The LORD Will Provide. And to this day it is said, "On the mountain of the LORD it will be provided."

God's instruction was unimaginable. The son born to Abraham and Sarai in their old age, the only hope of God's promise to make Abraham a great nation, the dearly loved son was to be put to death as a sacrifice. The request was out of character and seemed out of bounds. But Abraham obeyed without hesitation.

God's desire, however, was not for Isaac to die. He wanted Abraham to die . . . to self. God wanted to make sure that Abraham's total allegiance was to him. Seeing Abraham's willingness to obey the unthinkable test, God showed Abraham what had been there all along . . . a ram caught in the thicket. Abraham sacrificed God's provision instead of his son. He called the place Jehovah-Jireh meaning "The Lord Will Provide."

Is there anything that has stolen your heart away from God? A relationship? Job? Hobby? Dream? Child? Spouse? Money? Even good things can become an idol. But no one or no thing can stand between you and God. God will not put you through the same test he required of Abraham. He wants your total allegiance just the same. Put him first and he will provide everything you need. Remember, His name is Jehovah-Jireh.

Father, thank you for being our Jehovah-Jireh. We depend on you to provide all we need. Show us what has stolen our heart away from you, and give us the courage to take the action to place you on the throne of our hearts. In Jesus' name. Amen

reflection

RG - Jehovah-Jireh = The Lord will provide

further suggested reading:

Genesis 21-24

14

Eternal Inheritance

Genesis 25:24-26

When the time came for [Rebekah] to give birth, there were twin boys in her womb. The first to come out was red, and his whole body was like a hairy garment; so they named him Esau. After this, his brother came out, with his hand grasping Esau's heel; so he was named Jacob.

The twins could not have been more dissimilar. Esau was hairy; Jacob had smooth skin. Esau was impulsive; Jacob was reflective. Esau was boisterous; Jacob was quiet. Esau was an outdoorsman; Jacob was a homebody. Esau was a skilled hunter; Jacob could cook a mean pot of stew. The father, Isaac, loved Esau; the mother, Rebekah, loved Jacob. The rivalry started at birth with Jacob grabbing Esau's heel as they came out of the womb. But years later, Jacob really tripped up Esau.

As the oldest son, Esau was the heir apparent of the covenant promises that God gave to Abraham and passed down to Isaac. But one day, after coming in famished from hunting, Esau sold his birthright to Jacob for . . . ready for this . . . a piece of bread and a bowl of lentil stew! Esau treated the rights and privileges that God had given him with disdain. The writer to the Hebrews calls Esau "godless" for his actions (Hebrews 12:16).

Through the work of Jesus, believers have an eternal inheritance that will "never perish, spoil or fade - kept in heaven for you" (1 Peter 1:4). Our rebirth comes with powerful privileges. While the true believer cannot sell or forfeit these rights, we can ignore them and take them for granted. While being a child of God, we can live "godless" lives. Let's learn from Esau. Let's not despise our spiritual blessings.

Father, thank you for the great blessings we have through Jesus. Help us not to take them for granted. In Jesus' name. Amen.

RG

reflection

further suggested reading:

Genesis 25-26

El Shaddai

Genesis 28:3

May God Almighty bless you and make you fruitful and increase your numbers until you become a community of peoples.

In Isaac's prayer of blessing for Jacob, he addressed the heavenly Father as "God Almighty" (in the Hebrew "El Shaddai"). According to the *Bible Knowledge Commentary,* scholars suggest that "shaddai" means breast or mountain or both. Some words used for parts of the body were also used to describe geological formations. Understanding this word with its double meaning provides a powerful description of God.

First, as a mother nourishes her child, so God richly supplies all that we need. His "food" enables us to grow and stand strong. With him we are always spiritually satisfied. Second, God's strength is like a majestic mountain. He is powerful, immovable and unshakable.

If you are spiritually hungry . . . if your world feels like it is coming apart . . . if you are running on empty . . . if your foundations are quaking underneath your feet . . . then call on El Shaddai. He will meet your deepest need . . . not only for today but for all eternity.

Dear El Shaddai, some reading this today desperately need to be encouraged. They are spiritually depleted and need to be nourished. Their lives have been shaken, and they need to move to higher ground. Oh, El Shaddai, give them your strength and show them your power. In Jesus' name. Amen.

reflection

RG El Shaddai = God Almighty

further suggested reading:

Genesis 27-31

Plant Trees

January 12

Genesis 35:6-7

Jacob and all the people with him came to Luz (that is, Bethel) in the land of Canaan. There he built an altar, and he called the place El Bethel, because it was there that God revealed himself to him when he was fleeing from his brother.

It would be many years before Joshua led the children of Israel across the Jordan River into the Promised Land. But in our passage today, God placed a stake in Canaan. Even though Jacob would later move his family to Egypt to survive a famine, and Israel would stay there for 400 years before God sent Moses to deliver them, an altar called "Bethel" (House of God) was standing in the Promised Land. The promise given to Abraham continued.

Sometimes God's promises are not fully realized in our lifetime. Sometimes we are simply the ones who plant the seeds so that those who come after us can enjoy the harvest. Someone has said that the true meaning of life is to plant tree under whose shade you do not expect to sit.

In our "What are the benefits for me right now?" world, few are willing to make an investment that will not benefit them. But those on the journey of faith have a different mindset. We are willing to invest in eternal things. We must be willing to plant trees so that those who come after us can enjoy the shade . . . and plant trees of their own.

Father, shake us loose from "what's in it for me" thinking. Encourage us to make the sacrifices today that will impact people tomorrow. In Jesus' name. Amen.

reflection

_____

_____

_____

_____

_____

_____

_____

_____

_____

further suggested reading:

Genesis 32-36

The Sin Game

January 13

Genesis 37:1-2

Jacob lived in the land where his father had stayed, the land of Canaan. This is the account of Jacob's family line. Joseph, a young man of seventeen, was tending the flocks with his brothers, the sons of Bilhah and the sons of Zilpah, his father's wives, and he brought their father a bad report about them.

Sir Walter Scott wrote, "Oh what a tangled web we weave, when first we practice to deceive." I don't know if he was thinking of Joseph's brothers, but he could have been. Jealous of their father's favorite son, the brothers threw Joseph in a cistern and then sold him into slavery. In order to cover up the deed, they dipped Joseph's multi-colored robe in goat's blood and told Jacob that his son had been torn to pieces by a ferocious animal. A pretty busy day for the brothers!

"Sin" is bad enough in the singular, but it normally shows up in the plural. One sin is added to another to cover for the one before it. When we play the sin game, we dig deeper and deeper into a dark hole.

But even if you are living in the lonely sin-hole of your own digging, you don't have to stay there. "The Lord is gracious and compassionate, slow to anger and rich in love" (Psalm 145:8). Don't run from him; run to him! God promises that if we confess our sins, he "is faithful and just and will forgive us our sins and purify us from all unrighteousness" (1 John 1:9). It's time to come out of the darkness into the wonderful light of God's grace.

Father, give the person living in the dark, lonely pit of the hole they have dug the courage to cry out to you. In Jesus' name. Amen.

reflection

_____

_____

_____

_____

_____

_____

_____

_____

_____

further suggested reading:

Genesis 37-40

God Never Wastes Our Time

Genesis 41:41-43

So Pharaoh said to Joseph, "I hereby put you in charge of the whole land of Egypt." Then Pharaoh took his signet ring from his finger and put it on Joseph's finger. He dressed him in robes of fine linen and put a gold chain around his neck. He had him ride in a chariot as his second-in-command, and people shouted before him, "Make way!" Thus he put him in charge of the whole land of Egypt.

From our vantage point, life does not always move along smoothly according to our plans. Illness hits. A job goes away. A relationship is strained or lost. A loved one dies. A spouse leaves. And sometimes we wonder, "God, what in the world are you doing?"

That thought must have crossed Joseph's mind a time or two. One day he was enjoying the status of a favorite son. The next day his brothers sold him into slavery. One day he was Potiphar's favorite assistant, entrusted with the care of everything the official owned. The next day he was in prison, falsely accused of improper advances on Potiphar's wife. But God never wastes our time. Even with that question, "God, what in the world are you doing?" ringing in Joseph's mind, God was at work. In his time, God brought Joseph out of prison and put him in charge of the whole land of Egypt.

God's ways are not our ways, and his schedule is seldom synced with the calendar on our smart phone. But you can be sure of this: God never wastes our time. He is using today to prepare you for tomorrow. He has some great things for you to do. And he will show you what they are . . . in his time.

Father, even when we know the theological truth of your sovereignty, it is still hard to put our full trust in you. When we wonder, "God, what in the world are you doing?" calm us and remind us that you never waste our time. In Jesus' name. Amen.

reflection

_____

_____

_____

_____

_____

further suggested reading:

Genesis 41-42

God Is Real and Raw

January 15

Genesis 43:30

Deeply moved at the sight of his brother, Joseph hurried out and looked for a place to weep. He went into his private room and wept there.

The birth of Joseph's brother was bittersweet. The new life cost his mother hers. As Rachel was dying, she named her second son Ben-Oni ("son of my trouble"). But her husband, Jacob, renamed him Benjamin ("son of my right hand"). Joseph and Benjamin shared their mother and her memories.

But life separated the brothers. Joseph had been sold into slavery, sent to prison and then, through God's intervention, placed in charge of Egypt, second in power only to Pharaoh. When his brothers came to buy food in the midst of a famine, Joseph went to great lengths to make sure Benjamin was being treated well. In the process, he was overcome with emotion.

Woven into the story of God's sovereign work that saved and secured the nation of Israel, we see the overwhelming emotion of two brothers being reunited. God's Word is simply amazing. Throughout Scripture, God shows us that he is powerful and personal. The Bible is his story in the realness and rawness of human life. And . . . don't forget, he is still at work in the realness and rawness of your life today.

Father, thank you for your Word. And thank you for the reminder that you are just as much at work in my life when I am weeping as you are when I am worshipping. In Jesus' name. Amen.

reflection

further suggested reading:

Genesis 43-44

Greatness Is Knowing God

January 16

Genesis 45:5

And now, do not be distressed and do not be angry with yourselves for selling me here, because it was to save lives that God sent me ahead of you.

In his book, *Knowing God,* J. I. Packer says that people who know God personally have great thoughts of him, great energy and boldness for him and great contentment in him. That certainly describes Joseph.

Joseph's brothers stood before him speechless and terrified as they learned the one they had sold into slavery was now the second most powerful man in the most powerful nation of the world. No doubt, the thought "We are toast!" didn't just cross their minds but lodged itself in the part of the brain that says, "Be really scared now!" But through Joseph's journey, he had become intimately acquainted with God. He assured the brothers that it was God who sent him ahead "to preserve for you a remnant on the earth and to save your lives by a great deliverance."

How about you? What are you learning about God and yourself on the journey? Are you thinking great thoughts of God? Is your energy to follow hard after him increasing? Are you becoming bolder in telling others about him? Are you finding contentment in him alone? Packer's words describe Joseph. Do they describe you?

Father, the journey you've placed us on will take some serious twists and turns. Help us to see you at work in every circumstance. Remind us that you never waste our time. In Jesus' name. Amen.

reflection

further suggested reading:

Genesis 45-47

God Is at Work

January 17

Genesis 50:20

You intended to harm me, but God intended it for good to accomplish what is now being done, the saving of many lives.

Sometimes it's harder to accept forgiveness than it is to forgive. After their father died, Joseph's brothers were sure he would seek revenge for the harm they had done him. But Joseph reminded them (again!) that God used their intentions for his purposes. God never wastes our time.

Did you hear that? God never wastes our time.

- It may seem like it now as you live between jobs . . .
- It may seem like it now as you wait for God to bring the right mate into your life . . .
- It may seem like it now as you recover from another round of chemo . . .
- It may seem like it now as you live in the consequences of your sin . . .
- It may seem like it now as you go through the day with your broken heart . . .
- It may seem like it now as you recover from the death of a dream . . .
- It may seem like it now as your life has seemingly been placed on hold . . .

But . . . the Sovereign, Almighty, All-Powerful God never wastes our time.

So . . . (and I don't say this flippantly) . . . hang in there! God is using every minute to mold you into the person he needs you to be for the next leg of the journey. God is at work. He loves you with an unconditional love. He has given you an inheritance that can never perish, spoil or fade. He has purchased you with the precious blood of his Son. He has eternally invested in you! Ask him what he wants you to learn and how he wants you to respond to your present assignment. He is not wasting your time.

Father, for those who feel like they are stuck and their life is on hold, for those reeling from a difficult relationship or circumstance, please encourage them today with some tangible evidence that you are not wasting their time. In Jesus' name. Amen.

reflection

further suggested reading:

Genesis 48-50

God Is Always in Charge

January 18

Exodus 2:10

When the child grew older, she took him to Pharaoh's daughter and he became her son. She named him Moses, saying, "I drew him out of the water."

After Joseph and all his brothers died, God continued to bless the Israelites. They "became exceedingly numerous, so that the land was filled with them" (Exodus 1:7). This growth was seen as a threat by the new king. He enslaved the Israelites and ordered the midwives to kill all the newborn Israelite boys. When the midwives refused to carry out such a plan, the king ordered all the baby boys to be thrown into the Nile River.

But God protected a boy named Moses. After hiding him for three months, his mother placed him in a basket coated with tar and pitch and put him in the Nile. God sovereignly directed Pharaoh's daughter to find the child and raise him as her own. It was Moses whom God would use to deliver his people from slavery.

God's sovereignty is easy to see at the end of the story but not so evident when we are living in the middle of our situation. But don't get discouraged. God was just as sovereignly at work the day Moses' mom tearfully and fearfully placed him in the Nile as he was when Pharaoh's daughter drew him out of the water. Even when you don't know how the story ends, God is still in charge!

Father, thank you for writing and directing the story of our lives. Help us to trust you even when we don't know how the story ends. In Jesus' name. Amen.

reflection

_____
_____
_____
_____
_____
_____
_____
_____
_____
_____
_____

further suggested reading:

Exodus 1-2

23

Don't Resist God

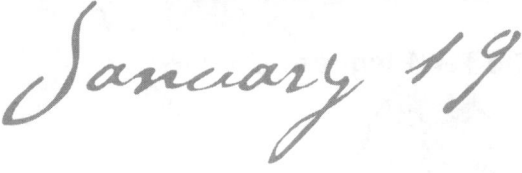

Exodus 4:13

But Moses said, "Pardon your servant, Lord. Please send someone else."

Let's do a little word association. Ready? What comes to your mind when you hear the name Moses? How about the following: **Courage** - confronting Pharaoh was not for the weak of heart. **Leader** - leading Israel out of slavery and across the Red Sea. **Ten Commandments** - just God and Moses on the mountain. With all that, somehow Exodus 4:13 doesn't fit into my picture of the great leader.

"O Lord, please send someone else to do it." That was Moses' first response to God's call. God said, "I want you to lead the Israelites out of slavery." Moses said, "Thanks, but no thanks. I'll pass. I'm happy where I am. I'd rather not be stretched. I like my schedule. I am content with the comfort of my life. What you're asking me to do is a bit risky. If it's all the same to you, Lord, let Charlton Heston play someone else in the movie." This response did not make God happy (unless I am missing the meaning of the phrase "the Lord's anger burned against Moses!").

Is there anything God is calling you to do that you are resisting? Anything that you are ignoring or putting off? A life calling? A career change? A new focus? Dealing with a sinful pattern? Dealing with an emotional scar? Getting help with your brokenness? Getting involved in a ministry? Are you reluctant to follow the call? Why? Look at what God did with Moses' reluctant heart. Think of what he could do with yours.

Father, forgive us for resisting your call and ignoring your instruction. Change our reluctant hearts to responsive ones. In Jesus' name. Amen.

reflection

_____
_____
_____
_____
_____
_____
_____
_____

further suggested reading:

Exodus 3-6

The Ten Plagues

January 20

Exodus 7:2-3

You are to say everything I command you, and your brother Aaron is to tell Pharaoh to let the Israelites go out of his country. But I will harden Pharaoh's heart, and though I multiply my signs and wonders in Egypt . . .

The ten plagues. Whom were they for? Well, certainly they were to convince Pharaoh to release Israel from slavery. But Pharaoh's was not the only hardened heart. I believe the ten plagues were primarily for the Israelites.

Israel had been in slavery for 400 years. Bondage was all they knew. They cried out to God for deliverance. But after such long time, many of the deliverance prayers were more liturgical lip service than heart-felt petitions. God used the plagues to show his people that he was present and powerful.

There is much discussion about God hardening Pharaoh's heart. But think about it. This was a tremendous act of God's grace. God simply kept the pagan king doing what his heart was already bent on doing - opposing the work of God. The multiple plagues showed the Israelites that God was to be feared and followed. The plagues gave them courage to leave all they had known and begin their journey into the unknown. Without the plagues, Moses may well have crossed the Red Sea alone.

Father, thank you for all your activity that goes along with your calling. Thank you for demonstrating your presence and power in our lives. Thank you for the courage to leave the familiar in order to follow you in faith. In Jesus' name. Amen.

reflection

further suggested reading:

Exodus 7-10

A Woven Masterpiece

Exodus 11:9

The LORD had said to Moses, "Pharaoh will refuse to listen to you - so that my wonders may be multiplied in Egypt."

Have you had time to read the morning paper or check out the news on your smartphone? Maybe you watched a morning news show while on the treadmill or elliptical machine or as you gulped down breakfast. Do you realize that when your favorite newsperson is describing the day's events, he or she is telling God's story?

Just as God was at work in the history of the world in Exodus 11, so he is at work in the history of the world today. The Proverb says, "The king's heart is like channels of water in the hand of the Lord; he turns it wherever he wishes" (Proverbs 21:1). From the Far East to the Middle East to Washington, D. C., God is directing the events of history.

And just as God is at work in the history of the world, so he is at work in the history of your world. That may be hard for you to believe right now. Your life may seem to be on hold or in chaos. But you can be sure that God is using every experience to weave a magnificent masterpiece with your name stitched at the top. Trust him. The colors of the thread he uses today will compliment and accent the colors he uses tomorrow.

Father, I thank you that you have not set the world spinning like a top and left to spin on its own. I thank you for the directing the affairs of man. And I thank you for directing the affairs of my day. In Jesus' name. Amen.

reflection

_____

_____

_____

_____

_____

_____

_____

_____

_____

further suggested reading:

Exodus 11

Nothing but the Blood

January 22

Exodus 12:13

The blood will be a sign for you on the houses where you are, and when I see the blood, I will pass over you. No destructive plague will touch you when I strike Egypt.

The final plague - the death of the firstborn - was the most costly. God's power over life and death would not only demonstrate his supremacy over the Egyptians' gods, it would bring the people who followed those gods to their knees.

But along with the plague, God offered a remedy. The death of a sacrificial lamb would appease. The blood of a sacrificial lamb applied to the top and sides of the door frame would be a sign for the Lord to keep the destroyer away. The blood of the lamb saved from death. It still does. Peter explained, "For you know that it was not with perishable things such as silver or gold that you were redeemed . . . but with the precious blood of Christ, a lamb without blemish or defect" (1 Peter 1:18-19).

The penalty of sin is death, a penalty that Jesus took on himself. "For Christ, our Passover lamb, has been sacrificed" (1 Corinthians 5:7b). Because of Jesus, eternal death passes over us, and we pass over from physical death to eternal life. It is not by our baptism, confirmation, first communion or good works that we are saved. In the words of the hymn, "What can wash away our sins? Nothing but the blood of Jesus!"

Father, thank you for the sacrifice of your Son, Jesus Christ. Words cannot express our gratitude.

reflection

further suggested reading:

Exodus 12

Waves of Fear and Doubt

January 23

Exodus 14:14

The LORD will fight for you; you need only to be still.

The twins of fear and doubt roll in like thirty-foot waves and crash onto the shore of our soul. They produce anxiety that leads to more fear and "what if" questions that leads to doubt.

Fresh from being delivered from slavery, the Israelites were caught between the powerful Egyptians and the Red Sea. No wonder they were terrified and cried out, "It would have been better for us to serve the Egyptians than to die in the desert." But Moses calmed them, "Do not be afraid. Stand firm and you will see the deliverance the Lord will bring you today . . . The Lord will fight for you; you need only to be still." You know the rest of the story.

So here they come rolling in . . . the waves of fear and doubt . . . caused by sickness, job loss, a relationship break-up, illness of a loved one, discouragement, death. You can't stand up under the force of the crashing wave. But you don't have to. The Lord will absorb the powerful force for you. You need only to be still.

Lord, I want to stand firm, but there are times when fear takes over. I want to live with faith, but there are times when doubt bursts through the doors of my heart. Oh, Father, help me to be still and watch you fight the battle for me. In Jesus' name. Amen.

reflection

further suggested reading:

Exodus 13-15

Keep the Banner
Lifted High

Exodus 17:15-16

Moses built an altar and called it The LORD is my Banner. He said, "Because hands were lifted up against the throne of the LORD, the Lord will be at war against the Amalekites from generation to generation."

The Amalekites were at it again. Those pesky enemies of Israel could never leave good enough alone. The Israelites, fresh from being delivered from Egypt, were still learning the ways of desert travel. The Amalekites took advantage of their vulnerable state and attacked God's people.

Moses sent Joshua to lead the troops into battle while he stood on the top of a hill to oversee the skirmish. When Moses raised the staff over his head symbolizing Israel's total dependence on God, the Israelites gained the advantage. But when Moses lowered his hands due to fatigue, the Amalekites started winning the battle. As a result the two men with Moses, Aaron and Hur, held up Moses' arms and the victory was secured. To thank God for deliverance, Moses built an altar and called it "The Lord is my Banner."

What banner do you hold high as you go into battle each day? If you hold the banner of self-sufficiency, independence or personal ambition, you will lose the battle every time. But if you hold high the name of the Lord, marching under his standard, he will give you the strength to defeat each foe. And one more thing . . . sometimes our arms grow tired. We need some people to help us keep the banner lifted high. Life is one battle you cannot fight alone.

Father, we depend on you and you alone. We are not strong enough on our own to defeat any foe. With you we can conquer each one. Help us to hold your banner high. And give us others to help us when our arms grow tired. In Jesus' name. Amen.

reflection

_____
_____
_____
_____
_____
_____
_____
_____

further suggested reading:

Exodus 16-18

Exodus 19:4

You yourselves have seen what I did to Egypt, and how I carried you on eagles' wings and brought you to myself.

For a young eagle, flying is an acquired skill with some potential failures along the way. Learning to walk is treacherous enough, but a stumble simply sends the toddler to the ground. A "stumble" for a young eagle learning to fly sends it plummeting to a deadly landing. So the mother eagle flies under her young with her wings spread out in order to catch them when they "stumble" or tire.

God uses that beautiful picture of love, care and protection to describe his relationship with Israel. God reminded Israel of his powerful acts in Egypt and of his demonstration of the same love, care and protection as the mother eagle in delivering them from slavery and through the Red Sea.

Our spiritual flight has many ups and downs. The wind currents of life lift us up and drag us down. The atmosphere of sin causes us to stumble and fall. We grow weary from the journey and start a dangerous descent. But God is there every time. Like the mother eagle, he carries us on his all-powerful wings.

Father, thank you for bringing us to yourself. And thank you for never letting your children plummet to the ground. Thank you for your constant love, care and protection. In Jesus' name. Amen.

reflection

further suggested reading:

Exodus 19-20

No Other God

Exodus 23:24

Do not bow down before their gods or worship them or follow their practices. You must demolish them and break their sacred stones to pieces.

Other gods have always been a problem for God's people. Beginning with the first commandment, God clearly warned against spiritual adultery. Bowing down before other gods is foolish, of course. They are temporal images made of stone, wood, metal, and sometimes, skin and bones. So why are the gods of this world so tempting?

For starters, humans have a problem with any god, even God. Sin has short-circuited God's wiring in our hearts. Sin turns our original purpose of honoring and serving the Creator into the worship of ourselves and the creation. The living, personal, eternal God is a threat. But we can control the gods of the world.

The question for today is the following: Are you bowing down before any god other than God? That god can come in the form of a person, possession or position. It may be something you are living with, living in or living for. Whatever it is, it's a pathetic substitute for the real thing. Get rid of it and bow before the One who loves you so much that he sent his Son to die on your behalf.

Father, show me before what I am really bowing down. Help me to demolish my worship of that thing and bow down before you. In Jesus' name. Amen.

reflection

_____

_____

_____

_____

_____

_____

_____

_____

_____

_____

_____

further suggested reading:

Exodus 21-24

31

Worship Through Giving

Exodus 25:1-2

The LORD said to Moses, "Tell the Israelites to bring me an offering. You are to receive the offering for me from everyone whose heart prompts them to give."

God's instructions to build the tabernacle were detailed and precise. God said, "Make this tabernacle and all its furnishings exactly like the pattern I will show you" (Exodus 25:9). Then in the following chapters, God clearly explained the measurements and needed material. But notice in today's passage that the contributions were left entirely to the worshipper.

God did not command people to give, nor did he provide a suggested donation. The monies to build the tabernacle and furnishings were to come from "everyone whose heart prompts them to give." Giving is an act of worship and forced worship is not worship at all.

This worship principle is repeated in the New Testament. As Paul collected an offering for the struggling church in Jerusalem, he instructed each person to "give what he has decided in his heart to give, not reluctantly or under compulsion, for God loves a cheerful giver" (2 Corinthians 9:7). From the Old Testament to the New, giving is an act of individual worship. Giving out of compulsion, legalism, manipulation or force is not worship at all.

Father, remind us that you own all things. All we have is a gift from you. All we have is to be used for you. Help us to give back to you willingly. In Jesus' name. Amen.

reflection

_____

_____

_____

_____

_____

_____

_____

_____

_____

_____

further suggested reading:

Exodus 25-27

God-Centered Relationships

Exodus 29:45-46

Then I will dwell among the Israelites and be their God. They will know that I am the LORD their God, who brought them out of Egypt so that I might dwell among them. I am the LORD their God.

What god but the living God says to humans, "I will dwell among" you. Gods of religion are so far removed from creation that man spends his life in a futile effort to somehow work his way to the deity. But God says, "I'll come to you. I want you to know me. I want you to know how much I love you. I want you to know the things I do for you. I want to live among you." Amazing!

Religions of the world focus on man working his way to God. But Christianity is not a man-centered religion, but a God-centered relationship. Religion is all about man. Christianity is all about God. A personal relationship with the living God is initiated by God the Father, made possible by God the Son and enabled by God the Holy Spirit. Amazing!

God so loved the world that he sent his Son. Jesus, fully-God and fully-man, died on the cross as the penalty for our sin. When we trust in the Son, the Father accredits Christ's righteousness to us and declares us "not guilty." God the Spirit takes up residence in us and enables us to live a life that pleases God. Life with God is amazing! What are you waiting for?

Father, for anyone reading this who does not know Jesus as Savior, please bring that person to yourself today. Show him his sin and separation from you. Show her the utter futility of trying to be good enough for you. Let them see your amazing promise that you will take up residence in your people and will never leave them. In Jesus' name. Amen.

reflection

_____

_____

_____

_____

_____

_____

_____

_____

further suggested reading:

Exodus 28-29

33

We Cannot
Do It Alone

Exodus 31:13

Say to the Israelites, 'You must observe my Sabbaths. This will be a sign between me and you for the generations to come, so you may know that I am the LORD, who makes you holy.'

Not long ago, I visited the Statue of Liberty and Ellis Island. The experience was very moving. As we took in the sights, I tried to imagine the emotions of the immigrants as they saw Lady Liberty after weeks at sea. What were they thinking and feeling as they walked up the steps to enter the immigration building on Ellis Island to begin the process of becoming citizens of the new country? These were special people who, with little or no money, made their way in the new world.

But when it comes to our relationship with God, no person can make his or her own way. We are sinners to the core, and our best effort on our best day is far below God's standard. We can't pull ourselves up by our own spiritual bootstraps because when it comes to a relationship with God, we have no spiritual boots!

Only God can make us holy. Maybe that has been one of your struggles. You have been trying to make yourself good enough for God. Good luck with that. But here's the good news - Jesus came to do for us what we could not do for ourselves. Jesus died for our sins so that through our trust in him, we could be made holy. Jesus walked in our boots and pulled us up by his sacrifice on the cross. Trust in him as the One - the only One - who makes you holy.

Father, thank you for sending your Son. I pray for the person trying to make himself or herself good enough for you. I pray that you will help them to see the futility of their efforts. I pray that they will trust in Jesus today as the One who makes them holy. In Jesus' name. Amen.

reflection

_____

_____

_____

_____

_____

_____

further suggested reading:

Exodus 30-31

His Character

Exodus 34:5-6

Then the LORD came down in the cloud and stood there with him and proclaimed his name, the LORD. And he passed in front of Moses, proclaiming, "The LORD, the LORD, the compassionate and gracious God, slow to anger, abounding in love and faithfulness . . ."

In Exodus 34, God invited Moses to bring two stone tablets to Mt. Sinai for the giving of the law. This was the second trip up the mountain for Moses. The first time he returned to find the Israelites dancing around a golden calf. In his anger, he threw the tablets to the ground "breaking them into pieces." God graciously invited him back and promised to write "the words that were on the first tablets, which you broke."

Early in the morning Moses made his way up the mountain. The Lord came down from a cloud, stood with Moses and proclaimed his name and his character. He introduced himself as the "Lord" ("Yahweh" in Hebrew), which explains that God depends on no one or no thing for his existence. Then God described his character. He is compassionate, gracious, patient, loving and faithful. Those were words Moses needed to hear . . . and words we need to hear.

Today, thank God for his compassion - his affection that leads to action. Thank God for his grace - acceptance without condition. Thank God for his patience - his slowness to become angry. Thank God for his love - the love that sent Jesus to the cross to pay the penalty for your sin. Thank God for his faithfulness - he will always keep his promises. Thank God that through his Holy Spirit, he is standing with you right now.

Father, thank you for who you are and what you do for us. Thank you for your attributes described in today's passage. May we live a life that demonstrates our gratefulness for your great generosity. In Jesus' name. Amen.

reflection

_____

_____

_____

_____

_____

_____

_____

further suggested reading:

Exodus 32-34

What Generosity!

Exodus 36:5-7

And said to Moses, "The people are bringing more than enough for doing the work the LORD commanded to be done." Then Moses gave an order and they sent this word throughout the camp: "No man or woman is to make anything else as an offering for the sanctuary." And so the people were restrained from bringing more, because what they already had was more than enough to do all the work.

"Stop giving! We have too much money already. We don't even know how we are going to use the funds we have. So from now on, we are not going to pass the plates. Cancel your online giving. And please, no special gifts. We have more than enough to do all the work God has for us to do."

Have you heard that from your pastor lately . . . or ever? I promise you have never heard that from me. But here in Exodus, as the people "continued to bring freewill offerings morning after morning" to build the Tabernacle and its furnishings, the builders said, "Enough already." And the people were "restrained from bringing more."

What a response to God! What generosity! Remember these were "freewill offerings" the people were giving. They were giving voluntarily from a heart of worship in response to God's amazing love and grace. How are you doing with your freewill offerings?

Father, remind us that all things belong to you. All things we have are a gift from you. Help us to use your gifts to us in a way that honors you. Help us to do so with grateful and generous hearts of worship. In Jesus' name. Amen.

reflection

_____

_____

_____

_____

_____

_____

_____

_____

further suggested reading:

Exodus 35-40

Preparing Us for Jesus

February 1

Leviticus 1:3-4

If the offering is a burnt offering from the herd, you are to offer a male without defect. . . . You are to lay your hand on the head of the burnt offering, and it will be accepted on your behalf to make atonement for you.

Sometimes an Old Testament passage may make you wonder, "What in the world does that have to do with me and my life?" That may have come to mind as you read today's passage. Interestingly, Leviticus was the first book studied by a Jewish child. It was important because it showed that "sacrifice was given by God as the only sufficient means for Israelites to remain in harmonious fellowship" with God (*Bible Knowledge Commentary*, David C. Cook, 1989, p.164).

Note today's instruction regarding the burnt offering. First, the offering had to be a male "without defect." A deficient sacrifice would not do. Second, the person laid his hands on the head of the burnt offering. This identified the worshipper with the animal as his personal substitute. Third, the animal was sacrificed in order to "make atonement" for the individual. Atonement means that reconciliation between God and man was achieved through the sacrifice.

God's sacrificial system in the Old Testament was a picture and preparer for the coming Lamb of God. Jesus came "without defect." By faith we lay our hands on him identifying ourselves with the substitute. The death of Jesus on our behalf brings forgiveness and reconciles us with the Holy God. Amazing, isn't it? Wherever you are in the Old Testament, God the Father is preparing us for God the Son.

Father, thank you for preparing us for Jesus. Thank you for the atonement that he provides by his death on the cross. By faith we identify ourselves with him and receive your forgiveness and reconciliation. Thank you! In Jesus' name. Amen.

reflection

further suggested reading:

Leviticus 1-3

37

Speak Up!

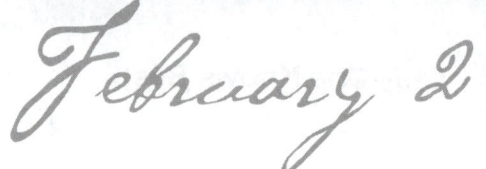

Leviticus 5:1

If anyone sins because they do not speak up when they hear a public charge to testify regarding something they have seen or learned about, they will be held responsible.

Information is power. Sharing it, or not sharing it, can change the course of a person's life. In today's passage, we find that refusing to share needed information is as much of a sin as sharing false information.

Let's say that a person you know is facing a public charge. People are dependent on the testimony of those who have the facts. And you have the facts. You may be an eyewitness or you may have learned all the details from a credible source. The question is will you speak out? If not, you will be held responsible for this sin.

Now, the issue may not be a public charge. It may be a nasty rumor or attempted character assassination in your office, school, circle of friends or home. Or it may be a person getting by with something for which he should be held accountable. The same principle applies. If you have what is needed information, speak out! When you don't, your silence is sin.

Father, someone reading this has some information about a person that needs to be shared. Give that person the courage to speak out. In Jesus' name. Amen.

reflection

further suggested reading:

Leviticus 4-7

Only One Knows Best

Leviticus 10:1

Aaron's sons Nadab and Abihu took their censers, put fire in them and added incense; and they offered unauthorized fire before the LORD, contrary to his command.

The key words in today's passage are the following: "contrary to his command." The new office of the Old Testament priest had just been established. Moses had explained God's instructions with great care and detail. But when it came time for Nadab and Abihu to perform their priestly duties, they knew better and "offered unauthorized fire before the Lord" and paid dearly for their sin (Leviticus 10:1-2).

Do you think you know better? When it comes to running your business? When it comes to leading your family? When it comes to your marriage? When it comes to personal and spiritual disciplines? Anytime we act contrary to God's instructions we are living as if we know better. I must admit that I know God knows best, but sometimes I act like I know better.

God's commands are based on his omniscience and his perfect will. There are always consequences when we refuse to follow his instructions. True worship and submission to God begins with an attitude of "Lord, you know best. Please give me the strength and determination to follow your instruction."

Father, that's our prayer. You know best. Please help me to live like I truly believe that today. Help me to submit and follow your instruction in all the areas of my life. In Jesus' name. Amen.

reflection

_____

_____

_____

_____

_____

_____

_____

_____

_____

_____

further suggested reading:

Leviticus 8-10

A Life Set Apart

Leviticus 11:45

I am the LORD, who brought you up out of Egypt to be your God; therefore be holy, because I am holy.

To be holy means to be set apart. It does not mean to run off and hide in a cave so as not to have contact with the world. To be holy means to live in purity and moral integrity as we go about the business of our life. To be holy means that we strive to live apart from the things that oppose God and the things that God opposes.

Our standard for holiness is not a set of rules or an abstract religious system. Our standard is not our mentor or a strong Christian friend. Our standard for holy living is God himself. He alone is holy.

Now it's true that absolute holiness cannot be achieved in this life. In our humanity, we will miss the mark. But it should be the believer's desire to be in a process of spiritual growth - conforming our lives to God's holy standard. This is done as we continually depend on the Spirit to control our attitude, thinking, desires and actions. While we will never live sinless lives on this earth, it is possible, by the strength of the Spirit, to sin less and obey more. That's the high standard to which God has called his children. And that's the desire of his children.

Father, today we pinpoint a sin that seems constantly to trip us up. We depend on you to resist it day by day, moment by moment. Help us to see that sin be less of a threat to our walk with you. Then help us to pinpoint another sin. In Jesus' name. Amen.

reflection

_____
_____
_____
_____
_____
_____
_____
_____
_____

further suggested reading:

Leviticus 11-13

Clean or Unclean

Leviticus 14:54-57

These are the regulations . . . to determine when something is clean or unclean.

The Bubonic Plague raged throughout Europe in the middle 1300s, killing an estimated 25 million people. In a three-year period, one-fourth of Europe's entire population was wiped out. Finally, it was discovered that the disease was carried by flea infested rats. But poor sanitation and the devastation of war allowed the epidemic to take its deadly toll.

As the people of Israel begin to get their footing as a nation freshly freed from Egypt, God revealed to them his civil, ceremonial and moral law. In that instruction were certain "regulations" that addressed hygiene and ways to avoid the spreading of disease. God knew how fast infection could spread. These regulations were an act of grace. In them God was protecting his people.

Now I'll admit that reading through the dietary and hygienic regulations in Leviticus doesn't provide the most moving morning devotional. But don't miss God's deep love and care within these practical rules and guidelines. Just as God provided a way to stop the spread of sin, so he instructed his people how to avoid the spread of infection and disease. Reading through these regulations gives me a new appreciation for God's gracious care, his thorough protection and his practical love.

Father, sometimes your instruction is deeply theological; sometimes it is downright practical. Thank you for loving us so much that you sent your Son. And thank you for loving us so much that you provided practical hygienic instruction to the Old Testament believer and practical instruction in the New Testament for believers today. In Jesus' name. Amen.

reflection

_____
_____
_____
_____
_____
_____
_____
_____

further suggested reading:

Leviticus 14-15

Blood, Sacrifice, Atonement

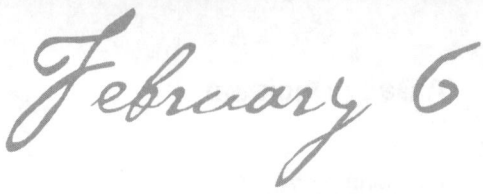

February 6

Leviticus 17:11

For the life of a creature is in the blood, and I have given it to you to make atonement for yourselves on the altar; it is the blood that makes atonement for one's life.

In the Old Testament, God gave his people a civil, ceremonial and moral law. Within the ceremonial law was a way for sins to be forgiven. God's justice demanded death for sin. God's love provided a substitute to die instead of the sinner.

The substitute was to be a male animal without defect. Identifying himself with the sacrifice, the worshipper would lay his hand on the animal's head. Then he, along with the priests, would kill the animal. The life of the animal was in the blood (Leviticus 17:14). As the blood left the body and death came, the worshiper experienced the death of the substitute that provided him atonement - forgiveness and reconciliation with God.

While the system of sacrifice was needed for the Old Testament believer, it was only a "shadow of the good things" to come (Hebrews 10:1). God was preparing his people for the perfect one-time-for-all-time sacrifice of Jesus. "God made him who knew no sin to be sin for us, so that in him we might become the righteousness of God" (2 Corinthians 5:21). Jesus is the only one who can make atonement for our sins.

Father, just as the Old Testament believer identified himself with the sacrifice, I pray that you will lead a person reading this to identify with Jesus today by trusting in his work on the cross as his or her own. Thank you for the atonement that only Jesus provides. I pray in Jesus' name. Amen.

reflection

_____

_____

_____

_____

_____

_____

_____

_____

further suggested reading:

Leviticus 16-17

A Daily Decision

February 7

Leviticus 20:7-8

Consecrate yourselves and be holy, because I am the LORD your God. Keep my decrees and follow them. I am the LORD, who makes you holy.

The word holy means "to be set apart." It describes something that is not for common use but is dedicated and devoted to God. There are two critical truths found in our passage today. Let's break them down.

Positional Holiness: On our best day with our best efforts we cannot make ourselves holy. It is the Lord "who makes you holy." Jesus Christ, the Righteous One, died on our behalf. When we trust in the work of Jesus as our own, God imputes or accredits Christ's righteousness to us. Covered with the righteousness of Jesus, we are set apart, made holy, as sons and daughters of the living God. Nothing can ever change our position in Christ.

Practical Holiness: While our holy position is secure, we still have the responsibility to live a life that is set apart to God. We need to keep his "decrees and follow them." Nothing can change our position of holiness, but we can choose to live a life that is set apart. Practical holiness is a partnership with the Holy Spirit. We ask him to control our lives (words, thoughts, actions) every moment of every day. The practice of holiness produces spiritual growth and fruit.

Both positional and practical holiness are critical to living a life that pleases God. It all begins by being set apart as his son or daughter and continues as we choose to live a life set apart to him instead of immersed in the world. Our position is set. Every day there awaits a practical decision.

Father, thank you for making us holy. May we live a life set apart every hour of every day to you. In Jesus' name. Amen.

reflection

further suggested reading:

Leviticus 18-20

43

Feasts of Focus

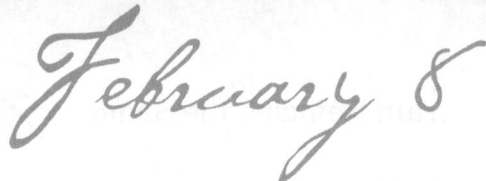

February 8

Leviticus 23:1-5

The LORD said to Moses, "Speak to the Israelites and say to them: 'These are my appointed festivals, the appointed festivals of the LORD, which you are to proclaim as sacred assemblies.'"

In Leviticus 23, God instructed his people to reserve certain dates in their calendar for times of national public worship. The length of these festivals ranged from a one-day event to a feast that lasted several days. The purpose of each feast varied from the rest, to remembering the poor, to remembering God's deliverance, to showing joy and thankfulness for God's blessings.

While these feasts are not reinstituted in the New Testament, they are very instructive for the believer. The feasts provided a time to break away from everyday activities and focus on the Lord. They provided a time of praise and worship. They were times to make things right with God. And the feast provided a great time for families to come together and enjoy food and fellowship.

The feasts show me a side of God I often miss. He desires me to take a break. He wants me to get away and reconnect with him. And he must smile when he sees us enjoying food and fellowship with other believers. We don't need to reinstitute the feasts. But we do need to reserve dates on our calendars, other than Sunday morning, to get away, enjoy our heavenly Father and have fun with other believers.

Father, help us to schedule times of retreat, relaxation and fellowship. Pry us away from our busy lives and allow us to reconnect with you and other believers. In Jesus' name. Amen.

reflection

_____
_____
_____
_____
_____
_____
_____
_____
_____
_____

further suggested reading:

Leviticus 21-23

Truth Remains the Same

Leviticus 26:12-13

I will walk among you and be your God, and you will be my people. I am the LORD your God, who brought you out of Egypt so that you would no longer be slaves to the Egyptians; I broke the bars of your yoke and enabled you to walk with heads held high.

Get ready to be impressed by some "useful" info I ran across. Ready?

- *The kings in a deck of cards are named Alexander, Caesar, Charles and David. Didn't know that, did you?*
- *The modern hamburger on a bun got its start at the St. Louis World's Fair in 1904.*
- *The ZIP in Zip Codes stands for Zone Improvement Plan and was introduced by the post office in 1963. Now you know.*
- *It takes 110 domestic silkworms' cocoons to make a man's tie and 630 to make a blouse. Talk about sacrifice!*

I could go on and on (really I could), but the point I want to make is this. **Most of the time we don't need new information; we need to use the information we have.**

Samuel Johnson said, "People need to be reminded more often than they need to be instructed." That's what God does in the book of Leviticus. While there is much instruction, he weaves this reminder into the teaching 49 times throughout the book as he states, "I am the Lord your God." In today's passage, he reminds the people that he will walk among them, he broke the chains of their slavery and he brought them out of Egypt.

God tells his people that because of who he is and what he has done, they can "walk with their heads held high." And so can we! The creator of all things is the Lord our God. He has broken the bars of sin's slavery. He has delivered us from the land of sin. In him there is forgiveness for the past, power for the present and a great promise for the future. Believers, because the Lord is our God, we can walk with our heads held high!

Dear Father, thank you for your deliverance! Enable us to walk with our heads held high. In Jesus' name. Amen.

further suggested reading:

Leviticus 24-27

A Demonstration of Love

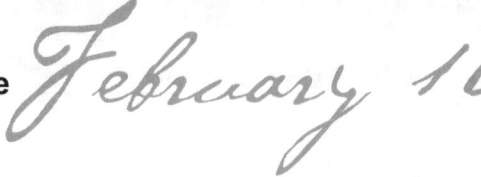

Numbers 1:1-2

The LORD spoke to Moses in the tent of meeting in the Desert of Sinai on the first day of the second month of the second year after the Israelites came out of Egypt. He said: "Take a census of the whole Israelite community by their clans and families, listing every man by name, one by one."

The English name for the book of Numbers comes from the Septuagint, the Greek translation of the Old Testament, and is based on the census in Chapters 1 and 26. But the contents of this book detail the 38 years of Israel's wanderings in the desert. The Hebrew name of this book is "beimdbar," meaning "in the desert," and better describes what the book is about.

The book of Numbers shows that God is the Lord of Israel. He entered into a covenant with them. He delivered them from Egypt. He calls them his "treasured possession" (Exodus 19:5). He gave them the law and graciously provided a way of worship. But this book also describes God's wrath when Israel ignores his instruction and promises.

We don't like to think of God's wrath. Yet it is the inevitable response to God's righteousness. God always says and does what is right. He is the standard. Sin not only misses the standard but destroys the lives of his children. God's wrath regarding sin is a demonstration of his love, care and protection. If God never demonstrated his wrath, he would not be righteous.

Father, thank you for loving us and caring for us so much that you demonstrate your wrath on sin. Thank you for your protection. In Jesus' name. Amen.

reflection

_____

_____

_____

_____

_____

_____

_____

_____

further suggested reading:

Numbers 1-4

Numbers 6:22-27

The LORD said to Moses, "Tell Aaron and his sons, 'This is how you are to bless the Israelites. Say to them: The LORD bless you and keep you; the LORD make his face shine on you and be gracious to you; the LORD turn his face toward you and give you peace.' So they will put my name on the Israelites, and I will bless them."

Do you ever have trouble knowing how to pray for your children? I do. My prayers too often default into worn out requests that lack specifics. But today's passage gives great help in putting some power into the prayers for our kids.

The prayer was given to Moses for Aaron. It is called the "Priestly Blessing" or sometimes the "Aaronic Benediction." Notice that God's name Yahweh (LORD) is repeated three times in this short prayer. This repetition emphasizes the person and work of God. There are seven requests made in this prayer. Let's consider three today and the remaining four tomorrow.

The Lord bless you . . . The word "bless" means to "provide favor or benefit." *Father, we pray that for our children. You are the eternal God. Please place your great kindness and advantage on those we love. May they be approved and favored by you.*

. . . and keep you . . . The Hebrew word "keep" means to "watch, guard, defend." This is a prayer for protection. *Father, my children are not perfect. They are going to make mistakes. But please watch over them and guard them against mistakes of youth that are unalterable. Please defend them against temptation. Protect them against Satan who desires to devour them.*

. . . the LORD make his face shine upon you . . . This is a request for God's presence. *Father, as a parent I know that I can't be with my children all the time, but you can. Just like they feel the warmth of the sun shining on them, please allow them to experience your presence. Thank you for being with them wherever they go. In Jesus' name. Amen.*

reflection

_____

_____

_____

_____

further suggested reading:

Numbers 5-6

A Holy Mark

Numbers 6:22-27

The LORD said to Moses, "Tell Aaron and his sons, 'This is how you are to bless the Israelites. Say to them: The LORD bless you and keep you; the LORD make his face shine on you and be gracious to you; the LORD turn his face toward you and give you peace.' So they will put my name on the Israelites, and I will bless them."

Aaron's "Priestly Blessing" is a great prayer to pray for our children. I introduced this prayer yesterday and considered the first three requests. Here are the final four.

*. . . **and be gracious to you** . . .* Grace is God's undeserved favor. He gives us what we don't deserve. *Father, thank you for your gift of grace. I pray that gift to be poured out on my children. Following that great gift of salvation, please show them your kindness and love in all the endeavors of their lives.*

*. . . **the Lord turn his face toward you** . . .* Here is a request for God's fellowship. *Father, thank you, that because of their trust in Jesus, the Holy Spirit lives in my children. Please walk with them in a powerful way. Enable them to submit to the Spirit's control day by day and moment by moment.*

*. . . **and give you peace.*** The Hebrew word for peace used here is "shalom." It means "completeness, wholeness and contentment." *Lord, please calm my children's fears; soothe their anxious souls. Keep them complete and whole in their thinking, emotions, desires and actions.*

So they will put my name on _____ (the name of your child/children). This is a request of identification. *Lord, please place your holy mark on my children. Set them apart to be used by you. I love them but you love them more. You love them with an everlasting love. May they represent you well on their earthly journey. And when their journey is completed, welcome them home to live forever with you. In Jesus' name. Amen.*

reflection

_____

_____

_____

_____

further suggested reading:

Numbers 7-8

The Disease of Doubt

February 13

Numbers 11:23

The LORD answered Moses, "Is the LORD's arm too short? Now you will see whether or not what I say will come true for you."

God's gracious provision of manna was getting old for some of the Israelites. "If only we had meat to eat!" they complained. "We remember the fish we ate in Egypt at no cost, but now we never see anything but this manna!" How easy it is to take God's gracious provisions for granted.

God promised a month's worth of meat for Israel, but Moses doubted God's ability to supply that much meat for 2,000,000 Israelites. Moses asked sarcastically, "Would they have enough if all the fish in the sea were caught for them?" God responded to Moses, "Is the LORD's arm too short?"

Doubting God is a disease that continues to infect the human heart. God provides sin's sacrifice; we proclaim self-sufficiency. God provides forgiveness; we carry our sin. God promises never to leave us; we feel alone. God promises to give us what we need; we're not convinced he'll come through. God promises the Spirit's power; we live in our human weakness. To all who question his ability to deliver, he answers, "Is the LORD's arm too short? Now you will see whether or not what I say will come true."

Father, forgive our doubts. We acknowledge that you are more than able to reach down and meet our needs. Thank you for your patience with us. In Jesus' name. Amen.

reflection

further suggested reading:

Numbers 9-12

An Uncomfortable Desire

February 14

Numbers 14:24

But because my servant Caleb has a different spirit and follows me wholeheartedly, I will bring him into the land he went to, and his descendants will inherit it.

Note the word "wholeheartedly" in today's passage. It describes Caleb, a man who followed hard after God. When everyone else was struck by fear, Caleb stood his ground and obeyed without reservation or hesitation. How does one acquire such a full-out faith?

At this point in history, Israel was only two years out of Egypt. Caleb had lived 38 of his 40 years in slavery. No doubt he prayed that God would deliver his people. And then one day Moses came. Caleb saw the plagues, experienced the Passover, marched through the Red Sea and then turned to watch the walls of water envelop the Egyptians. Caleb was there at the giving of the Ten Commandments when the earth shook with the presence of God. He gathered the manna day after day as God supplied the food. Caleb had seen God at work.

How does one acquire such a full-out faith? I believe the answer is this: a firsthand experience of God's power and faithfulness. You cannot live a wholehearted life just by hearing the stories of God's great work. You have to experience it up close and personal. You will never feel God's power until you are in a position to need it. You will never experience God's faithfulness until you are in a position where the only thing left is to trust him.

Father, life is too comfortable for many of us to place ourselves in a position where we must trust in you to provide. Help us realize that meaningful faith is not developed on the left-over experiences of others. Help us to put ourselves in situations that stretch us and make us depend on you. In Jesus' name. Amen.

reflection

_____
_____
_____
_____
_____
_____
_____

further suggested reading:

Numbers 13-16

Emotionally Fried and Unguarded

February 15

Numbers 20:12

But the LORD said to Moses and Aaron, "Because you did not trust in me enough to honor me as holy in the sight of the Israelites, you will not bring this community into the land I give them."

Moses was emotionally fried. He had just buried his sister, Miriam, and the people of Israel were quarreling with him again. "Why did you bring [us] into this desert that we . . . should die here? And there is no water to drink!" they complained. Moses and Aaron went before the Lord. God directed them to go to a certain rock and "speak to that rock before their eyes and it will pour out its water."

But as I said, Moses was emotionally fried. He stood before the rock and said, "Listen, you rebels, must we bring you water out of this rock?" Then, instead of speaking to the rock as God had instructed, Moses "raised his arm and struck the rock twice with his staff." God did not approve of or appreciate his disobedience. In fact, that act of disobedience kept Moses from entering the Promised Land.

Do you know when the rock-striking incident happened? The 40th year after the exodus! The years of wandering in the desert were almost over! But in an unguarded emotional moment, Moses blew it. And so can we. Each of us is only one unguarded, emotional, regrettable step away from doing something really foolish; one step away from blowing up our family, ruining our reputation and not honoring God as holy. It happened to the great leader of Israel; it can happen to us. Guard your hearts!

Father, this passage puts fear into my heart. Please place your protection around my life. Protect me especially when I am emotionally fried. Keep me from unguarded moments. Don't let me follow this part of Moses' life. In Jesus' name. Amen.

reflection

further suggested reading:

Numbers 17-20

Between the Wrinkles

February 16

Numbers 23:19

God is not human, that he should lie, not a human being, that he should change his mind. Does he speak and then not act? Does he promise and not fulfill?

Human beings are all about change. We change from a wrinkly faced baby to a wrinkly faced old man. Okay, maybe it ends up the same, but a lot of change takes place between the wrinkles. We grow physically. We develop intellectually. We mature emotionally. Things we held to passionately at one point in life are jettisoned at another. We change our mind regarding decisions and opinions.

But God is not human. He cannot go from better to worse or worse to better. He is perfectly holy. He cannot become holier than he has always been. Certainly, he cannot change for the worse, for then he would no longer be God. A. W. Tozer says, "All that God is he has always been, and all that he has been and is he will ever be. . . . In God no change is possible; in men change is impossible to escape" (*Knowledge of the Holy, Harper Collins*, 1992, p. 50).

What's the truth we can learn from God's immutable nature? God will do whatever he says. God will fulfill whatever he promises. No action of God will be left undone. No promise of God will dangle without complete accomplishment. God is the Rock that never settles or shifts. My Savior is "the same yesterday and today and forever" (Hebrews 13:8).

Father, thank you for never changing! Thank you for never changing your mind! Thank you for doing what you say you will do! Thank you for the constancy of your love and grace even when I fail to follow your instruction. In Jesus' name. Amen.

reflection

_____

_____

_____

_____

_____

_____

_____

_____

_____

_____

further suggested reading:

Numbers 21-25

Don't Wander

February 17

Numbers 26:65

For the LORD had told those Israelites they would surely die in the wilderness, and not one of them was left except Caleb son of Jephunneh and Joshua son of Nun.

Soon after God delivered Israel from slavery in Egypt, Moses sent twelve undercover agents to scope out the Promised Land. The men came back with differing views. Two men said, "Let's go take possession of the land! We can do it!" Ten said, "Not so fast. The people are powerful. The cities are fortified. No way can we defeat these people." The majority report was accepted, and Israel refused to trust in God's ability to conquer the enemy.

Israel's actions resulted in a tough penalty. God said that every person twenty years of age would die in the desert. Not one of them would enter the Promised Land except Caleb and Joshua. Forty years later, God gave Joshua the privilege of leading the people into the land of promise. Regarding Caleb, God said, "because my servant Caleb . . . follows me wholeheartedly, I will bring him into the land . . . and his descendants will inherit it."

The obstacles you face today may seem as undefeatable as the cities and people seemed to the ten spies. You may feel small and weak compared to your problems. And you know what? You are! But God isn't. The God you call your Father is with you. And he is bigger and more powerful than any obstacle in your life. He can be trusted. Here's the question: Will you trust him?

Father, there is stuff in our life that seems insurmountable. It's tempting to shrink back in fear. But give us the faith of Joshua and Caleb. Help us to follow you wholeheartedly. Don't leave us to wander in the desert and miss your promises. In Jesus' name. Amen.

reflection

_____
_____
_____
_____
_____
_____
_____

further suggested reading:

Numbers 26-30

Unreserved Focus, Direction and Trust

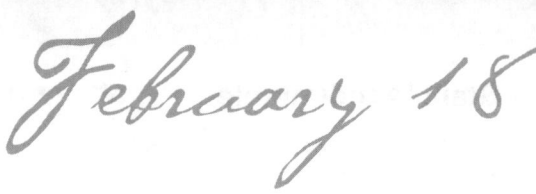

Numbers 32:11-12

Because they have not followed me wholeheartedly, not one of those who were twenty years old or more when they came up out of Egypt will see the land I promised on oath to Abraham, Isaac and Jacob-not one except Caleb son of Jephunneh the Kenizzite and Joshua son of Nun, for they followed the LORD wholeheartedly.

Soon after God delivered Israel from slavery in Egypt, Moses sent twelve spies to scope out the Promised Land. All agreed that the land was "flowing with milk and honey," but ten of the undercover agents were convinced that the land was also filled with a large number of strong men who could not be defeated. Only two were ready to take the land. As a result, the doubters died in the desert. Only Caleb and Joshua were allowed to enter the land of promise.

Notice how God describes these two men - "they followed me **wholeheartedly**." What does it mean to follow God wholeheartedly?

- **Focus.** The majority of the spies focused on the strength of the enemy. The result? Fear. Joshua and Caleb focused on the strength of their God. The result? Faith.
- **Direction.** Fear always causes retreat. Faith always leads the charge.
- **Trust.** At some point we have to determine who or what we really trust. Will it be our abilities, training, position, portfolio or the living God? The answer is simple on paper, but the application is hard in practice.

I don't know about you, but I can't think of a better description of a life well-lived. "He/She followed God wholeheartedly." Do you want that on your tombstone? Then you have to start writing the inscription today.

Father, it is so easy for me to lose my focus, take the wrong direction and trust the worthless stuff of this world. Please help me to follow you wholeheartedly and to enjoy the fruits of your promises today and forever. In Jesus' name. Amen.

reflection

_____
_____
_____
_____
_____

further suggested reading:

Numbers 31-32

Stand Accountable

February 19

Numbers 32:23

But if you fail to do this, you will be sinning against the LORD; and you may be sure that your sin will find you out.

Our sins are pesky little things, aren't they? We fondle them in secret, and then when we least expect it, they show up decorated in bright flashing lights. We meet them in private; they return in public. We engage them in the dark; they emerge in the light.

The Apostle Paul reminded Timothy, "The sins of some men are obvious, reaching the place of judgment ahead of them; the sins of others trail behind them" (1 Timothy 5:24). Whether our sin is waiting for us with its sinister greeting, or tracks us down like a heat seeking missile, you can be sure that "your sin will find you out."

Maybe you are different. Maybe this passage doesn't apply to you. Maybe you believe you are one of those people who can wallow in a pile of manure and come out smelling like a rose. And maybe you will be able to go to your grave with a great secret sin. But remember there is life after the grave. God says that nothing in all creation is hidden in his sight. "Everything is uncovered and laid bare before the eyes of him to whom we must give an account" (Hebrews 4:13). You may pull the wool over the eyes of men, but nothing is hidden from God.

Father, please don't allow me to think that my secret sin will not eventually show up in public or that what I do in darkness is somehow hidden from you. Remind me often that one day I will stand accountable before you. In Jesus' name. Amen.

reflection

further suggested reading:

Numbers 33

55

The Many Gates of Our Temple

February 20

Numbers 35:34

Do not defile the land where you live and where I dwell, for I, the LORD, dwell among the Israelites.

It's an amazing truth! An astounding truth! The Spirit of God lives in the believer. Just as God dwelt among the Israelites in the Old Testament, now God lives in the person who trusts in Christ. The Apostle Paul said that each believer is a "temple of God . . . the Spirit of God dwells in you" (1 Corinthians 3:16).

In the Old Testament, the Israelites were not to defile the land where God dwelt. Now the believer needs to take care of his "temple" where God dwells. When I was growing up, many used this instruction to teach against the use of alcohol and tobacco. And I certainly agree that the abuse of these (and overeating and lack of exercise) defiles the "temple." But it doesn't stop there.

Defiling the land and defiling our "temple" today includes more than the physical dangers. We must also guard the gate of our eyes . . . what we watch and look at. The gate of our mind . . . the things we think about. The gate of our emotions . . . the things we desire. The gate of our will . . . the mission of our life. If only it were as easy as simply refraining from alcohol or tobacco.

Father, by your Spirit help us to guard all the gates of our life where the enemy stands ready to invade. By your Spirit help us to stand strong in our areas of weakness. Please protect us from defiling your dwelling place. In Jesus' name. Amen.

reflection

further suggested reading:

Numbers 34-36

A Continuing Work

February 21

Deuteronomy 3:22

Do not be afraid of them; the LORD your God himself will fight for you.

Nelson Henderson said, "The true meaning of life is to plant trees, under whose shade you do not expect to sit." That's what Moses was doing in today's passage. An act of disobedience had disqualified him from leading Israel into the land of promise. As a result, he is encouraging the next generation with the truths that he has personally experienced. That's the job of every godly leader.

Godly leaders leave more than a business or an inheritance to the next generation. They pass on certain confidence and tenacious trust in God. They know that since God does not change, the way he worked in their life will continue to be the way he works in the next generation.

When a godly leader has truly lived a life of faith, he can say to those who come after him, "Do not be afraid . . . the Lord your God himself will fight for you."

Father, remind us that we must plant seeds today that grow trees under whose shade we do not expect to sit. Give us a vision that outlives us. Give us the wisdom to pass confidence in you to those who come after us. In Jesus' name. Amen.

reflection

further suggested reading:

Deuteronomy 1-4

The Curse of Compartmentalization

February 22

Deuteronomy 6:6-7

These commandments that I give you today are to be upon your hearts. Impress them on your children. Talk about them when you sit at home and when you walk along the road, when you lie down and when you get up.

Compartmentalization is a curse that impacts many Christians. This happens when our walk with Christ is separated from instead of merged with all the other areas of our life. Jesus becomes the subject of the songs we sing on Sunday and the person in whose name we pray but is seldom invited into our marriage, family, business and recreation. But remember, Jesus lives in the believer! He is with us in every area of our life.

Check out today's passage. We are to live out our walk with Christ whether at home or conducting business. The truth of God's Word and his presence should be woven into the interactions of my day from morning until night.

This spiritual wholeness is how God wants me to impress who he is on my children. They shouldn't see God as someone who lives in a church building. Spiritual wholeness teaches our children that God is alive and active in every area of life.

Lord, cure us from compartmentalization. Grow us in wholeness. Don't allow us to leave you out of any part of our life. In Jesus' name. Amen.

reflection

further suggested reading:

Deuteronomy 5-7

Ready, Set, Live!

February 23

Deuteronomy 10:12-13

And now, Israel, what does the LORD your God ask of you but to fear the LORD your God, to walk in obedience to him, to love him, to serve the LORD your God with all your heart and with all your soul, and to observe the LORD's commands and decrees that I am giving you today for your own good?

What does the Lord ask of you? That's a great question, isn't it? What does God really want me to do? Here are five answers from today's passage.

Live in Awe. The fear of God is not a trembling terror but rather a respectful awe. This involves an overarching attitude toward God that saturates our being and shows through in our actions.

Live in Obedience. Obeying God is not restricted to our morning "Quiet Time." As we live through our day, we are to submit ourselves to God's instruction.

Live in Love. Living in the fear of God can seem somewhat intimidating and submitting to his instruction somewhat restricting. But the opposite is true. Appreciation for who God is bursts out in love.

Live out Service. Service provides a God-ordained outlet to use our God-given abilities in a God-honoring way. Service is not a half-hearted effort with distracted minds and left over energy. God deserves our best . . . a service with all our heart and soul.

Read, study and live out his Word. The Lord's commands, found in his Word, are not random rituals purposed to see if we are willing to jump through holy hoops. God's instruction is always for our own good. When we follow his ways, we are doing the very thing that is best for us.

Father, thank you for giving us instruction that is for our best. Help us to read your Word, learn your commands and get them done in a way that honors you. In Jesus' name. Amen.

reflection

_____

_____

_____

_____

further suggested reading:

Deuteronomy 8-11

Deliverance, Provision, Protection

February 24

Deuteronomy 16:16-17

Three times a year all your men must appear before the LORD your God at the place he will choose: at the Festival of Unleavened Bread, the Festival of Weeks and the Festival of Tabernacles. No one should appear before the LORD empty-handed: Each of you must bring a gift in proportion to the way the LORD your God has blessed you.

Each year, the Old Testament worshipper observed three Old Testament festivals. The Feast of the Unleavened Bread began with the Passover and celebrated Israel's deliverance from Egypt. Seven weeks later, The Festival of Weeks marked the climax of the wheat harvest. The Festival of Tabernacles was an annual reminder of God's protection and provision during the forty years in the wilderness.

These were times of looking back and looking ahead. Israel had seen God's deliverance, provision and protection in the past, and he would certainly provide it in the future. In gratitude to what God had done and would do, the worshipper was not to come "empty-handed." His freewill offering was not a set amount. It was to be in proportion to God's blessings.

The same instruction applies to New Testament believers. Giving is not to be legalistic or burdensome. It is an act of worship when we bring our offering to him. Someone has well said, "Give according to God's blessing; lest he bless according to your giving."

Father, may we know this truth: you own all things. Everything we have is from your hand. Everything we have must be used to honor you. May we not only know this truth but live it out in our lives. In Jesus' name. Amen.

reflection

further suggested reading:

Deuteronomy 12-16

Christian Leader

February 25

Deuteronomy 17:18-20

When he takes the throne of his kingdom, he is to write for himself on a scroll a copy of this law, taken from that of the Levitical priests. It is to be with him, and he is to read it all the days of his life so that he may learn to revere the LORD his God and follow carefully all the words of this law and these decrees and not consider himself better than his fellow Israelites and turn from the law to the right or to the left. Then he and his descendants will reign a long time over his kingdom in Israel.

Today's passage provides instruction for the kings of Israel and applies to all Christian leaders. Whether you were the Old Testament king of Israel or leading in some capacity today, God's principles never change.

Responsibility: The leader was to "write for himself on a scroll" a copy of the law. The act of writing it out was an act of personal responsibility and ownership.

Devotion: The powerful position of a leader is always under the leadership of the Lord. Without continued awe and devotion to the Lord, the leader's life is out of order.

Obedience: Reading the Word of God is not enough. The leader must carefully follow God's instructions. The leader must not "turn from the law to the right or to the left."

Humility: The leader is not to consider "himself better than" those he is leading. God's philosophy of servant-leadership was clearly explained and powerfully exemplified by Jesus.

How are you doing, Christian leader? These principles are challenging and continuing. At the end of the day, these are the areas in which we will be judged.

Lord, leadership - whether at church, work or home - is a weighty responsibility. By your Holy Spirit who lives in us, give us the desire and determination to be a leader led by you. In Jesus' name. Amen.

reflection

further suggested reading:

Deuteronomy 17-18

Our God Is Stronger

Deuteronomy 20:1

When you go to war against your enemies and see horses and chariots and an army greater than yours, do not be afraid of them, because the LORD your God, who brought you up out of Egypt, will be with you.

Are you fighting a pretty tough battle? Does the enemy seem bigger, faster and stronger than you? Do you feel fear and even panic? Stop right there! If you were fighting the battle alone, I'd say, "Run!" But you are not alone. The Lord your God is with you! He is bigger than any enemy. Let me say that again. He is bigger than **any enemy** you will ever face.

When the armies of Israel were about to go into battle, the priest addressed the army. Standing before the fearful soldiers, he said, "Do not be fainthearted or afraid; do not be terrified or give way to panic. For the Lord your God is the one who goes with you to fight for you and against your enemy to give you victory." Read those last four words again. God is fighting for you **to give you victory.**

Chris Tomlin sings a song that drives home today's passage. The name of the song is *Our God*. If you are facing a tough battle, I encourage you to download the song and make it a part of your playlist. Here are some of the words.

> *Our God is greater, our God is stronger,*
> *God you are higher than any other.*
> *Our God is Healer, awesome in power,*
> *Our God! Our God!*
>
> *Our God is greater, our God is stronger,*
> *God you are higher than any other.*
> *Our God, is Healer, awesome in power,*
> *Our God! Our God!*
>
> *And if Our God is for us, then who could ever stop us*
> *And if our God is with us, then what could stand against?*
> *And if Our God is for us, then who could ever stop us*
> *And if our God is with us, then what could stand against?*

Heavenly Father, you are our God! And we welcome you into our lives. We know you are with us. We acknowledge that you are greater, stronger and higher than any other. If you are with us, then what can stand against us? We love you for who you are and how you work in our lives. In Jesus' name. Amen.

further suggested reading:

Deuteronomy 19-20

Two Are Better Than One

February 27

Deuteronomy 22:1-4

If you see your fellow Israelite's ox or sheep straying, do not ignore it but be sure to take it back to its owner. If they do not live near you or if you do not know who owns it, take it home with you and keep it until they come looking for it. Then give it back. Do the same if you find their donkey or cloak or anything else they have lost. Do not ignore it. If you see your fellow Israelite's donkey or ox fallen on the road, do not ignore it. Help the owner get it to its feet.

Today's passage addresses the need for us to look out for one another. If a fellow Israelite saw a brother's ox or sheep straying, he was to take it back to its owner. If he did not know to whom the animal belonged, he was to care for it until the owner came. If a donkey or ox had fallen, the Israelite was to help the owner get the animal back on its feet. These are simple and straightforward instructions based in the theology of community.

The Christian life is not to be lived alone. God created us for community. Solomon said, "Two are better than one, because they have a good return for their labor: If either of them falls down, one can help the other up. But pity anyone who falls and has no one to help them up (Ecclesiastes 4:9-10).

We need each other on the journey. Traveling alone is not only lonely; it is also foolish. There will be times when we'll need to help pack for a move, mow a lawn for someone who is sick, do some grocery shopping for a shut-in or provide some words of encouragement for someone going through a tough stretch. And there are many things on the journey that will cause us to trip and fall. Pity anyone who falls and has no one to help him or her up.

Heavenly Father, thank you for community. Help us to never think we are better off alone. Help us to find the right people to go with us on the journey. In Jesus' name. Amen.

reflection

_____

_____

_____

_____

_____

_____

_____

further suggested reading:

Deuteronomy 21-26

The Path That Leads to Life

February 28

Deuteronomy 30:19-20

This day I call the heavens and the earth as witnesses against you that I have set before you life and death, blessings and curses. Now choose life, so that you and your children may live and that you may love the LORD your God, listen to his voice, and hold fast to him. For the LORD is your life, and he will give you many years in the land he swore to give to your fathers, Abraham, Isaac and Jacob.

The sovereign God gives us choices. Through his Word, he clearly explains the two roads we can take. One leads to death; the other to life. His desire is that we choose the path that leads to life. This choice not only produces blessing for us but for our children after us.

The life that God offers is found in himself. . . . "for the Lord is your life." He sent his Son to provide that life for us. Jesus said, "I have come that [you] may have life, and have it to the full" (John 10:10b). Through Jesus we can love God, hear his voice and hold fast to him. It is Jesus who brings us to the Father and keeps us there. A personal relationship with God comes only through Jesus.

What road are you on? Are you headed to the destination of death or life? Have you trusted in Jesus alone as the only One who can place you into a loving, personal, eternal relationship with God? If not, I encourage you to pray the prayer below. Simply praying the prayer will not save you. But if you have a true desire to know God, let this prayer be your guide.

Dear God, I know that I am on the wrong path. I admit that I am a sinner on the road headed away from you. I want to turn around and journey with you on the road to eternal life. I know that I cannot do that by myself. I know that you sent your Son, Jesus Christ, to die for my sins. Right now, I trust in Jesus as the only one who can provide true life, the life that is found in you. I trust in Jesus as the One who did for me what I cannot do for myself. I trust in Jesus as the only One who can place me in an eternal relationship with you. In Jesus' name. Amen.

reflection

_____

_____

_____

_____

_____

_____

further suggested reading:

Deuteronomy 27-30

64

Something To Hold Onto

February 29

Deuteronomy 32:3-4

I will proclaim the name of the LORD. Oh, praise the greatness of our God! He is the Rock, his works are perfect, and all his ways are just. A faithful God who does no wrong, upright and just is he.

Do you feel like your life has been shaken? Your health is failing, the prodigal child has not come home, your marriage is going through tough times, your job is going away? Those things and many others can cause our world to shake and our legs to weaken. During these times we need something to hold onto. We need a rock . . . like our God.

He will never be shaken by circumstances or shift with the inevitable challenges of life. Security is found in him alone. All his works are perfect. He does not make mistakes. "Oops!" is not in his vocabulary. All his ways are just. "Unfair" can never describe him. He is faithful. He will never leave us nor forsake us. He will always have your back.

Do you feel like your life has been shaken? Let me introduce you to the Rock. He is the loving God who desires an eternal relationship with you. He is the gracious God who longs to show you favor. He is the caring God who wants to protect you. He is the One who brings light to the darkness, calmness to anxiety, courage to a heart filled with fear. Don't you think it's time to quit trusting in yourself and cling to the Rock?

Heavenly Father, we proclaim your name. We praise your greatness. You are our Rock. Your works are perfect. Your ways are just. You are the faithful God who does no wrong. You are upright and just. We love you! We are privileged to be called your children. In Jesus' name. Amen.

reflection

further suggested reading:

Deuteronomy 31-34

Cross the Jordan

Joshua 1:10-11

So Joshua ordered the officers of the people: "Go through the camp and tell the people, 'Get your provisions ready. Three days from now you will cross the Jordan here to go in and take possession of the land the LORD your God is giving you for your own.'"

God is omnipotent! Nothing can thwart his plan. Yet, at the same time, he gives us the privilege of participating in his work on earth. He allows us to be used as instruments to carry out his plan. We can't do it without him; he chooses not to do it without us. I love the way Jerry Bridges explains this. Comparing our partnership with God to farming he says, "Farming is a joint venture between God and the farmer. The farmer cannot do what God must do, and God will not do what the farmer should do" (*The Pursuit of Holiness,* NAV Press, 1966, p.9).

In our verse today, it is clear that God is the One giving his people the land. But he instructs them to get the supplies ready. He gives them a timeline to physically cross the Jordan. He will be with them as they go into the new land and do the physical work of taking possession.

Are you doing your part in the joint venture with God? Certainly, you must follow God's direction and depend on his strength. But he expects you to get the supplies ready. It's time to move forward and cross your "Jordan." It's time to take possession of the great things that God has for you. What are you waiting for? Get up and get going! There are some great things in store on the other side of the Jordan!

Father, give us the confidence to know that we are following you and your plan. Then give us the strength and courage to get up and get the job done. In Jesus' name. Amen.

reflection

further suggested reading:

Joshua 1-5

Breaking Down the Walls

March 2

Joshua 6:20

When the trumpets sounded, the army shouted, and at the sound of the trumpet, when the men gave a loud shout, the wall collapsed; so everyone charged straight in, and they took the city.

The Art of War, written by Sun Tzu in 6 century BC, is one of the oldest books on military strategy. Each of its thirteen chapters is devoted to one aspect of warfare. Great military leaders like General Douglas MacArthur claim to have been inspired by the work. As comprehensive as the book is, there is no strategy recommended like the one God had for the defeat of Jericho.

For six days the fighting men of Israel were instructed to walk around the walled city of Jericho one time. On the seventh day, they were to walk around the city seven times. After the march the trumpeters were to "sound a loud blast," and all the people were to "give a loud shout." After that exercise, God promised that the wall of Jericho would collapse, and the people could go straight into the city.

Do you have any walls that need to be collapsed in your life? It's very possible you won't find a successful strategy online or in a bestselling "How To" book. Block out some time, and openly talk to the Lord about all the things keeping you from following hard after him. Believe me, he is an expert at breaking down the walls.

Father, I pray that each of us will spend time with you regarding the barriers in our lives that keep us from a more intimate and powerful relationship with you. Allow us to see the walls collapse. In Jesus' name. Amen.

reflection

_____
_____
_____
_____
_____
_____
_____
_____
_____

further suggested reading:

Joshua 6-8

Decisions Require Prayer

Joshua 9:14

The Israelites sampled their provisions but did not inquire of the LORD.

When God brought the Israelites across the Jordan into the land of promise, the word spread. The surrounding countries knew two things. First, Israel was going to try to conquer them, and second, the God of Israel was a powerful God. One country, Gibeon, decided on a plan of deception.

Pretending to be from a distant country, the leaders of Gibeon came to Israel. Although they lived next door, they dressed in old clothes, patched sandals and came with donkeys loaded with worn-out sacks and old wineskins. When they asked for a treaty, the Israelites "sampled their provisions" and agreed to a treaty of peace. But God's people "did not inquire of the Lord."

I was convicted when I read today's passage. How many times do I make decisions without spending time in prayer? How many times do I decide to do or not to do something by simply "sampling the provisions" (spreadsheets, test-drives, investment returns, outward appearance, etc.). Decisions require prayer. I know that, but knowing and not doing is a formula for failure.

Father, forgive me for depending on a "sampling of provisions." Forgive me for making decisions without spending needed time in prayer. Help me to depend on you and not on myself to make the choices that will honor you. In Jesus' name. Amen.

reflection

further suggested reading:

Joshua 9

God Listens to Man

Joshua 10:14

There has never been a day like it before or since, a day when the LORD listened to a human being. Surely the LORD was fighting for Israel!

Joshua led his entire army on an all-night march and caught the kings of the Amorites by surprise. The Lord threw the Amorites into confusion, "hurled large hailstones down on them from the sky," and in answer to Joshua's prayer for more fighting time, caused the sun to stop "in the middle of the sky." Indeed, "the Lord was fighting for Israel!"

Amazingly, God altered the creation pattern of day and night. But the most amazing thing in this story is not the sun stopping in the middle of the sky. It is the fact that the holy eternal God listens to man. And you know what? He still does.

Our prayers are not for the alteration of the sun's pattern, but they involve God's miraculous work just the same - salvation of a loved one, physical healing, strength to be a good witness through an illness, the determination to resist a temptation or the restoration of a relationship. And the miracle is that the holy God hears and answers our prayers. As the prophet says, "Surely the arm of the Lord is not too short to save, nor his ear too dull to hear" (Isaiah 59:1).

Oh LORD, I call to you; come quickly to me. Hear my voice when I call to you. May my prayer be set before you like incense; may the lifting up of my hands be like the evening sacrifice (Psalm 141:1-2). In Jesus' name. Amen.

reflection

_____

_____

_____

_____

_____

_____

_____

_____

_____

_____

further suggested reading:

Joshua 10-12

Sold Out

Joshua 14:11

I am still as strong today as the day Moses sent me out; I'm just as vigorous to go out to battle now as I was then.

One of my favorite characters in all of Scripture is a man named Caleb, a member of the twelve undercover agents sent by Moses to check out the Promised Land. While ten from the team convinced Israel that the land was unconquerable, Caleb, along with Joshua, said, "We should go up and take possession of the land, for we can certainly do it" (Numbers 13:30). Four decades later, Joshua and Caleb, the only ones left from the faithless generation, entered the Promised Land. At eighty-five years old, Caleb was as strong and vigorous and visionary as ever.

The word Scripture uses to describe this choice servant is "wholehearted" (Numbers 14:24; Joshua 14:8, 9, 14). He was a man whose heart was ignited with a passion to follow hard after God. He held nothing back. He didn't doubt God's promises or power. He was sold out, all in, ready to go wherever God called him to go and do whatever God called him to do.

We are in desperate need of more wholehearted servants like Caleb. We need men and women who are not sliding for home but rather are using all their gifts and resources to serve God until he calls them home. There is no such thing as retirement in the service of the Lord. Whether you are 15, 25, 45 or 85 - PRESS ON!

Heavenly Father, give us physical, emotional and spiritual strength to follow hard after you all the days of our lives. Never let us retire from your service. May the addition of years produce vigor and vision. May we be described as wholehearted servants of the living God. In Jesus' name. Amen.

reflection

_____

_____

_____

_____

_____

_____

_____

further suggested reading:

Joshua 18-21

Life Is Uncertain

Joshua 21:45

Not one of the Lord's good promises to the house of Israel failed; every one was fulfilled.

There are many things in life that change and take us by surprise. Illness barges in like an uninvited intruder. Death hits us hard like a rogue wave and bowls us over with grief. A separation and divorce was the last thing we thought would ever happen to us. We planned on retiring from the company; then the job went away. One thing is certain; life is uncertain.

But there is one thing that we can be sure of, one thing that will come to pass. We can live with the confidence of knowing that every promise of God will be fulfilled; not one of them will fail. "God is not a man, that he should lie, nor a son of man, that he should change his mind. Does he speak and then not act? Does he promise and not fulfill?" (Numbers 23:19).

Without God, life is a roller coaster of emotions. Without God, unexpected changes will blow us in every direction. Without God, our life is foundationless, like a house built on sand. But a relationship with God through his Son Jesus Christ changes everything. He is our constant. He is our anchor. When we know God, we will be able to say with Joshua, "[I know with all my heart and soul] that not one of all the good promises the Lord [my] God gave [me] has failed."

Father, thank you for all your promises. And thank you for keeping every one of them. In Jesus' name. Amen.

reflection

_____
_____
_____
_____
_____
_____
_____
_____
_____
_____
_____

further suggested reading:

Joshua 18-21

Stake of Commitment

March 7

Joshua 23:6; 24:15

Be very strong; be careful to obey all that is written in the Book of the Law of Moses without turning aside to the right or to the left. But if serving the Lord seems undesirable to you, then choose for yourselves this day whom you will serve . . . But as for me and my household, we will serve the Lord.

Many years had passed since God told Joshua to cross the Jordan River and lead the Israelites into the land of promise. Joshua, now "old and well advanced in years," stood before the people to give his farewell address. Here Joshua echoes what God told him many years earlier when the heavy responsibility of leadership was placed on his shoulders. Then Joshua drives a stake of commitment regarding the leadership of his family. The echoes are just as relevant today as they were the day Joshua gave this address to the leaders of Israel. And the commitment is needed today more than ever.

Be very strong. The journey of life is filled with winding roads and unexpected turns. There is continual temptation to give in and give up. We are always one bad decision, one unguarded moment, from a life-altering decision. We must rely on the Holy Spirit's strength. We must stay strong.

Obey the Word. God's Word is the GPS for the journey. But unlike the annoying voices of GPS's, his voice is strong and encouraging. As we read his Word, he speaks to our heart. Be still, listen to his voice and do what he tells you to do.

Don't compromise. There will always be opportunities for shortcuts on our journey. If we take the shortcuts of sin, we will always end up on the path to a dangerous destination. Stay on the path clearly marked by the Word. At times it may seem that you are the only one on the road of obedience. But don't compromise. Drive the stake of commitment - for me and my house, we will serve the Lord!

Father, remind us that you always provide the strength to handle all the twists and turns of life. Speak to us clearly through your Word. By your grace, keep us on the well-marked path all the way to eternity. In Jesus' name. Amen.

reflection

further suggested reading:

Joshua 22-24

Judges 2:10

After that whole generation had been gathered to their ancestors, another generation grew up, who knew neither the LORD nor what he had done for Israel.

After Joshua, "another generation grew up, who knew neither the Lord nor what he had done for Israel." Unbelievable! A group of people passed from childhood to adulthood without effectively being taught about the person of God and without being exposed to the experiences that would allow them to see God's power firsthand. How does that happen?

Well, a better question would be, Is that happening in your home with your children? Are you teaching your children about the Lord and backing it up with your life? What you say becomes irrelevant when your walk and talk don't jive. Are you placing your children in situations where they can experience God's faithfulness - stretching experiences where they have to depend on God? Are you giving your children the opportunity to own their faith? Faith is not an heirloom that we pass down. A living faith must be personally and powerfully experienced.

The fact is that we are not going to get out of this life alive. One day, all too soon, we will be gone. When our children leave our grave and walk to their cars, will they do so in the power of the Spirit or with meaningless religious remnants? What we say and do today will determine the answer to that question.

Lord, help us to pass on the power of a personal relationship with you. Don't let us leave behind a Judges 2:10 generation. In Jesus' name. Amen.

reflection

_____
_____
_____
_____
_____
_____
_____
_____

further suggested reading:

Judges 1-5

The Lord Is Peace

Judges 6:24

So Gideon built an altar to the LORD there and called it The LORD is Peace.

Gideon was minding his own business or trying to. Israel's enemy, the powerful and oppressive Midianites, had driven them into hiding. Gideon was threshing wheat in a hidden location. But God had bigger plans for Joash's son.

When God called Gideon to lead the Israelites against their enemy, he didn't jump at the opportunity. Gideon asked, "But Lord, how can I save Israel? My clan is the weakest in Manasseh, and I am the least in my family." God, however, makes a habit of using little people to do big things. To confirm the calling, God gave Gideon a sign delivered by the angel of the Lord (the pre-incarnate Christ). When Gideon realized who it was, he exclaimed, "Ah, Sovereign Lord! I have seen the angel of the Lord face to face!" But God reassured him, "Peace! Do not be afraid. You are not going to die." That's when Gideon built the altar and named it "The Lord is Peace."

No one, on his own, can see God and live. But there is One who intercedes for us. Jesus stands between the holy God and sinful man and by his death bridges the great separation. Paul writes, "Therefore, since we have been justified through faith, we have peace with God through our Lord Jesus Christ" (Romans 5:1). Only Jesus can deliver peace. Do you have that peace with God through Jesus?

Lord Jesus, thank you for giving us peace with God. Thank you for the price you paid in order to bring us to the Father. You are our peace! In your name we pray. Amen.

reflection

_____

_____

_____

_____

_____

_____

_____

_____

_____

_____

further suggested reading:

Judges 6-8

Open Arms

Judges 10:15-16

But Israel said to the Lord, "We have sinned. Do with us whatever you think best, but please rescue us now." Then they got rid of the foreign gods among them and served the Lord. And he could bear Israel's misery no longer.

Judges can be summed up with the book's last six words, "everyone did as he saw fit." The account describes seven cycles of Israel running from God, paying the consequences and then running back home.

In today's passage Israel had, once again, run from God and served pagan gods. Once again, sin's consequences caused them to cry out for help. Once again, God is merciful to his children "And he could bear Israel's misery no longer."

There are two truths that echo throughout this book, truths we cannot forget. First, running from God is a futile journey that dead ends in a cul-de-sac of consequences. Before we start down the path of sin, let's not be ignorant as to what waits at the end. Second, God is gracious. Regardless of how far we have gone, how long we have been gone or how much damage we've done, the loving Father waits with open arms to welcome his child (prodigal though he or she may be) back home.

Father, thank you for your great grace. We are sinners so often determined to do as we see fit. But when we crash and cry out, you hear our prayer, forgive us and welcome us back home. Lord, as we are so thankful for your grace of forgiveness, please help us to follow closely to you so that the cul-de-sac of consequences becomes a more rare experience in our lives. In Jesus' name. Amen.

reflection

_____

_____

_____

_____

_____

_____

_____

_____

_____

further suggested reading:

Judges 9-10

God Will Not Be Used

March 11

Judges 11:1

Jephthah the Gileadite was a mighty warrior. His father was Gilead; his mother was a prostitute.

Jephthah was a mighty warrior, but he was also the son of a prostitute. His brothers, by his father Gilead's legitimate wife, kicked him out of the house and wanted nothing to do with him until they needed a mighty warrior to lead them into battle. Funny how those things work.

But before an important battle with the Ammonites, Jephthah did a foolish thing. Instead of depending on God to fight for Israel, he made a bargain with God. Jephthah promised that if God would secure the victory, he would sacrifice as a burnt offering whatever came out of the front door of his house upon his return. Unfortunately, when he arrived, out came his daughter dancing to the tunes of a victory song. Jephthah was devastated.

One commentator wrapped up the story this way, "Thus all [Jephthah's] efforts to assure for himself a position of power in Israel by manipulating God backfired. God will not be used!" Jephthah's tragedy is a lesson for us all. Trying to manipulate God always backfires. He will not be used.

Father, forgive us for making deals with you as if your care and protection can be bought. Forgive us for trying to bargain for the things we want. Remind us often of the truth that your ways are founded in unconditional love, and you always have our best interest at heart. In Jesus' name. Amen.

reflection

further suggested reading:

Judges 11-12

What Am I Doing for the Sake of Christ?

March 12

Judges 16:28

Then Samson prayed to the Lord, "Sovereign Lord, remember me. God, please strengthen me just once more, and let me with one blow get revenge on the Philistines for my two eyes."

PBS's documentary on former President Bill Clinton is a four-hour treatment of his eight years in the White House. Unfortunately, many of those years (starting with his first campaign) were filled with scandal. Looking back on the time they served with him, many of his cabinet members and closest advisers celebrated the accomplishments but wondered what might have been accomplished without all the distractions.

Samson's twenty years of service in the nation of Israel was yet another administration filled with distractions. From his demand to marry a Philistine woman, to their "kind of" wedding, from high stake riddles to victory poems, from great physical strength to emotional immaturity, from Delilah to the sharing of his great secret, Samson's life was a bit of a train wreck . . . a life of "what could have been." Finally, it all ended in the Philistine temple, when Samson, performing a strong man's circus act, literally brought the house down.

Sad, isn't it, when a person wastes so much potential? Hmm . . . but . . . I have the Spirit of the living God living in me. I have the resurrection power right in my person. What am I doing for the sake of Christ? How are life's distractions keeping me from being all God wants me to be?

Father, keep me from the distractions that keep me for living full out for you. Help me understand and apply the power of your Holy Spirit. Don't let me waste my life. In Jesus' name. Amen.

reflection

_____
_____
_____
_____
_____
_____
_____
_____
_____

further suggested reading:

Judges 13-16

Train Wreck

March 13

Judges 21:25

In those days Israel had no king; everyone did as they saw fit.

You have to admit, the book of Judges is a tough read. Don't get me wrong. It is the inerrant Word of God and is "useful for teaching, rebuking, correcting and training in righteousness." But these years of Israel's history reported in this book can best be described in two words: "Train Wreck!"

Judges describes a generation "who knew neither the Lord nor what he had done for Israel." There are a few highlights like Deborah, but even the well-known characters are greatly flawed. Gideon was not only known for his fleece but also for the idol he made at the end of his life that became a "snare" to him and his family. Samson lived a reckless life ending in one last demonstration of strength that killed 3,000 Philistines and himself. And the story of the Levite and his concubine . . . well, it makes your stomach turn.

But that's just the point. This was a time in Israel's history when the people did not know God. There was no godly leader to give guidance. Everyone did as he saw fit. The same thing happens today. When we do what is right in our own eyes, our life can be described in two words: "Train Wreck!"

Father, please let this book be a warning to us. Keep us from self-counsel and rationalization. Keep us from doing the things that seem right in our own eyes. Keep us in your Word, following your instructions. Keep us on the road that leads to blessing and life. In Jesus' name. Amen.

reflection

further suggested reading:

Judges 17-21

Ruth 1:20-21

"Don't call me Naomi," she told them. "Call me Mara, because the Almighty has made my life very bitter. I went away full, but the LORD has brought me back empty. Why call me Naomi? The LORD has afflicted me; the Almighty has brought misfortune upon me."

Naomi was convinced that God had made her life miserable. Honestly, she had good reasons for such feelings. Her husband had died. Then her two married sons died, leaving no heir to carry on the family name. To express the feelings of her heart, Naomi changed her name to Mara, which means "bitter."

When a famine forced Naomi to return to her home in Judah, she kissed her daughters-in-law good-bye and started the long journey. But one daughter-in-law refused to leave Naomi. Ruth, so aligned with Naomi in spirit, left her family of origin and went with her mother-in-law. The rest is a story of God's love and grace. God had prepared a relative named Boaz who was waiting back home. Through Boaz, God redeemed Ruth and Naomi from their situation. Boaz married Ruth, and God blessed them with a son to carry on the family name. Through this line God sent King David and, later, his Son to redeem us from sin.

I admit that I don't always understand how God works. When Naomi changed her name to Mara, she wasn't exactly saying, "I know God loves me and will somehow work all this out for my good." But her story is yet another reminder that he always does. When you feel like changing your name to convey your feelings about God, just remember that he never changes his. God's name is always faithful. He will never leave you nor forsake you.

Father, for those whose hearts feel bitter toward you, surround them with your faithful love. When we can't understand, give us that peace that passes human understanding. Remind us that you are always faithful. In Jesus' name. Amen.

reflection

_____

_____

_____

_____

_____

_____

_____

further suggested reading:

Ruth 1-4

Make a Promise

1 Samuel 1:24-28

After he was weaned, she took the boy with her, young as he was, along with a three-year-old bull, an ephah of flour and a skin of wine, and brought him to the house of the LORD at Shiloh. When the bull had been sacrificed, they brought the boy to Eli, and she said to him, "Pardon me, my lord. As surely as you live, I am the woman who stood here beside you praying to the LORD. I prayed for this child, and the LORD has granted me what I asked of him. So now I give him to the LORD. For his whole life he will be given over to the LORD." And he worshiped the LORD there.

Hannah desperately wanted a child and prayed fervently for God to grant her request. In passionate prayer, she "poured out [her] soul before the Lord." She knew that every child was a miracle from God, not simply the product of a biological function. If God would grant her request, Hannah promised to "give [the child] to the Lord for all the days of his life." God finally gave Hannah a son, and now it was time to make good on her promise.

Hannah took her son, around three-years-old, and left him at the temple to live his life for the Lord. There had been tears as she prayed for a child. You can bet there were more tears that day as she left her son and made the lonely journey back home with empty arms. It's one thing to make a promise; it's another thing to keep it. But Hannah kept her promise even when it hurt.

John and Betsy were one of the first couples we met in Pittsburgh. They were fellow Oklahomans, and we bonded quickly. When their daughter, Lauren, was in high school, she wanted to take a lengthy summer mission trip to a difficult part of the world. Letting her go was not an easy decision. As they struggled with this, I remember Betsy saying, "When she was little, we dedicated her to the Lord and told him to use her in any way he wanted. Now we have to keep that promise." Today Lauren and her husband serve the Lord "undercover" in a country on the other side of the world. It's one thing to have a nice baby dedication with family and friends. But, parents, are you willing to follow through on your commitment? It's one thing to make a promise; it's another thing to keep it.

Father, we want our children live for you. Help us not to restrict their service by being overly protective or possessive. Keep us from keeping our children from following hard after you. Remind us that as much as we love them, you love them more. Use them for Christ's sake. Amen.

reflection

further suggested reading:

1 Samuel 1-3

Be Careful What You Pray For

1 Samuel 8:19-20

But the people refused to listen to Samuel. "No!" they said. "We want a king over us. Then we will be like all the other nations, with a king to lead us and to go out before us and fight our battles."

Samuel governed Israel throughout his life, and God blessed the nation with peace. But when the prophet grew old, Israel wanted a change.

The nation was tired of having an old prophet riding around the country on a donkey. They wanted to be like the other nations with a king riding in a chariot flanked by soldiers. In their desire to be like the other nations, Israel was not rejecting Samuel. God said, "They have rejected me as their king." As a result, God gave Israel their first king, a reluctant leader named Saul.

In the story of Israel's first king we learn an important lesson. Sometimes God answers your prayers, and you live to regret it. And from this lesson we learn an important application. Be very careful what you pray for.

Father, keep us in your Word and walking close to you so that our desires match yours. Protect us from prayers we pray when we are disconnected from you. In Jesus' name. Amen.

reflection

_____

_____

_____

_____

_____

_____

_____

_____

_____

_____

_____

_____

further suggested reading:

1 Samuel 4-8

The Appearance Trap

1 Samuel 9:2

Kish had a son named Saul, as handsome a young man as could be found anywhere in Israel, and he was a head taller than anyone else.

When it came time for Israel to choose their first king, what kind of criteria do you think they used? What were they looking for in the man who would lead them? Honesty? Integrity? Leadership? Not quite. Check out today's verse. Israel got caught in the trap of appearance.

But then again, the appearance trap is still snapping shut on many victims today. More than a few young men and women have fallen in love with a face or a body before they ever saw the person's heart. Presidential elections have become more about camera presence than political substance. Maybe it's a coincidence, but in the twenty-eight presidential elections since 1900, the shorter candidate has won only seven times. And then, maybe it's not a coincidence.

Here's the problem - Saul was great to look at but a train-wreck to follow. The lesson is a simple one: Don't choose a king by his cover (or a wife, husband, friend, president for that matter). Beautiful bodies lose their lure when they house a shriveled heart.

Father, help us to be discerning enough to not be caught in the appearance trap and live to regret it. In Jesus' name. Amen.

reflection

further suggested reading:

1 Samuel 9

A Reluctant Leader

1 Samuel 10:21-24

But when they looked for him, he was not to be found. So they inquired further of the LORD, "Has the man come here yet?" And the LORD said, "Yes, he has hidden himself among the supplies." They ran and brought him out, and as he stood among the people he was a head taller than any of the others. Samuel said to all the people, "Do you see the man the LORD has chosen? There is no one like him among all the people." Then the people shouted, "Long live the king!"

This verse always makes me chuckle. Israel wanted a king but got caught in the trap of appearance. They chose a man who was handsome and tall. But when it came time for the coronation, he was hiding "among the supplies." Saul was a reluctant leader.

Be leery of reluctant leaders. These are people placed in positions that they are not ready for or prepared for. Someone (parent, friend, management team or congregation) pushed them to the front when they wanted to stand in the back. Leaders were made to lead. Reluctant leaders were made to do something else, just as important, but something other than leading.

Be leery of reluctant leaders. Their skin is not thick enough, their roots aren't deep enough and their commitment is not strong enough. You can be on the right bus but in the wrong seat. And when reluctant leaders like Saul are behind the wheel, get ready to hear the screams of a busload of people going off the road and over the cliff.

Father, may we not push people to the front who shouldn't be there. Help us not to impose our will on others. May we seek your will in the lives of those we love. In Jesus' name. Amen.

reflection

further suggested reading:

1 Samuel 10-12

Turn to God

March 19

1 Samuel 14:6

Jonathan said to his young armor-bearer, "Come, let's go over to the outpost of those uncircumcised men. Perhaps the LORD will act in our behalf. Nothing can hinder the LORD from saving, whether by many or by few."

King Saul was sitting under a pomegranate tree. A few days earlier, his army was 3,000 soldiers strong, but due to his impatience and disobedience, 2,400 had deserted. The remaining soldiers were not anxious to go up against the Philistines' 3,000 chariots, 6,000 charioteers, and "soldiers as numerous as the sand on the seashore." Sitting under the pomegranate tree seemed like a safe thing to do.

But Saul's son, Jonathan, was not comfortable sitting in the shade. Check out today's passage. He was ready to take on the entire Philistine army with God. When God gave him the okay, he climbed up a cliff to the waiting Philistines (not good military strategy) with his armor bearer behind him (really bad military strategy) and routed the Philistines as God struck panic in the whole army with his presence and an earthquake.

It's amazing what you can do when God is on your side. Giants fall. Armies flee. The ground shakes. Strength for obedience is given. Peace replaces panic. His presence is actually felt and experienced. Are you facing an impossible situation? Turn to God. "Perhaps the Lord will act on [your] behalf. Nothing can hinder the Lord from saving, whether by many or by few."

Father, thank you for acting on our behalf by sending your Son to the cross. Since you didn't spare Jesus for us, we know you will give us everything we need. In Jesus' name. Amen.

reflection

_____
_____
_____
_____
_____
_____
_____
_____

further suggested reading:

1 Samuel 13-15

Only a Boy Named David

1 Samuel 17:33

Saul replied, "You are not able to go out against this Philistine and fight him; you are only a young man, and he has been a warrior from his youth."

"Only a boy named David, only a little sling." Remember that song? "Only a boy named David but he could pray and sing." Sing it with me. "Only a boy named David, only a rippling brook. Only a boy named David but five little stones he took." Still singing? "And one little stone went in the sling, and the sling went round and round (repeat this line and then sing round and round several hundred times). Finally, David let the rock fly "and the giant came (slow and in a deep voice) tumb . . . ling . . . down!" One more time . . . this time with all the motions! Ready? (I was never big on motions. The giant tumbling down part was cool, but the "rippling brook" motion bothered me. You hold your hands out in front of you, wiggle your fingers and then move your hands from side to side. For some reason, I felt like boys should not be caught dead doing that motion.)

In our passage today, Saul sold David short. The statement "You are only a boy," while certainly a fact, was also Saul's assessment of David's ability. You're not big enough. You're not strong enough. You're not experienced enough. Goliath has been fighting since he was a boy and David, you are a boy! Let the men handle this situation. Trouble was that the men were not handling the situation. Every time the giant took one small step forward, they took one giant leap backwards. God chose to work through a boy to demonstrate his mighty power.

Don't sell our children short. God does big work in small packages. Always has . . . always will.

Father, thank you for our children. May we honor them for your work in their lives. May we be the mentors and models that encourage them to step up against the giants. In Jesus' name. Amen.

reflection

_____
_____
_____
_____
_____
_____
_____
_____

further suggested reading:

1 Samuel 16-19

Love the Lord Your God

 *March 21*

1 Samuel 20:16-17

So Jonathan made a covenant with the house of David, saying, "May the LORD call David's enemies to account." And Jonathan had David reaffirm his oath out of love for him, because he loved him as he loved himself.

The story of David and Jonathan is one of true friendship. The bond they shared was a healthy, deep and binding love based on the same purpose for life and the same passion for God. It was a love stronger than blood, deeper than royal privilege and threaded with a true sense of justice.

Jonathan's love for David was genuinely sacrificial. He lost so David could win. He risked so David could reign. He stepped aside so David could step up. Protecting David from his jealous father meant no throne for Jonathan. Yet he knew that neither tradition nor lineage could stand in God's way. He was determined to obey God rather than men.

Jonathan had the second greatest commandment down: Love your neighbor as yourself. No doubt that started with a heart committed to the greatest commandment: Love the Lord your God with all your heart, soul, mind and strength. When we start by loving God with our whole being it flows from there. If you are having trouble with the second greatest commandment, start with the first.

Father, give us the desire and commitment to love you with all our heart, soul, mind and strength. Then let that love flow to those whom you place in our lives. In Jesus' name. Amen.

reflection

_____

_____

_____

_____

_____

_____

_____

_____

_____

_____

_____

further suggested reading:

1 Samuel 20-23

An Emotional Furnace

1 Samuel 25:21-22

David had just said, "It's been useless all my watching over [Nabal's] property in the wilderness so that nothing of his was missing. He has paid me back evil for good. May God deal with David, be it ever so severely, if by morning I leave alive one male of all who belong to him!"

Have you ever overreacted? Blown up? Experienced an emotional tsunami? You were hanging in and hanging tough through a difficult time, but then something happened . . . the proverbial straw that broke the camel's back . . . and you let loose. That's what happened to David in today's passage.

David and his ragtag army were running from Saul in the Desert of Moan. A wealthy man, named Nabal, lived in the area, and David sent a few of his men to request some food. When Nabal refused, David detonated! He sent 400 armed soldiers to kill Nabal and his shepherds. Talk about killing a gnat with a sledgehammer! Thankfully, Nabal's wife, Abigail, intervened and stopped the massacre.

During the journey of life each of us spends some time on the emotional edge. We cannot escape fatigue, disappointment and stress. These are dangerous times. Reactions (and overreactions) can cause much collateral damage. But our trust in God, even in the heat of pressure cooker situations, makes all the difference. You can trust him and depend on him . . . even in the midst of an emotional furnace.

Father, someone reading this today is going through a very difficult time. Life presents challenges from without and within. In the midst of the heat, cool them with the calm of your Spirit. In Jesus' name. Amen.

reflection

further suggested reading:

1 Samuel 24-26

Self-Counsel

1 Samuel 27:1

But David thought to himself, "One of these days I will be destroyed by the hand of Saul. The best thing I can do is to escape to the land of the Philistines. Then Saul will give up searching for me anywhere in Israel, and I will slip out of his hand."

There are times when I can convince myself of almost anything. I can rationalize my decisions. When I give myself advice, it's exactly what I want to hear. Self-counsel is like emotional comfort food. It is rich and savory, but it clogs our spiritual arteries.

After running from Saul for over eight years, David was worn out. Coming off a great spiritual victory in which he refused to kill Saul, David "thought to himself." He forgot (or doubted) God's promises and took matters into his own hands. The future king of Israel sought protection in the land of the Philistines. The next sixteen months, living in the land of the enemy, did not make David's life highlight film.

Self-counsel leads to self-directed actions and leaves God out of the picture. An excerpt from the devotional *Jesus Calling* sums it up well. "When your thoughts flow freely, they tend to move toward problems. Your focus gets snagged on a given problem, circling round and round it in attempts to gain mastery. Your energy is drained away from other matters through the negative focus. Worst of all, you lose sight of me" (*Jesus Calling*, Sarah Young, Thomas Neison, 2004).

Lord Jesus, guard us from self-counsel. Please help us to never lose sight of you. In your name we pray. Amen.

reflection

_____
_____
_____
_____
_____
_____
_____

further suggested reading:

1 Samuel 27-31

True Friendship

2 Samuel 1:25-26

How the mighty have fallen in battle! Jonathan lies slain on your heights. I grieve for you, Jonathan my brother; you were very dear to me. Your love for me was wonderful, more wonderful than that of women.

For ten years David had been running from Saul. Now the fugitive life was over. But David was not in the mood for celebration. Saul and his son Jonathan were dead. David wrote a lament and ordered that the men of Judah be taught the words. David wanted the former king and his son remembered and honored.

David had never known a kindred spirit like Jonathan. They had the same purpose in life and the same passion for God. More than once, Jonathan saved David's life. Although he was the king's son, Jonathan acknowledged David as the next king and made the sacrifices for that to happen.

Some read today's passage and conclude that an inappropriate relationship existed between David and Jonathan. But that is not the case. Neither is David suggesting that marital love is inferior to a friendship. David is drawing attention to Jonathan's great sacrifice and self-denying commitment. David had never known a friend like Jonathan. And as he took the throne, he never would again.

Father, help us develop friendships that are built on the same purpose for life and the same passion for God. Help us to be friends that demonstrate the great sacrifice and self-denying commitment of Jonathan. In Jesus' name. Amen.

reflection

_____
_____
_____
_____
_____
_____
_____
_____
_____
_____

further suggested reading:

2 Samuel 1-2

Blind Spot

2 Samuel 3:1-5

The war between the house of Saul and the house of David lasted a long time. David grew stronger and stronger, while the house of Saul grew weaker and weaker. Sons were born to David in Hebron: His firstborn was Amnon the son of Ahinoam of Jezreel; his second, Kileab the son of Abigail the widow of Nabal of Carmel; the third, Absalom the son of Maakah daughter of Talmai king of Geshur; the fourth, Adonijah the son of Haggith; the fifth, Shephatiah the son of Abital; and the sixth, Ithream the son of David's wife Eglah. These were born to David in Hebron.

Way to go, David! You are the newly appointed King of Judah! You are off to a great start and learning the ropes of running a country. You are developing a strong military. The house of Saul is toast. David, you have just been blessed with six, count 'em, six sons! But David, David, David! What's up with the six wives? What were you thinking?

Blame it on the culture. Blame it on the "times." Blame it on the hardness of hearts. Blame it on whatever you want, but David was living with a blind spot. When it came to marriage, David missed some pretty important instruction, don't you think? Like one man, one woman, one flesh. Blind spots . . . in the life of the man after God's own heart. Amazing, isn't it?

Do you have any blind spots? Any areas of obedience you overlook or just flat miss? I bet you do. You can bet I have mine. Better deal with them. Ask your spouse or a trusted friend to point them out. Ask God to bring light to the dark area. Take off the blinders and deal with your blind spots before you get blindsided.

Father, please give us the humility and discernment to ask others to point out in our life what we can't see ourselves. In Jesus' name. Amen.

reflection

_____

_____

_____

_____

_____

_____

further suggested reading:

2 Samuel 3-4

You Are God

2 Samuel 7:28-29

Sovereign LORD, you are God! Your covenant is trustworthy, and you have promised these good things to your servant. Now be pleased to bless the house of your servant, that it may continue forever in your sight; for you, Sovereign LORD, have spoken, and with your blessing the house of your servant will be blessed forever."

People respond to a "No" from God in many different ways. Some become bitter. They conclude God cannot be trusted. Some become paralyzed. They conclude God should not be served. Some become cynical. They conclude God must not love them. But check out David's response in today's passage, right after God told the king that he was not the man to build the temple.

David recognized God's work in the past. God's gracious hand had established the nation in strength. David acknowledged God's promises. Then David summed up his prayer with this declaration, "Sovereign Lord, you are God!" (2 Samuel 7:28a).

God didn't answer your prayer? Yes, I know it is very disappointing. Yes, I know the request was truly the desire of your heart. But can I encourage you? Can I encourage you to get on your knees before God? Thank him for his past "yes's." Thank him for all his future promises. And then from the depth of your being, make this declaration, "Sovereign Lord, you are God!" Don't ask God to change his answer; ask him to change your heart.

Father, I admit that I am disappointed when your answer is "No." But today I declare that you are God, and I am not. In Jesus' name, Amen.

reflection

_____

_____

_____

_____

_____

_____

_____

_____

further suggested reading:

2 Samuel 5-7

Great Grace

2 Samuel 9:6-7

When Mephibosheth son of Jonathan, the son of Saul, came to David, he bowed down to pay him honor. David said, "Mephibosheth!" "At your service" he replied. "Don't be afraid," David said to him, "for I will surely show you kindness for the sake of your father Jonathan. I will restore to you all the land that belonged to your grandfather Saul, and you will always eat at my table."

In one moment his life was changed permanently. Fearing for her life, his nanny had scooped up the five-year-old and had run for safety. He fell out of her arms. The fall must have been vicious. The boy's feet were irreparably injured. He grew up as an invalid in a time when kindness was seldom shown to the physically handicapped. But one man was intent on showing kindness to this last son of Jonathan. The story of David and Mephibosheth is a story of great grace.

Mephibosheth could offer nothing. Yet David gave him "everything that belonged to Saul and his family." Mephibosheth could not walk. Yet everyday he sat in a seat of privilege and honor at David's table. Mephibosheth was the recipient of great grace.

Are you involved in a story of great grace? How about giving to someone who can offer nothing in return? How about serving a person in need? How about taking food to a local mission? How about doing something for which you will receive nothing? When you experience your story of grace, you'll find that the simple act of showing grace turns out to be the most powerful experience.

Father, I pray that today you will help us write a story of grace. Help us to do one thing for which we will receive nothing in return. In Jesus' name, Amen.

reflection

_____
_____
_____
_____
_____
_____
_____
_____

further suggested reading:

2 Samuel 8-10

Check Your Heart

2 Samuel 11:2-3

One evening David got up from his bed and walked around on the roof of the palace. From the roof he saw a woman bathing. The woman was very beautiful, and David sent someone to find out about her.

What Eve did in the Garden and Achan did in Jericho, David did in Jerusalem. Like a lamb going to slaughter, he followed the three-part pattern of temptation - he saw, he wanted and he took. While each part of temptation is luring, it's the sum of the three that equals sin. And sin, even forgiven sin, always carries consequences.

After that night with Bathsheba, things were never the same. David's son, Absalom, killed another son, Amnon. Absalom conspired to take the throne from his father, and David had to run for his life. While he was gone, Absalom had sexual liaisons on the roof of the palace for all to see. Finally, Absalom was killed in battle. Certainly, damage was done to David's reputation. As one has said, "The beard of reputation once shorn is hard to grow back."

Ask God to check your heart. Examine your sexual temptations that lead to the sins of lust, pornography and adultery. Examine your materialistic tendencies that lead to the sins of greed and avarice. Examine your areas of personal pride that always go before a fall. Each part of temptation is dangerous enough. Don't let them add up to sin.

Search me, God, and know my heart; test me and know my anxious thoughts. See if there is any offensive way in me, and lead me in the way everlasting. In Jesus' name. Amen.

reflection

further suggested reading:

2 Samuel 11-14

Monument to Self

2 Samuel 18:18

During his lifetime Absalom had taken a pillar and erected it in the King's Valley as a monument to himself, for he thought, "I have no son to carry on the memory of my name." He named the pillar after himself, and it is called Absalom's Monument to this day.

You've heard the phrase "memo to self." Have you heard the phrase from today's passage "monument to self?" Here's what it looks like.

It is a tall pillar erected with pride and greed, decorated with lust and power. Blowing in the breeze at the top are banners of momentary pleasure and self-gratification. There, for all to see, chiseled in big letters, is the name of its maker. But one of the big problems with a monument to self is its foundation. It is never dug deeply enough to hold the thing upright. It is only a matter of time before someone yells, "Timber!" or "Fore!" or whatever one yells for a falling monument. Monuments to self always come crumbling down.

There is only one "monument" that can stand - a life transformed by Jesus. It is erected by grace through faith, "decorated" by the atoning blood of the Perfect Sacrifice. And there in its deep solid foundation is chiseled the name of its Maker. This life will stand forever.

Father, show us now if we have erected any monuments to self. If so, help us tear them down. May your great name be chiseled on our hearts. In Jesus' name. Amen.

reflection

_____

_____

_____

_____

_____

_____

_____

_____

_____

further suggested reading:

2 Samuel 15-18

Consequences of Sin

2 Samuel 19:6

You love those who hate you and hate those who love you. You have made it clear today that the commanders and their men mean nothing to you. I see that you would be pleased if Absalom were alive today and all of us were dead.

David's emotions were raw. His son, Absalom, had betrayed him and chased him from the palace. David's men, fighting for their king, killed his son. David grieved the loss. He wept and mourned for Absalom, covered his face and "cried aloud, "O my son Absalom! O Absalom, my son, my son!'" The victorious soldiers "stole into the city that day as men steal in who are ashamed when they flee from battle." Can you imagine the emotion? You won the battle by killing your son.

But there was a bigger burden on David's heart. Absalom's rise to power, insurrection and death were all a consequence of David's sin with Bathsheba. Sin is never to be treated in a flippant manner. What a man sows, he also reaps.

Today's passage issues a strong warning. Sin always brings consequences. It may be pleasurable for a time. You may think that your rebellion was hidden from God. You may even think that because the consequences were not immediate, they are not coming. But here is the solemn truth. Be sure your sins will find you out. All of us need to think about the outcome of sin before the act of sin.

Father, keep our hearts tender toward you. Keep us close to your side. Draw us in when we start to stray. Protect us from sin and its consequences. We pray in Jesus' name. Amen.

reflection

_____

_____

_____

_____

_____

_____

_____

_____

_____

_____

further suggested reading:

2 Samuel 19-20

Who Is God Besides the Lord?

March 31

2 Samuel 22:31-32

As for God, his way is perfect: The LORD's word is flawless; he shields all who take refuge in him. For who is God besides the LORD? And who is the Rock except our God?

David's life was not a bed of roses. His twenties were spent running from the jealous King Saul. His thirties were spent uniting a divided kingdom. In his fifth decade, there was that little problem with Bathsheba. After that, consequences to his sin sprouted like unwelcome weeds. But in the midst of all his challenges, even the self-inflicted ones, this man after God's own heart never wandered far from God. The following are some of the truths that David took to the grave:

- **The holy God is perfect.** Following the holy God will always have you walking on the right path.

- **The Lord's word is flawless.** Everything God says is right. His promises are always true.

- **God is a shield.** He is our protector in the midst of every storm and attack.

- **God is our Rock.** He is immovable and unchangeable, the firm foundation.

No one sails on glassy, calm waters all the way home. Our ship will get rocked! But today's passage gives us some truths to nail down. And as we sail for home, we can say with David, "Who is God besides the Lord?"

Father, thank you for your perfect way, your flawless word and your constant protection. You are our solid foundation. There is no God besides you. Thank you in Jesus' name. Amen.

reflection

_____

_____

_____

_____

_____

_____

_____

further suggested reading:

2 Samuel 21-24

Words Every Leader Needs To Hear

1 Kings 2:1-3

When the time drew near for David to die, he gave a charge to Solomon his son. "I am about to go the way of all the earth," he said. "So be strong, act like a man, and observe what the LORD your God requires: Walk in obedience to him, and keep his decrees and commands, his laws and regulations, as written in the Law of Moses."

Today's passage records some of King David's last words. This charge was spoken to his son, Solomon, who would follow him as Israel's leader. Absent is the poetry that is found in many of David's psalms. His message to Solomon is straightforward and to the point. They are words every leader needs to hear.

Be strong. I am sick of leaders acquiescing at the sign of any opposition. Leaders have to stand for what they believe regardless of the cost.

Act like a man. The feminization of men is seen throughout our culture. It is time for men to provide the leadership that God calls us to. David did not call Solomon to act like a "caveman" but a godly man.

Observe what the Lord your God requires. A godly man submits to the Lord and his requirements. He is determined to "walk in obedience" and to follow God's instruction.

Men, I don't know what will need to change in your life to apply this instruction, but I am asking you to pray for the courage to make any changes necessary. Generations will be impacted by your commitment to be strong, act like a man and walk in obedience.

Father, help us be men who are morally strong, who provide godly leadership and who follow hard after you in obedience. In Jesus' name. Amen.

reflection

_____

_____

_____

_____

_____

_____

further suggested reading:

1 Kings 1-4

Counterfeit Gods

April 2

1 Kings 8:22-23

Then Solomon stood before the altar of the LORD in front of the whole assembly of Israel, spread out his hands toward heaven and said: "Lord, the God of Israel, there is no God like you in heaven above or on earth below - you who keep your covenant of love with your servants who continue wholeheartedly in your way."

It was a great day of celebration. Israel was at peace, and the temple was complete. The priests brought the ark of the Lord's covenant to its place in the inner sanctuary. Solomon stood before the people and professed, " . . . there is no God like you in heaven above or on earth below." We know that to be true, but far too often our actions tell a different story.

In his book, *Counterfeit Gods*, Timothy Keller writes, "A counterfeit god is anything so central and essential to your life that, should you lose it, your life would be hardly worth living. A [counterfeit god] is whatever you look at and say in your heart of hearts, 'If I have that, then I'll feel my life has meaning, then I'll know I have value, then I'll feel significant and secure.'" Keller then lists counterfeit gods ranging from family and children, to secure and comfortable circumstances, to political and social causes. Convicting, isn't it?

Everyone follows someone or something. As believers, we have to make sure the one true God holds that central and essential part of our lives. There is no one like him in heaven above or earth below. Make the adjustments and changes in your life to demonstrate you follow him alone.

Father, show us if we are following counterfeit gods, point out what they are and help us make the changes to follow you and you alone. In Jesus' name. Amen.

reflection

further suggested reading:

1 Kings 5-8

Fully Devoted

1 Kings 11:4

As Solomon grew old, his wives turned his heart after other gods, and his heart was not fully devoted to the LORD his God, as the heart of David his father had been.

"He had it all!" For most people, that statement is an exaggeration. For Solomon, it's an understatement. When the Queen of Sheba says after seeing your kingdom, "not even half was told me; in wisdom and wealth you have far exceeded the report I heard," you know you have arrived. But having everything you want is not always the best thing for the heart.

Along the journey of amassing great wealth, Solomon accumulated a few wives - 700 to be exact. He added 300 concubines to the mix just to make things interesting. And you think you have trouble remembering your wife's birthday. Some of these marriages were for political gain; others came from the desires of an undisciplined heart. But in the end, his pagan wives turned his heart after pagan gods. Solomon's father, David, was "fully devoted." Solomon was fully divided. And after Solomon, the kingdom was divided as well.

I am pretty sure none of you reading this has 700 spouses, let alone 300 concubines. But do you have anything that turns your heart away from God? It doesn't matter if it is one thing or many things. God does not entertain rivals. You are either fully devoted to him or you're not. Which is it?

Father, please examine my heart and highlight anything that is causing divided allegiance. Then give me the courage to get rid of any other god. In Jesus' name. Amen.

reflection

_____

_____

_____

_____

_____

_____

_____

_____

further suggested reading:

1 Kings 9-11

Self-Counsel

1 Kings 12:26

Jeroboam thought to himself, "The kingdom will now likely revert to the house of David."

Self-counsel. It will get you into trouble every time. Left to ourselves, we can rationalize just about anything . . . even sin. Here are some examples of self-counsel that did not end well.

- Running from Saul and exhausted, David **thought to himself,** "One of these days I will be destroyed by the hand of Saul. The best thing I can do is to escape to the land of the Philistines" (1 Samuel 27:1). Don't do it, David! Joining forces with the enemy is not a good idea. To make a long story short, the whole episode ended with David's men almost stoning him to death.

- Haman, whose plan was to eliminate the Jews, thought he was going to receive high honor from the king. He **thought to himself,** "Who is there that the king would rather honor than me?" But in the end he was "honored" with a hanging. (See Esther 6).

- Jesus told a parable about a rich fool who had more crops than barns. The man **thought to himself,** "What shall I do? I have no place to store my crops." He solved the problem by building bigger barns, but God had other plans for the man. "You fool! This very night your life will be demanded from you. Then who will get what you have prepared for yourself?" (See Luke 12).

In today's passage, Jeroboam, who was contending for leadership in the turmoil following Solomon's death, convinced himself that another person would be crowned king. To keep this from happening, he built golden calves for the people to worship instead of the living God. Not a good idea.

Self-counsel. It will get you in trouble every time.

Father, may we be wise enough to learn from the mistakes of others without making the mistakes of others our own. Lord, may we be wise enough to learn from past mistakes and not repeat them. In Jesus' name. Amen.

reflection

further suggested reading:

1 Kings 12-16

Worn Out by Obedience

1 Kings 19:3-4

Elijah was afraid and ran for his life . . . He came to a broom bush, sat down under it and prayed that he might die. "I have had enough, LORD," he said.

Let's face it. There are times when obedience will flat wear you out. Ask the teenager determined to remain sexually pure when his hormones feel like the grand finale of a Fourth of July fireworks display. Ask the young adult who is committed to wait for God's choice when her friends are hooking up with their choices. Ask the husband and wife who vowed "for better, for worse" and are experiencing a long stretch of "worse." Ask the business person whose peers are getting ahead by making promises that they can't keep and products that won't work. You can love God with a "Crazy Love" - but don't forget that the spiritual journey is made up of stepping stones of obedience, and obedience is hard. Just ask Elijah.

Right before today's passage, Elijah had one of his greatest victories. In the showdown at Mt. Carmel, God demonstrated his power through Elijah in a miraculous way, and the prophet demolished (literally) 450 prophets of Baal. After the great victory, he heard that Jezebel was out to kill him. Amazing, isn't it? Standing up for God in Chapter 18 and running for his life in Chapter 19. Obedience can wear you out.

God told Elijah to take a deep breath and stand in his presence. God sent a microburst that shattered rocks around the prophet, then shook the ground with an earthquake and finally sent a fire. But the Lord was not in the wind, quake or fire. Then came God's "gentle whisper" that calmed Elijah's fears and reinvigorated his spirit. Worn out by obedience? Listen, shhhh, for God's gentle whisper.

Father, we are busy, tired and distracted. Obedience is hard. Help us to calm ourselves in you. We wait for your gentle whisper. In Jesus' name. Amen.

reflection

---

further suggested reading:

1 Kings 17-19

God Is the God of the Hills and the Valleys

April 6

1 Kings 20:28

The man of God came up and told the king of Israel, "This is what the LORD says: 'Because the Arameans think the LORD is a god of the hills and not a god of the valleys, I will deliver this vast army into your hands, and you will know that I am the LORD.'"

God's promise proved to be true. It always does. Just as God said, Israel's King Ahab and his army defeated the Arameans soundly. Thus, Ben-Hadad, King of Aram, took a year to rebuild his army and then went at Israel again but this time with a different strategy.

Ben-Hadad's advisors told the king that the "gods" of Israel were the "gods of the hills." They convinced their leader that fighting in the hills had led to their previous defeat. This time, they would meet Israel on the plains. Look again at today's passage. God said that he would prove himself to be the God of the hills and the valleys. Then everyone "will know that I am the Lord."

It's true, isn't it? God is the God of the hills and the valleys. During the great hilltop blessings, God is there. We enjoy his presence and stand in awe of his work. During the deep valley experiences, he is there as well. We depend on his strength and help to make it through the troughs of life. He is the God of the hills and the valleys.

Thank you, Father, for never leaving or forsaking us. Help us to enjoy the hilltop blessings and handle the valley challenges knowing that you are with us regardless of the terrain. In Jesus' name. Amen.

reflection

_____
_____
_____
_____
_____
_____
_____
_____
_____
_____

further suggested reading:

1 Kings 20-22

Trusting God

2 Kings 1:3

But the angel of the LORD said to Elijah the Tishbite, "Go up and meet the messengers of the king of Samaria and ask them, 'Is it because there is no God in Israel that you are going off to consult Baal-Zebub, the god of Ekron?'"

Israel's king, Ahaziah, took a fall. While walking in his upper room, he fell through the lattice covering a window. More than likely, he fell to the ground because his injuries were serious. Before calling lawyers to sue the builders and instead of praying to God for healing, he sent messengers to consult Baal-Zebub, god of Ekron. Did I mention that this guy was the king of Israel?

God sent the prophet Elijah to intercept the messengers and ask them, "Is it because there is no God in Israel that you are going off to consult" a pagan god? What in the world was Ahaziah thinking? By ignoring God, the king's actions resulted in his death.

I find that question a bit convicting. We depend on many things other than God to bring healing and success into our lives. We depend on many things other than God to provide security and confidence. Is it because we can't or won't trust God that we place our trust in all this other stuff? I believe there is a big lesson to learn from Israel's king, Ahaziah.

Father, forgive us for trusting in other "gods" to find what we are looking for. Remind us of the absolute futility of trusting in anything but you. In Jesus' name. Amen.

reflection

_____

_____

_____

_____

_____

_____

_____

_____

_____

_____

further suggested reading:

2 Kings 1

A Bold Request

2 Kings 2:9

When they had crossed, Elijah said to Elisha, "Tell me, what can I do for you before I am taken from you?" "Let me inherit a double portion of your spirit," Elisha replied.

Think teacher - student, coach - player, mentor - mentee. That was the relationship between the two prophets. Elisha was privileged to serve and learn from the great prophet, Elijah. But then God scheduled a day to take Elijah to heaven - one of the few who went directly to heaven without passing through death.

Before the chariots of fire came to take Elijah away, the teacher asked his student, "Tell me, what can I do for you before I am taken from you?" Elisha's response is one of the most bold and instructive requests in the Bible. Speaking to the powerful prophet, Elisha said, "I want twice as much strength and power as you have." I want a "double portion of your spirit." And God granted the request.

When Jesus was taken into heaven, he promised to send the Holy Spirit. When we trust in Jesus, the Spirit makes his home in our heart. Be assured the moment that we believe, we are indwelt by the Holy Spirit in full. But how bold would it be to make a request like Elisha's? Let's try it. Ready? Let's pray.

Lord Jesus, I know that your Spirit lives within me in his fullness. But today I pray that you will help me to experience his presence like never before. Today I pray that you will help me experience twice as much strength and peace and resurrection power. Give me a "double portion" of all I need to do what you have called me to do. In your name. Amen.

reflection

_____

_____

_____

_____

_____

_____

_____

_____

further suggested reading:

2 Kings 2-3

God Is for Us

April 9

2 Kings 6:16

"Don't be afraid," the prophet answered. "Those who are with us are more than those who are with them."

Elisha kept foiling the king's plan. Every time the king of Aram set strategic traps for the Israelite army, the prophet revealed his hiding places. The enraged king discovered Elisha's location, surrounded the city and planned the attack. The next morning, when Elisha's servant saw an army with horses and chariots surrounding the city, he said, "Oh, my lord, what shall we do?"

Look at today's passage. There was no panic in Elisha. He saw something his servant didn't. When the Lord opened the servant's eyes, "he looked and saw the hills full of horses and chariots of fire all around Elisha." There is no need to panic when God is on your side.

Paul says it this way, "If God is for us; who can be against us?" (Romans 8:31). John says, "The one who is in you is greater than the one who is in the world" (1 John 4:4). I wonder what we would see if we really opened our eyes?

Heavenly Father, please give us eyes to see your strength and power around us and let that drive anxiety and panic from our hearts. In Jesus' name. Amen.

reflection

further suggested reading:

2 Kings 4-8

Our Whole Heart

2 Kings 10:28-29

So Jehu destroyed Baal worship in Israel. However, he did not turn away from the sins of Jeroboam son of Nebat, which he had caused Israel to commit - the worship of the golden calves at Bethel and Dan.

Jehu was a man on a mission. After Elisha had him anointed as king of Israel, he wasted no time. Driving his chariot from place to place "like a madman," he took care of the existing leaders in short order. Then he went after Jezebel. Right after she painted her face and arranged her hair, he had her thrown from the city wall. Then he killed all of Baal's prophets and destroyed Baal's temple. Let's just say that Jehu did not stand around letting the grass grow under his feet.

But the devil is in the details. There were some things he didn't get around to doing. He flattened Baal's temple but let the golden calves stand. Scripture says that, "Jehu was not careful to keep the law of the Lord, the God of Israel, with all his heart." His twenty-eight year reign ended with mixed reviews.

Some people, like Jehu, are passionate and adamant about certain things. They live their lives on a mission to make sure good things get done for God. But like Jehu, there are some glaring spiritual deficiencies. God wants our whole heart. Anything less is a life of mixed reviews.

Father, what would it really look like if we held nothing back? What would it look like if we were careful to follow you with all our heart? By your grace, help us to realize a full-out following of Jesus. Don't let us go to the grave with mixed reviews. In Jesus' name. Amen.

reflection

_____

_____

_____

_____

_____

_____

_____

_____

_____

_____

further suggested reading:

2 Kings 9-12

Idols in Your Life

April 11

2 Kings 17:41

Even while these people were worshiping the LORD, they were serving their idols.

Today's passage chronicles Israel's sad demise when they were captured and deported to Assyria. All this took place "because the Israelites sinned against the Lord their God, who had brought them up out of Egypt. They worshiped other gods and followed the practices of the nations the Lord had driven out before them."

It was not that Israel stopped worshiping God. The problem was that they worshiped God and in blatant disobedience to Commandments #1 and #2 worshiped other gods. They never quite got the "no other gods before me" and no "idol in any form" instruction. But then, do we?

I know it's a worn out question, but do you have any idols in your life? The question is worn out because from 2 Kings to the present day, "idols" continue to make us stumble. Jobs, possessions, relationships, money, hobbies and a host of other things serve as the "add on" for many worshipers. It's sad that today's passage described Israel. But having been warned of sin's consequences, it's even more tragic if this passage describes us today.

Father, examine my heart. Point out anything and everything that I serve . . . along with you. Please help me to tear down idols before, like Israel, it is too late. In Jesus' name. Amen.

reflection

_____
_____
_____
_____
_____
_____
_____
_____
_____

further suggested reading:

2 Kings 13-17

Stumbling at the End

April 12

2 Kings 20:19

"The word of the LORD you have spoken is good," Hezekiah replied. For he thought, "Will there not be peace and security in my lifetime?"

Hezekiah was a king who "did what was right in the eyes of the Lord." He "trusted in the Lord, the God of Israel" and "held fast to the Lord." In a strange turn of events, a flaw surfaces.

Hezekiah became deathly ill, and God graciously answered his prayer for healing and added fifteen years to his life. But when well-wishers from Babylon showed up, Hezekiah, thankful for their visit, became an open book. There was "nothing in his palace or kingdom" that he did not show them. God was not pleased and told Hezekiah that his descendants would be "eunuchs in the palace of the king of Babylon." Hezekiah's response is found in today's passage. In essence he said, "Well, at least things will be good during my lifetime."

Stumbling at the end is a danger for everyone. Unfortunately, last impressions are lasting ones. It is not just about our life; it's about the legacy we leave. We thank God when things are good during our lifetime, and we don't want to hinder good things for the lives of those who follow.

Father, keep us holding fast to you until the day you call us home. Help us not to stumble as we near the finish line. In Jesus' name. Amen.

reflection

further suggested reading:

2 Kings 18-21

God Sees Your Heart

April 13

2 Kings 23:25

Neither before nor after Josiah was there a king like him who turned to the LORD as he did - with all his heart and with all his soul and with all his strength, in accordance with all the Law of Moses.

It's been said that youth is wasted on the young. But that statement does not hold true for King Josiah. He was only eight-years-old when he became king! During his thirty-one year reign, the Book of the Law was rediscovered, and the covenant to follow God was renewed.

Josiah did the hard work of weeding out many pagan practices. But notice in today's passage that a leader's success starts on the inside. Josiah followed God with all his heart (his thinking, desire, will), with all his soul (his whole being), and with all his strength (his actions). The king submitted himself to God's commands and instructions.

Long before people see your actions, God sees your heart. Here's the question. When he looks inside, does he like what he sees?

Father, help us to turn to you like Josiah and follow you with all our heart, soul and strength. In Jesus' name. Amen.

reflection

further suggested reading:

2 Kings 22-25

Bold Prayers

1 Chronicles 4:9-10

Jabez was more honorable than his brothers. His mother had named him Jabez, saying, "I gave birth to him in pain." Jabez cried out to the God of Israel, "Oh, that you would bless me and enlarge my territory! Let your hand be with me, and keep me from harm so that I will be free from pain." And God granted his request.

The Prayer of Jabez took the Christian community by storm and sold a gazillion copies (give or take a few zillion). This two sentence prayer - turned into a bestselling book - had Christians everywhere praying, "Oh Lord, enlarge my territory."

But there is one problem when I take Jabez's request and make it my own - God's will for Jabez may not be God's will for me. And the other problem is that if God doesn't answer my prayer like he did Jabez's, I may become disappointed . . . even disillusioned with him.

We can learn three things from this prayer.

1. Pray great prayers. Ask God to show his favor on your life.
2. Pray personal prayers. God has something great just for you.
3. Pray according to God's will. That's where his blessing will be and where great things will happen in your life.

Father, thank you for this man Jabez and his bold prayer. Lord, following Jabez's example, give us bold prayers of our own. In Jesus' name. Amen.

reflection

_____

_____

_____

_____

_____

_____

_____

_____

_____

further suggested reading:

1 Chronicles 1-4

They Trusted in Him

1 Chronicles 5:20

They were helped in fighting them, and God delivered the Hagrites and all their allies into their hands, because they cried out to him during the battle. He answered their prayers, because they trusted in him.

Are you in a battle? A battle to keep your marriage together? A battle with a wayward child? A battle with disease? A battle with doubt? An internal struggle to follow the right path when everything within you is screaming to take the detour? Come to think of it, all Christians are in a battle! We constantly fight against the allied forces of the world, the flesh and the devil.

Check out today's passage. God helped his people in their battle because they cried out to him "during the battle." God worked on their behalf because "they trusted in him." He will do the same for you.

Right now, in the midst of your battle, cry out to him. Let him know that you are in desperate need of his help. Let him know that you are in desperate need of his strength. Let him know that you trust him. God "answered their prayers because they trusted in him." He'll do the same for you!

Father, I pray for all of us in a battle today. We cry out to you in the midst of the battle! We trust you in the midst of the battle! Come to our aid and give us your strength and deliverance. In Jesus' name. Amen.

reflection

_____

_____

_____

_____

_____

_____

_____

_____

_____

_____

_____

further suggested reading:

1 Chronicles 5-9

Doing Great Things . . . The Wrong Way

1 Chronicles 13:9-10

When they came to the threshing floor of Kidon, Uzzah reached out his hand to steady the ark, because the oxen stumbled. The LORD's anger burned against Uzzah, and he struck him down because he had put his hand on the ark. So he died there before God.

David and his men were celebrating with all their might before the Lord. Finally, the ark of God, representing the presence of God, was headed back to Jerusalem. The ark was on a cart pulled by oxen with Uzzah and Ahio guiding it. But then the oxen stumbled, and when Uzzah reached out to steady it, he was struck down because he put his hand on the ark. Hmm . . . this needs some explanation.

God gave very specific instructions regarding the transport of the ark. Anytime it was moved, it was to be carried by the Levites with poles put through the rings on the side. The Levites were to carry the ark with the poles on their shoulders. David was bringing the ark back to Jerusalem, a great thing . . . but in the wrong way.

Many believers think that as long as they are obeying God in the "big" stuff, all is well. But God calls for obedience even in the details. His instruction is not optional. His commands are not suggestions. Check your heart to see if you are doing great things for God in the wrong way.

Father, search my heart and show me if I am doing good . . . even great . . . things for you but in the wrong way. Give me courage to obey you even in the details. In Jesus' name. Amen.

reflection

_____

_____

_____

_____

_____

_____

_____

_____

_____

_____

further suggested reading:

1 Chronicles 10-16

What's the Cost?

1 Chronicles 21:24

But King David replied to Araunah, "No, I insist on paying the full price. I will not take for the LORD what is yours, or sacrifice a burnt offering that costs me nothing."

Have you ever done something you regretted? Yes? Then you have something in common with King David.

In response to David's disobedience, God told him to build an altar "on the threshing floor of Araunah the Jebusite" and make a sacrifice for his regrettable sin. David asked Araunah for the floor and said, "Sell it to me at the full price." But Araunah told David to take the floor and do whatever he wanted. "No," David replied, "I insist on paying the full price. I will not . . . sacrifice a burnt offering that costs me nothing."

The Christian life is a blessed life. Forgiven. Made righteous. Reconciled to God. Indwelt by the Holy Spirit. God has given us everything that we need to do everything he has called us to do. Along with the blessings come the cost. Here's the question. What is it costing you to serve Jesus? I mean, really? What sacrifices are you making for the One who gave it all for you?

Father, we love your blessings. Help us to accept the cost. In Jesus' name. Amen.

reflection

_____
_____
_____
_____
_____
_____
_____
_____
_____
_____
_____

further suggested reading:

1 Chronicles 17-21

What Are You Planting?

1 Chronicles 22:5

David said, "My son Solomon is young and inexperienced, and the house to be built for the LORD should be of great magnificence and fame and splendor in the sight of all the nations. Therefore I will make preparations for it." So David made extensive preparations before his death.

David desired to build a great temple for God. But God told him, "You are not the one to build me a house to dwell in." That job was for David's son, Solomon.

How would you have responded? Your dream denied. Your desire squelched. Your effort to show love for God given to the next generation. Would you have become angry, discouraged or have thrown a spiritual tantrum? Would you have taken your marbles and gone home? Many people respond to God's "no" in similar ways. But check out David's response in today's passage.

David spent the rest of his days making plans for a structure he would never see. David didn't spend his golden years at the golf course, tennis court or card table. He was willing to use his experience, influence and time to make preparations for a great house for the Lord, in spite of knowing he would not be around for the grand opening. How about you? What are you planting today that you will never see grow?

Father, help us to live our lives investing in things that will outlive us. In Jesus' name. Amen.

reflection

_____

_____

_____

_____

_____

_____

_____

_____

_____

_____

_____

_____

further suggested reading:

1 Chronicles 22-27

God's Word in Real Life

April 19

1 Chronicles 28:20

David also said to Solomon his son, "Be strong and courageous, and do the work. Do not be afraid or discouraged, for the LORD God, my God, is with you. He will not fail you or forsake you until all the work for the service of the temple of the LORD is finished."

The greatest thing parents can pass on to their children and mature leaders can pass on to younger leaders is found in today's passage. It does not involve a hefty inheritance or the corner office. It is not written in a will or a succession plan. It comes from a life that has been tested and tried and remains standing. The greatest thing that can be passed along is the assurance of God's presence and strength from one who has truly experienced both.

David's journey from the sheep pens to the palace had a few detours along the way. One minute David was holding Goliath's head and welcomed as a hero; the next minute he was dodging the jealous king's spear and running for his life. In his decade as a fugitive, David learned much about himself and more about God. Now he passed that knowledge to his son, not as verses from a Scripture memory packet, but as God's Word experienced in real life.

What do I have to pass on to those who follow? I pray it is confidence in the living God based on the living Word fleshed out in real life. I want to make sure the truth in my head is passed on with the passion of my heart.

Father, please help us not to be hearers of the Word only but also doers. Help us to follow you on rocky and winding roads, so that we will know that you are a guide who delivers us home regardless of the tough terrain. Help us to share with those who follow more than just words. In Jesus' name. Amen.

reflection

further suggested reading:

1 Chronicles 28-29

What Do You Need?

2 Chronicles 1:7-10

That night God appeared to Solomon and said to him, "Ask for whatever you want me to give you." Solomon answered God, "You have shown great kindness to David my father and have made me king in his place. Now, LORD God, let your promise to my father David be confirmed, for you have made me king over a people who are as numerous as the dust of the earth. Give me wisdom and knowledge, that I may lead this people, for who is able to govern this great people of yours?"

Imagine God appearing before you and saying, "Ask for whatever you want me to give you." Can you even imagine? I would start singing that song I learned as a kid, "He owns the cattle on a thousand hills; the wealth in every mine." My face would break out in smiles. No more ministry fund-raising, no more capital campaigns . . . my mind would start spinning with things on my wish list! But Solomon showed great discernment.

Solomon acknowledged that the people in his charge belonged to God. He acknowledged that God made him their leader. He humbly confessed his need for wisdom and knowledge in order to lead them well.

What things do you request from God to lead effectively the people he has placed in your life? That question deserves some reflection, doesn't it?

Father, I often only ask for what I want. Please give me the discernment to know what I need. In Jesus' name. Amen.

reflection

_____

_____

_____

_____

_____

_____

_____

_____

_____

_____

further suggested reading:

2 Chronicles 1-5

Posture of Your Heart

2 Chronicles 6:13-14

He stood on the platform and then knelt down before the whole assembly of Israel and spread out his hands toward heaven. He said: "LORD, the God of Israel, there is no God like you in heaven or on earth - you who keep your covenant of love with your servants who continue wholeheartedly in your way."

After years of planning and two decades of construction, the temple was ready to be devoted to God. Today's passage includes the opening words of Solomon's prayer of dedication.

Notice Solomon's posture. The great king, whose wisdom was known throughout the world, humbly dropped to his knees. This was not a time for sitting or standing. Solomon bowed before the God of heaven and earth. And notice his hands. They are not hanging limp at his side or stuffed in his pockets. His hands are lifted toward the Person whom he is praising.

Posture or the position of our hands during prayer or praise is not a measure of our spirituality. But many times the posture of our body reveals the posture of our heart. There is something humbling about bowing down. There is something freeing about lifting our hands. During his time of great praise, Solomon chose to do both. Here's the main question for us: During our times of prayer or praise, what is the posture of our heart?

Lord Jesus, may our posture of worship never be all about outward appearance, and may our posture never hold back a heart of humility and praise. In your name. Amen.

reflection

_____

_____

_____

_____

_____

_____

_____

_____

further suggested reading:

2 Chronicles 6-7

No One Like God

2 Chronicles 6:13-14

He stood on the platform and then knelt down before the whole assembly of Israel and spread out his hands toward heaven. He said: "LORD, the God of Israel, there is no God like you in heaven or on earth - you who keep your covenant of love with your servants who continue wholeheartedly in your way.

Solomon is on his knees - a posture of humility - with his hands reaching up toward God. After twenty years of construction, the temple is completed. Our passage today includes the first words of Solomon's prayer of dedication where he focuses on two attributes of God.

Uniqueness: Make a careful search over all the earth. If possible, take a fact-finding trip through the heavens. You know what you would find? Nothing like our God. The eternal, omnipresent, omnipotent, omniscient God is unique. There is no one like him.

Faithfulness: Our God is a covenant-keeping God. His "gifts and his call are irrevocable" (Romans 11:29). When we belong to him, nothing "in all creation, will be able to separate us from the love of God that is in Christ Jesus our Lord" (Romans 8:39).

There is no one like our covenant-keeping God. Only one thing left to do - kneel down, lift your hands to the heavens and praise him for his love and work in your life.

Father, I acknowledge that you alone are God; there is no one like you. All the gods of the nations are idols, but you made the heavens. Thank you for opening my eyes and heart to see my sin and need for a Savior. Thank you for introducing me to Jesus. Thank you that nothing can separate me from you because of Christ Jesus my Lord. [Keep thanking God for his work in your life.]

reflection

_____

_____

_____

_____

_____

further suggested reading:

2 Chronicles 8-9

A Leader's Decision

April 23

2 Chronicles 10:8

But Rehoboam rejected the advice the elders gave him and consulted the young men who had grown up with him and were serving him.

After Solomon died, the people asked Rehoboam, Solomon's son and new leader, to reduce the amount of their labor and taxation. Rehoboam sought advice. First, he counseled with those who had served with his father. They said that if he would reduce the labor and taxes, the people "will always be your servants." But those who grew up with Rehoboam advised him to make a statement and increase the load. Rehoboam followed the advice of his contemporaries, the people rebelled and the kingdom was divided. Israel's history was altered by Rehoboam's decision.

The following are two important points to learn from this passage:

Lesson #1: In seeking advice, it is best to weigh heavily the words of people who have "been there and done that" rather than those going through it with you. Experience is a great teacher.

Lesson #2: Be careful when you ask for advice from people who "serve" you. They may feel that they have a lot to lose if they disagree.

Be careful with whom you consult, and weigh carefully what they say. A leader's decisions impacts lives.

Father, lead us to those who will give us good counsel. Help us to be wise enough to follow it. In Jesus' name. Amen.

reflection

further suggested reading:

2 Chronicles 10-12

119

Seek Help from the Lord

April 24

2 Chronicles 16:12

In the thirty-ninth year of his reign Asa was afflicted with a disease in his feet. Though his disease was severe, even in his illness he did not seek help from the LORD, but only from the physicians.

How does it happen? How does a person follow hard after God for many years and then blow it at the end? Do we start believing that success comes from us? Do we become worn out by obedience? When does pride drive out humility? Check out this story of Asa.

Asa, the King of Judah, was a bold reformer. He did "what was good and right in the eyes of the Lord." He led the people to enter into a covenant "to seek the Lord . . . with all their soul and all their heart." Asa even deposed his own grandmother "because she made a repulsive Asherah pole." Then something snapped . . . spiritually speaking. In his last years, he made a treaty with a pagan king. When God sent a prophet to confront him, Asa became "so enraged that he put [the prophet] in prison" and "brutally oppressed some of the people." Look at today's passage. In his illness, "he did not seek help from the Lord."

How does that happen? What causes the best days of one's life to be seen only in the rearview mirror? Asa is a great reminder that any one of us can blow it. In the words of the Apostle Paul, we need to strain toward what is ahead and "press on toward the goal to win the prize for which God has called me heavenward in Christ Jesus" (Philippians 3:14).

Dear Father, may it not be said of us that our best spiritual days are behind us. Please give us the strength and focus to press on to win the prize. Whatever has happened in our past, may our best spiritual days be in our future. In Jesus' name. Amen.

reflection

further suggested reading:

2 Chronicles 13-16

God Is on Your Side

2 Chronicles 20:15

This is what the LORD says to you: 'Do not be afraid or discouraged because of this vast army. For the battle is not yours, but God's.'

These words were spoken to King Jehoshaphat and his people as they prepared for battle. The people were not to be intimidated by their opponent's massive army. Regardless of soldiers and equipment, God's people held the trump card - he was on their side. God is still on the side of his people.

That's a truth that I need to remind myself of each day. Sometimes when I face my vast armies, I feel alone and defeated. I convince myself that the battle is lost before it even begins. I am certain that I can't deal with - much less defeat - the challenge ahead. I can never find the strength for victory when I look to myself. However, looking to myself for victory is the real problem, isn't it?

God reminds us that the battle is not ours to fight. He will be the One fighting for us. We simply need to trust him. Regardless of today's challenges - and granted, the challenges may look like a vast army - "the battle is not yours, but God's." In addition, I'll let you in on a little secret - he never loses!

Father, I pray that truth in today's passage drives fear and discouragement from our hearts. Thank you for taking our battles from us and fighting our battles for us. In Jesus' name. Amen.

reflection

_____

_____

_____

_____

_____

_____

_____

_____

_____

_____

_____

further suggested reading:

2 Chronicles 17-20

A Half-Baked Christian Life

2 Chronicles 25:2

He did what was right in the eyes of the LORD, but not wholeheartedly.

Today's verse describes King Amaziah, who was twenty-five years old when he became King of Judah and then reigned for almost three decades. I have to admit this verse haunts me.

I believe this verse describes the following:

- A person who comes to Christ early in his life but never really owns his faith.
- A person who is more into the stuff of church than love for Christ.
- A person whose insightful comments during the Bible study are seldom applied.
- A person who does good spiritual things while suffering from spiritual anemia.
- A person more concerned about pleasing people than God.
- A businessman who is "all about Christ" . . . kind of . . . and all about the almighty dollar . . . for sure.
- A spouse who stays in a marriage but does not honor God through the marriage.
- A parent who is more into coaching his child in a sport than mentoring his child for life.

This verse describes exactly what I don't want to do and exactly who I don't want to be. It describes a half-baked Christian life, a person who does the right things but not necessarily for the right reasons. Let make a deal. Let's not allow this verse to describe us.

Father, show me if this verse describes me. Help me to make the changes today so that this verse does not describe my life. In Jesus' name. Amen.

reflection

_____

_____

_____

_____

_____

_____

_____

further suggested reading:

2 Chronicles 21-25

Dangerous Success

April 27

2 Chronicles 26:16

But after Uzziah became powerful, his pride led to his downfall. He was unfaithful to the LORD his God.

How many times have you seen this under "Prayer Concerns" in the weekend bulletin?

Please pray fervently for the following people who desperately need our prayers:

- Tom - Received significant promotion
- Sue - Honored as her high school's Outstanding Student
- Bob - Selected to the All-State baseball team
- Esther - Named firm's new partner
- Tyler - Salesman of the year

I have never seen these in our church bulletin, yet I believe good times are more dangerous than challenging times. Just ask Uzziah. He came into power at age sixteen and reigned for fifty-two years. Uzziah defeated the Philistines, built towers for protecting his people, developed a well-trained army and designed cutting edge war machines. His fame spread far and wide "because he had become very powerful." But note today's passage. It was Uzziah's success that led to pride and that led to his downfall.

In his book *What Should I Do with My Life?* Po Bronson wrote, "Failure's hard, but success is far more dangerous. If you're successful at the wrong thing, the mix of praise and money and opportunity can lock you in forever." That thing that success can lock you into is pride. Pride always sits on the top of a very slippery slope.

Father, please don't let us turn your great blessings into the downfall of pride. Help us keep our eyes on you in our greatest challenge and our greatest success. In Jesus' name. Amen.

reflection

_____

_____

_____

_____

_____

further suggested reading:

2 Chronicles 26-28

The Hand of God

2 Chronicles 32:7-8

"Be strong and courageous. Do not be afraid or discouraged because of the king of Assyria and the vast army with him, for there is a greater power with us than with him. With him is only the arm of flesh, but with us is the LORD our God to help us and to fight our battles." And the people gained confidence from what Hezekiah the king of Judah said.

The arm of flesh versus the hand of God. Not much of a contest, is it? Even when the "vast armies" come against us (and they will!) "there is a greater power with us."

The arm of flesh versus the hand of God. Man makes great boasts and builds impressive stuff. Some of that stuff is threatening. But the Lord our God is with us "to help us and to fight our battles."

The arm of flesh versus the hand of God. Fear is a ready companion when the future looks bleak, when the test results report dreaded news, when she says, "It's over." But if God is for us, who can be against us?

The arm of flesh versus the hand of God. Be confident. God will have his way every time!

Father, thank you for the reminder that you are on our side . . . even when the enemy threatens, even when the day is dark, even when the valleys are deep. When you are on our side, we always win. In Jesus' name. Amen.

reflection

_____

_____

_____

_____

_____

_____

_____

_____

_____

_____

further suggested reading:

2 Chronicles 29-30

Does God Test Us?

2 Chronicles 32:31

But when envoys were sent by the rulers of Babylon to ask him about the miraculous sign that had occurred in the land, God left him to test him and to know everything that was in his heart.

Does God test us? Does God put things in our path to see how we will respond . . . to see if we'll keep walking with him? Check out this snapshot from Hezekiah.

Hezekiah was riding a spiritual roller coaster. One day he was ruling the country with authority. The next day he was about to die. God miraculously healed him, but Hezekiah twisted God's blessing into personal pride. The next day he repented. God wanted to see what was really in Hezekiah's heart, and he sent envoys from Babylon to ask him about the miraculous healing. Unfortunately, we learn in the corresponding passage (2 Kings 20) that the king failed the test.

Does God test us? Yes, but for this purpose: James says, "because you know that the testing of your faith develops perseverance. Perseverance must finish its work so that you may be mature and complete, not lacking anything" (James 1:3-4). The tests God sends are not meant to tear us down but to build us up. God is in the process of developing us today for what he wants us to do tomorrow.

Father, thank you for working in our lives to prepare us for your great plans. In Jesus' name. Amen.

reflection

_____

_____

_____

_____

_____

_____

_____

_____

_____

further suggested reading:

2 Chronicles 31-32

125

Time To Come Back Home

April 30

2 Chronicles 33:12-13

In his distress he sought the favor of the LORD his God and humbled himself greatly before the God of his ancestors. And when he prayed to him, the LORD was moved by his entreaty and listened to his plea; so he brought him back to Jerusalem and to his kingdom. Then Manasseh knew that the LORD is God.

Not every life begins well. In fact, many people experience times far from the Lord. But all heaven rejoices when a wayward child comes back home. That's what happened to King Manasseh.

Manasseh was a king who "did evil in the eyes of the Lord" and dragged his country down the path away from God. However, God got his attention by sending the king of Assyria to take him captive. More specifically, the Assyrian king "put a hook in [Manasseh's] nose, bound him with bronze shackles and took him to Babylon." In his distress, he humbled himself. God saw the sincerity of his heart and gave him back his kingdom.

Maybe you are a bit like Manasseh. You have made some mistakes in your life and have the scars to prove it. Today is the day to humble yourself before God. Today is the day to seek his forgiveness. Time to come back home, isn't it? What are you waiting for?

Father, thank you for reminding us through the story of Manasseh that there is no sin that you cannot forgive. Prod the wanderer to come back home. In Jesus' name. Amen.

reflection

further suggested reading:

2 Chronicles 33-36

God Rules Over All

May 1

Ezra 1:1

In the first year of Cyrus king of Persia, in order to fulfill the word of the LORD spoken by Jeremiah, the LORD moved the heart of Cyrus king of Persia to make a proclamation throughout his realm and also to put it in writing.

God rules over all. The teaching of his sovereignty throughout Scripture is clear. The hearts of the kings of the world are like "channels of water in the hand of the Lord; he turns it wherever he wishes" (Proverbs 21:1).

God built a great nation under King David and King Solomon, but after their reigns the kingdom divided. Due to the ongoing sins of the nation, God's people were overthrown by the Assyrians and Babylonians. The walls of Jerusalem were torn down and the temple destroyed. In his perfect timing, God "moved the heart of Cyrus king of Persia" to allow the Israelites to return to Jerusalem to rebuild the temple.

We will not always understand God's timing and ways, but we can be sure of this . . . God is sovereign over all. Nothing takes him by surprise. His perfect plan for nations and people will be carried out. As it is with nations, so it is with your life.

Father, we acknowledge you as the God who is in complete control. We trust you, your ways and your timing to carry out your perfect will in our lives. In Jesus' name. Amen.

reflection

_____

_____

_____

_____

_____

_____

_____

_____

_____

_____

_____

further suggested reading:

Ezra 1-3

Know What God Has Called You To Do

Ezra 4:4

Then the peoples around them set out to discourage the people of Judah and make them afraid to go on building.

Whatever you set out to do, someone will work to stop you. When God puts something in your heart, someone will try to convince you that you're mistaken. When God calls you to a great task, naysayers come out of the woodwork.

Years after God's people were overthrown and taken captive, God moved in the heart of the Persian king to let the Israelites return to Jerusalem and rebuild the temple. Of course, there was opposition. People set out "to discourage the people of Judah and make them afraid." They even "hired counselors to work against them and frustrate their plans."

Some things never change. Whenever God calls you to do something, get ready for the opposition. The pessimists will show up to let you know that it can't be done. The cynics will call to challenge your motives. The worrywarts will share their fear. When God is for us, who can stand against us? Know what God has called you to do and get 'r done!

Father, you call us to do great things for you. We want to do those great things. Please help us when people come to discourage us and cause us to be afraid. We follow and depend on you alone. In Jesus' name. Amen.

reflection

_____
_____
_____
_____
_____
_____
_____
_____
_____
_____

further suggested reading:

Ezra 4-6

Teaching God's Word

May 3

Ezra 7:10

For Ezra had devoted himself to the study and observance of the Law of the LORD, and to teaching its decrees and laws in Israel.

For years, I have claimed today's passage as my life verse. Let me share with you why this verse is so meaningful to me.

Devoted. I do not want to live a half-baked Christian life. Ezra was all in and going all out to do what God called him to do.

Study. All effective teachers of God's Word have to put in the hard work of understanding the passage. Our study cannot be shoddy.

Observance. A seminary professor was fond of saying, "You cannot impart what you do not possess." As another has said, "You can be in the Word with out the Word being in you." The teacher cannot miss the critical step of personal application.

Teaching. Teaching God's Word is a great privilege and responsibility. For the person with the gift of teaching, there is no greater thing than to stand and say, "Open your Bibles and turn to . . . " God promises that when his Word goes forth, it never comes back empty. It always accomplishes his purpose.

Father, on behalf of all those reading this who have the gift of teaching, we thank you. We thank you for the privilege of opening your inerrant Word to children, youth and adults. Thank you for the promise that your purpose is always accomplished when your Word goes forth. In Jesus' name. Amen.

reflection

_____
_____
_____
_____
_____
_____
_____
_____

further suggested reading:

Ezra 7-8

True Confession

Ezra 10:1

> While Ezra was praying and confessing, weeping and throwing himself down before the house of God, a large crowd of Israelites - men, women and children - gathered around him. They too wept bitterly.

True confession is not a flippant, "I'm sorry." Neither is it a regretful, "I'm sorry I got caught." It begins with an understanding that our sin is in direct opposition to the heavenly Father, who loves us so much that he sent his Son to die for us on the cross. It includes a deep remorse for knowing what God said to do and refusing to do it or knowing what he said not to do and doing it anyway.

Notice the emotion of today's passage. Ezra was praying, confessing, weeping and throwing himself on the ground prostrate before God. His sorrow for the sins of the people was deep, heartfelt and visible. Israel's sins had led them to captivity. Now after many had returned to rebuild the temple, Ezra wanted the people to restart with a clean slate.

What about you? Anything you need to bring before God in true confession? God is waiting with open arms for you to come with a heart of true confession.

Father, thank you for not only providing the remedy for our sin but also a way of confessing our sins before you and keeping a clean slate. Thank you for the promise that if we confess our sins to you, you will forgive us and cleanse us from all unrighteousness. In Jesus' name. Amen.

reflection

_____

_____

_____

_____

_____

_____

_____

_____

_____

_____

further suggested reading:

Ezra 9-10

Great Compassion

Nehemiah 1:3-4

They said to me, "Those who survived the exile and are back in the province are in great trouble and disgrace. The wall of Jerusalem is broken down, and its gates have been burned with fire." When I heard these things, I sat down and wept. For some days I mourned and fasted and prayed before the God of heaven.

What's the most important characteristic of a leader? Vision? Perseverance? Inspiration? All those are important, but from the great leader Nehemiah, we learn that one characteristic leads the way. In today's passage, note the great compassion Nehemiah had for his fellow Israelites.

As cupbearer to the king, Nehemiah had it made. However, when he heard that his kinsmen were in "great trouble and disgrace" and that the protective wall of Jerusalem had been demolished, he sat down and wept. His great compassion led to mourning, fasting and prayer. Nehemiah was a man who lived beyond himself. He was willing to leave the comfort of the palace in order to serve those in need.

Today we need strong leaders who are willing to stand firm even if they have to stand alone. We need leaders who possess and communicate God's vision that inspires people to get on board. Most of all, we need leaders who are not in it for themselves but are willing to make needed sacrifices to help others. We need leaders - like Nehemiah - with great compassion.

Father, raise up leaders who are willing to make personal sacrifices in order to build others up. Raise up leaders like Nehemiah. In Jesus' name. Amen.

reflection

further suggested reading:

Nehemiah 1

Great Things for God

Nehemiah 2:17-18

Then I said to them, "You see the trouble we are in: Jerusalem lies in ruins, and its gates have been burned with fire. Come, let us rebuild the wall of Jerusalem, and we will no longer be in disgrace." I also told them about the gracious hand of my God on me and what the king had said to me. They replied, "Let us start rebuilding." So they began this good work.

Nehemiah's compassion for his fellow Israelites led him to action. At great risk, he spoke to the king and was granted leave to lead in the rebuilding of Jerusalem's broken down walls. After surveying the damage and determining the size of the project, Nehemiah stood before the discouraged people and inspired them to begin the process. Notice that the people were encouraged by two things that Nehemiah said.

First, Nehemiah explained that God had graciously saved his life. A sad cupbearer not only lost his job; he lost his head. However, when Nehemiah had been unable to hide his sadness for Jerusalem in the king's presence, God graciously spared him. Second, the king was willing to participate in the rebuilding project. He gave Nehemiah timber from the royal forest and sent army officers and cavalry to ensure safe arrival. When the people heard how God had worked, they said, "Let us start rebuilding."

It's amazing how God works. He moved the heart of a pagan king to supply materials for rebuilding the wall of Jerusalem. He normally uses people in his great projects. Nehemiah was willing to risk his life. What are you and I willing to risk in order to do great things for God?

Father, thank you for the privilege of allowing us to be involved in your work. Give us the courage and willingness to be involved. In Jesus' name. Amen.

reflection

_____

_____

_____

_____

_____

_____

_____

further suggested reading:

Nehemiah 2

Finish the Work

May 7

Nehemiah 4:1-2

When Sanballat heard that we were rebuilding the wall, he became angry and was greatly incensed. He ridiculed the Jews, and in the presence of his associates and the army of Samaria, he said, "What are those feeble Jews doing? Will they restore their wall? Will they offer sacrifices? Will they finish in a day? Can they bring the stones back to life from those heaps of rubble - burned as they are?"

Are you ready to partner with God on a great endeavor? Are you ready for God to work through you to accomplish significant stuff? Then get ready for some opposition.

When Nehemiah returned to Jerusalem to rebuild the walls, not everyone was overjoyed. For Sanballat and his friends, rebuilt walls meant less power. They did all that they could to stop the project. In a series of mocking questions, Sanballat worked to deflate the workers' spirits and delivered paralyzing discouragement.

Whatever project God has you working on, don't be surprised when the opposition shows up. It may come from people who don't particularly like you or even from family and friends who think they are looking out for you. It may come from a personal setback or from Satan himself. However, God's work is too important to stop before it's finished. Hang in there and finish the work God called you to do.

Father, hearing ridicule or criticism is hard no matter the source. In the midst of opposition, help us to keep our eyes focused on you. Give us the strength and courage we need to complete great things for you. In Jesus' name. Amen.

reflection

_____

_____

_____

_____

_____

_____

_____

further suggested reading:

Nehemiah 3-4

Leading Out of Reverence for God

May 8

Nehemiah 5:15-16

But the earlier governors - those preceding me - placed a heavy burden on the people and took forty shekels of silver from them in addition to food and wine. Their assistants also lorded it over the people. But out of reverence for God I did not act like that. Instead, I devoted myself to the work on this wall. All my men were assembled there for the work; we did not acquire any land.

Nehemiah was a leader who cut his own course. Earlier leaders in Jerusalem lorded their power over the people with heavy burdens of taxation. Their greed was one reason the discouraged Israelites lived in disgrace. The wall of Jerusalem was not the only thing in shambles. The people lived with worn out bodies and broken spirits.

However, Nehemiah was a different kind of leader. He refused to take advantage of the people. He and his men engaged in the work on the wall. He didn't use his power to acquire personal wealth. In fact, each day "a hundred and fifty Jews and officials ate at his table" (Nehemiah 5:17).

Why did Nehemiah lead in such a way? Look at today's passage. Nehemiah said that his behavior was "out of reverence" for God. What a powerful statement! Nehemiah was not about to take advantage of the position that God had given him. He led differently because of his love, devotion and admiration of the holy God. Leading out of reverence for God . . . now that puts leadership in a true biblical perspective.

Father, please help us all to live and lead out of reverence for you. In Jesus' name. Amen.

reflection

_____

_____

_____

_____

_____

_____

_____

_____

_____

further suggested reading:

Nehemiah 5-7

Spiritual Renewal

Nehemiah 9:16-17

But then our ancestors became arrogant and stiff-necked, and they did not obey your commands. They refused to listen and failed to remember the miracles you performed among them. They became stiff-necked and in their rebellion appointed a leader in order to return to their slavery. But you are a forgiving God, gracious and compassionate, slow to anger and abounding in love. Therefore you did not desert them.

The walls were not the only thing in Jerusalem that needed to be rebuilt. The hearts of the people were in spiritual disrepair. Ezra was called on to lead the spiritual renewal. The people reviewed the deeds of their ancestors that had brought on the downfall of the nation and then proclaimed five characteristics of God. Take the time to thank God for the ways that he has demonstrated these attributes in your life.

Forgiveness: When we confess our sins, God is faithful to forgive us. Scripture says that he separates our sin from us as far as the east is from the west; he puts them behind his back; he throws them into the depth of the sea; he remembers our sins no more. God will forgive you, and then you can forgive yourself. *Father, thank you for forgiving my sins and remembering them no more.*

Grace: In God's mercy he holds back what we deserve. In his grace, he gives us what we don't deserve. Grace is not earned or deserved. It is absolutely free. If grace weren't free, it wouldn't be grace. *Father, thank you for giving me what I absolutely do not deserve.*

Compassion: God does not leave us in our state of sin. He has a deep sympathy for us and moves in to alleviate our desperate state. *Father, thank you for your great compassion!*

Slow To Anger: I am so thankful that God is patient with me. *Lord, I am such a slow learner. Thank you for being so patient with me.*

Love: God's love overflows in its abundance. He loves us so much that he gave his Son to die as our substitute on the cross. That is abounding love!

Father, thank you for showing your love by sending Jesus for me while I was still a sinner and had no intention of turning to you.

further suggested reading:

Nehemiah 8-10

135

A Daily Celebration

Nehemiah 12:43

And on that day they offered great sacrifices, rejoicing because God had given them great joy. The women and children also rejoiced. The sound of rejoicing in Jerusalem could be heard far away.

If you had led the rebuilding of the wall of Jerusalem, how would you have celebrated God's great work through his people? How about marching on top of the wall? That's what Nehemiah did. He had one choir singing and praising and marching in one direction and another choir singing and praising and marching in the opposite direction until they met to combine their praise in one awesome chorus. Then they climbed down from the wall to do more praising in the house of God. Singing so loudly that their voices "could be heard from far away," men, women and children joined together.

If the people of Jerusalem had something to rejoice about, we have so much more! Believers have been declared "not guilty" and made righteous! The Holy Spirit lives in us! Because of Jesus we can experience abundant life today and move to heaven forever! Our lives have been rebuilt, restored, redeemed!

Living for Christ is . . . or should be . . . a daily celebration. Let's live today in such a way that people take note of our deep joy and deliberate rejoicing.

Father, may our joy and rejoicing reflect the lives you have rebuilt through Jesus. In his name. Amen.

reflection

further suggested reading:

Nehemiah 11-13

His Sovereign Hand

May 11

Esther 2:17-18

Now the king was attracted to Esther more than to any of the other women, and she won his favor and approval more than any of the other virgins. So he set a royal crown on her head and made her queen instead of Vashti. And the king gave a great banquet, Esther's banquet, for all his nobles and officials. He proclaimed a holiday throughout the provinces and distributed gifts with royal liberality.

Xerxes knew how to throw a party! In the third year of his reign, he gave a bash for his nobles, officials, princes and military leaders that lasted for 180 days! Then a mere week long banquet was held for all the people from the least to the greatest. On day seven, after he had a little too much to drink, Xerxes sent for Queen Vashti to come and "display her beauty . . . for she was lovely to look at"(Esther 1:11). When Vashti refused to entertain the drunken nobles, she was banished from the king's presence, and the search began for a new queen.

That's the setting for the book of Esther, the only book of the Bible where God's name is not mentioned, but his sovereign hand is evident in every paragraph on every page. Esther, a Jewess, eventually became the new queen and saved her people from annihilation. And in a divine twist of events, the man who devised the annihilation plan was hung from the gallows that he built to hang Esther's uncle who refused to bow before anyone but God.

In this amazing book, we see that God is at work in all the events of life. He is the One who weaves the details of our days together to display his perfect plan. You might think that hearing a certain story, or sleep-depriving indigestion or your position in life are all mere coincidences. But in the book of Esther, what seems trivial today is tantamount tomorrow. We know that the same God who guided the events of Esther is guiding the events of our lives today.

Father, you never waste our time. Thank you for working all things together for good. In Jesus' name. Amen.

reflection

_____

_____

_____

_____

_____

_____

further suggested reading:

Esther 1-2

A Strategic Postion

Esther 4:14

For if you remain silent at this time, relief and deliverance for the Jews will arise from another place, but you and your father's family will perish. And who knows but that you have come to your royal position for such a time as this?

Haman's plan was not just to persecute the Jews; he set out to annihilate them. His hatred for Mordicai took such possession of his soul that he wanted Mordicai and all his people wiped from the face of the earth. Little did he know that Esther, the new queen, was a Jew. However, the position that God gives us means nothing unless we use it for his purposes.

Mordicai's words to Esther remind us that God will get his work accomplished. Although our refusal to participate may be detrimental to us, he'll find someone else to get the job done. But God places us in specific positions for strategic purposes. The all-powerful God chooses to use people in his sovereign work.

There is no doubt about it. God has placed YOU in a strategic position. No one has been gifted and resourced like you. No one else on earth has your network of family and friends. God has placed you right where you are for such a time as this. God wants to use you to accomplish his work! Don't sit still or remain silent.

Father, thank you for the privilege of partnering with you in eternal work. Give us the courage to stand up, speak out and accomplish it. In Jesus' name. Amen.

reflection

_____
_____
_____
_____
_____
_____
_____
_____
_____
_____

further suggested reading:

Esther 3

Man's Greatest Privilege

Esther 4:15-16

Then Esther sent this reply to Mordecai: "Go, gather together all the Jews who are in Susa, and fast for me. Do not eat or drink for three days, night or day. I and my attendants will fast as you do. When this is done, I will go to the king, even though it is against the law. And if I perish, I perish."

Partnering with God is man's greatest privilege - and it's not for the faint of heart. God's work is not insignificant stuff that we can take on as a hobby. It involves spiritual preparation. And it is not to be done alone. We need to know that others have our back.

Esther knew that asking the king to repeal the edict to annihilate the Jews might result in her death. In that day you didn't go before the king without a special invitation and then ask him to change his mind. Esther declared a three-day fast for spiritual preparation and strength. Notice that Esther did not declare the fast as a guarantee for success. After the fast she would go to the king, and say "if I perish, I perish." What courage!

Partnering with God is man's greatest privilege - and it's not for the faint of heart. We need strength, courage and others to journey with us. Like Esther, we must resign ourselves to God's sovereign plan.

Father, thank you for the privilege of partnering with you. Please give us the strength we need to do all you have called us to do. We leave the outcome to you. In Jesus' name. Amen.

reflection

_____
_____
_____
_____
_____
_____
_____
_____
_____
_____

further suggested reading:

Esther 4

The Great Director

Esther 6:1-2

That night the king could not sleep; so he ordered the book of the chronicles, the record of his reign, to be brought in and read to him. It was found recorded there that Mordecai had exposed Bigthana and Teresh, two of the king's officers who guarded the doorway, who had conspired to assassinate King Xerxes.

Was it indigestion? Or insomnia? Or was the king's sleeplessness caused by a gnawing question about the significance of his leadership? Who knows what God used to keep the king awake and in need of a bedtime story about the history of his reign. But through the reading, the wide-awake king learned that a man named Mordecai had exposed an assassination plot, and he decided to honor the man who saved his life.

In sweet irony, the king assigned wicked Haman, who was intent on killing Mordicai, to be the one to lead the honoring ceremony. Singing the praises of the man he absolutely despised, Haman led Mordicai around the town. God has a great sense of humor!

This passage is a reminder that God is at work in all the details of life. Think about it . . . God works through sleepless nights, flat tires and cancelled flights. God is there when the baby won't sleep, the car won't start and the bills won't stop. Do you think it's a coincidence that the job went away, the advancement didn't come or that another move is in the future? God is the Great Director, and he has a great part for you to play.

Heavenly Father, I acknowledge that you are sovereign over all! You are at work in my doubt, disappointments and sleepless nights. I trust you. Help me to trust you more. In Jesus' name. Amen.

reflection

_____

_____

_____

_____

_____

_____

_____

further suggested reading:

Esther 5-7

Eternal Deliverance

Esther 9:28

These days should be remembered and observed in every generation by every family, and in every province and in every city. And these days of Purim should never fail to be celebrated by the Jews - nor should the memory of these days die out among their descendants.

Every year, a Jewish friend makes me Hamantaschen, a special cookie in the shape of Haman's hat, to celebrate Purim. She is doing her part to make sure the memory of God's deliverance does not die out among the Jewish descendants.

This person is not just about Jewish traditions. She has a vibrant trust in the Messiah as her Savior and Lord. Despite a debilitating disease that has confined her to a wheelchair, she's been set free through Christ! Her forefathers celebrated their physical deliverance; she celebrates her spiritual one.

How about you? Can you celebrate the deliverance that Jesus brings . . . the eternal deliverance from sin and brokenness and separation from God? Knowing Christ is something that "should never fail to be celebrated."

Father, thank you for the eternal deliverance that comes from Jesus! May we celebrate that freedom every day of our lives. In Jesus' name. Amen.

reflection

further suggested reading:

Esther 8-10

Declare His Praise

Job 1:20-22

At this, Job got up and tore his robe and shaved his head. Then he fell to the ground in worship and said: "Naked I came from my mother's womb, and naked I will depart. The LORD gave and the LORD has taken away; may the name of the LORD be praised." In all this, Job did not sin by charging God with wrongdoing.

Standing by the freshly dug grave, I watched the heavy-hearted couple make their way up a steep hill. The father served as the lone pallbearer. Only one was needed to carry the casket holding the body of his infant son. He placed it on the nylon straps that would lower the small casket into the grave. What do you say to a couple who has lost a child? I remember only hugs and tears as we waited for the rest of the family to gather on the windy hillside.

I said a few words that seemed so inadequate. A relative spoke as well, and I was thankful for his personal and comforting remarks. Then the father spoke. His words were emotional but strong and right from Scripture. Over the sound of the wind blowing through the nearby trees, he said, "The LORD gave and LORD has taken away; may the name of the LORD be praised."

Here in this statement, first uttered by Job in his tragic loss, are words declaring the sovereignty of God and man's only proper response. With broken hearts, tearful eyes and quivering lips, we acknowledge that God is the giver of our first breath and the One who determines our last. Even through our pain we declare his praise.

Father, thank you for the example of that young grieving father on the hillside who declared your sovereignty. God, when we stand in brokenness and pain, may we too declare your praise. For Christ's sake. Amen.

reflection

further suggested reading:

Job 1-3

Spiritual Fatigue

May 17

Job 6:11

What strength do I have, that I should still hope? What prospects, that I should be patient?

These words of Job are often on the lips of those going through difficult times. Loss, grief and discouragement sap our strength. Hurt drives hope from our heart. When there is no forecast of a better tomorrow, waiting seems useless.

Maybe you can relate all too well to Job's questions. You are presently experiencing spiritual fatigue. Hope is lost. With no possible remedy in sight, waiting for God seems to be out of the question. You feel like you need to take matters into your own hands, but you have exhausted all possible solutions.

I don't say this glibly. Hang in there! Let's pray these promises together.

> *He gives strength to the weary and increases the power of the weak.*
> Isaiah 40:29

> *My soul, find rest in God; my hope comes from him. He is my rock and my salvation; he is my fortress, I will not be shaken.*
> Psalm 62:5-6

> *Since ancient times no one has heard, no ear has perceived, no eye has seen any God besides you, who acts on behalf of those who wait for him.*
> Isaiah 64:4

Father, give strength to the spiritually exhausted today. Deliver an overflowing measure of hope to the hopeless heart. For those who are ready to give up, help them to wait for you, as you act on their behalf. In Jesus' name. Amen.

reflection

_____

_____

_____

_____

_____

_____

further suggested reading:

Job 4-7

Forgetting God

Job 8:11-14

Can papyrus grow tall where there is no marsh? Can reeds thrive without water? While still growing and uncut, they wither more quickly than grass. Such is the destiny of all who forget God; so perishes the hope of the godless. What they trust in is fragile; what they rely on is a spider's web.

The words in today's passage were spoken by Bildad, a "friend" of Job. However, as the old saying goes, with friends like him, who needs enemies? While Job suffered, Bildad kept the ill-advised advice coming. But in the middle of his musings, he made a significant point. Hopelessness is the inevitable product of leaving God out of your life.

The destiny, Bildad says, of those who leave God out of their lives is as fragile as a dried up reed that withers "more quickly than grass." The things they rely on to provide security have the strength of a spider's web. Any hope the godless may have perishes with them.

Unfortunately, the godless are not the only ones who struggle in this area. Forgetting God is the believer's struggle. Self-assured and self-reliant, we go our own way doing our own thing. We believe that we are more than capable of handling life without God . . . until the bottom falls out . . . until we learn the hard way that trusting in ourselves is fragile . . . until we learn that what we trusted in fell apart like a spider's web. Thank God for his gracious welcome back when we humbly return from the land of forgetfulness.

Father, forgive us for forgetting you. Forgive us for trusting in fragile things. Help us to keep our trust placed solely in you. In Jesus' name. Amen.

reflection

_____
_____
_____
_____
_____
_____
_____

further suggested reading:

Job 8-10

His Ways Are Certain

Job 12:13-14

To God belong wisdom and power; counsel and understanding are his. What he tears down cannot be rebuilt; those he imprisons cannot be released.

It is one thing to make a statement like the one found in our passage today when things are going well. When the family is healthy, when the job is secure, when you are enjoying a great stretch of life, then it is easy to say, "To God belong wisdom and power." But when Job said these words, he was on a zipline headed down with no end in sight. He was mourning the loss of his children and his health. His wife had told him to curse God and die. To make matters worse, three friends had come to "help."

Yet read Job's words. Reread them. In the midst of grief and suffering, Job can still acknowledge God as sovereign. His ways are certain. When he tears something down, no one can rebuild it. When he binds something up, no one can release it. Wisdom, power, counsel and understanding belong to him.

I don't know your situation. I don't know if you are enjoying a great ride or if you are barely hanging on as your life spirals downward. I do know this. Whatever your situation, God is in control. He has not left you alone or forgotten you. Somehow (and I know this might be hard for you to believe right now) he is working all things together for your good. Can God be trusted? Yes! Can you trust God? I will let you answer that question.

Dear Father, You are close to the brokenhearted. Please make your presence known to those going through difficult times. Remind them that no matter what it "feels" like, you are in control and at work for their good. In Jesus' name. Amen.

reflection

_____

_____

_____

_____

_____

_____

_____

_____

further suggested reading:

Job 11-12

God Forgives Us Completely

Job 14:16-17

Surely then you will count my steps but not keep track of my sin. My offenses will be sealed up in a bag; you will cover over my sin.

Forgiveness. It's an area where many of us struggle. When someone hurts you, it's hard to let it go. We like to take the pain and coddle it, mull it over and relive the hurtful conversation or action. Soon the infection turns to bitterness. And bitterness turns the heart hard and away from God.

Sometimes the hardest person to forgive is ourselves. When we hurt others, the pain often ricochets. The disappointment turns inward. We are devastated by our own actions and words.

Look at today's passage. Job reminds us that God will not keep track of our sin. He seals it up in a bag, buries it in the ground and covers it over. He puts it behind his back. He throws it in the sea of forgetfulness. He puts it out of sight and out of mind. But be sure God does not take sin lightly. He sent his Son to pay sin's penalty on the cross.

God forgives us completely. We need to forgive others . . . and ourselves.

Father, thank you for your complete forgiveness. Help us show our gratitude by offering forgiveness to someone today. In Jesus' name. Amen.

reflection

further suggested reading:

Job 13-14

The Light Is Near

Job 17:11-12

My days have passed, my plans are shattered. Yet the desires of my heart turn night into day; in the face of the darkness light is near.

News flash! Not all of our plans work out. Things that we don't want to happen, do. Things that we do want to happen, don't. Stuff comes into our life unexpectedly. The expected stuff never seems to show up on time. Like Job, our days pass by; our plans and dreams are shattered.

Job experienced the worst of life in spades. Everything he owned - gone. His children - dead. His health - wiped out. Job's name is synonymous with suffering. Yet in the midst of his darkest night, Job never gave up hope. Sitting in the shreds of shattered dreams, the desires of Job's heart kept him going. Sitting in the loneliness of darkness, he knew that light was near.

Have your dreams been shattered? Don't give up hope. Keep the desires of your heart ignited. Don't let shattered plans become abandoned plans. It's the desire to keep pushing forward, to keep hoping, to keep trusting that turns night into day and reminds us that light is near. The light is near . . . hang on!

Father, there is someone reading this who is about to give up. By your spirit, infuse hope into the realms where hopelessness lives. For those living in darkness, remind them that the light is near. In Jesus' name. Amen.

reflection

_____
_____
_____
_____
_____
_____
_____
_____
_____
_____

further suggested reading:

Job 15-17

Our Redeemer Lives!

Job 19:25-27

I know that my redeemer lives, and that in the end he will stand on the earth. And after my skin has been destroyed, yet in my flesh I will see God; I myself will see him with my own eyes - I, and not another. How my heart yearns within me!

Today's passage is one of, if not the most, powerful profession of the hope found in Scripture. Let's break down Job's proclamation.

I know that my redeemer lives. Everything precious to Job was gone. His life was ebbing away. Yet Job clung to knowing God's existence and care.

And in the end he will stand on the earth. When it was all said and done, Job knew that God would be victorious.

And after my skin has been destroyed, yet in my flesh I will see God. Job was confident that he would see God after his death. Job was certain of a resurrected body.

How my heart yearns within me! Job had transitioned from clinging to life to yearning for heaven.

This passage gives tremendous encouragement to all facing death. Our Redeemer lives! We have the confidence that he will deliver us safely home.

Father, thank you for the certainty of eternal life. Remind us often that death is simply a transition to eternal life. Help our hearts to yearn for heaven. In Jesus' name. Amen.

reflection

_____
_____
_____
_____
_____
_____
_____
_____

further suggested reading:

Job 18-19

An Eternal Mindset

Job 21:7

Why do the wicked live on, growing old and increasing in power?

In the opening verses of this book, Job is described as a man who was "blameless and upright;" a man who "feared God and shunned evil." He was "the greatest man among all the people of the East." Then came his three tests. First, everything he owned was destroyed. Second, all his children were killed by a storm. Finally, Satan "afflicted Job with painful sores from the soles of his feet to the top of his head." But "in all this, Job did not sin in what he said."

Most of the book of Job deals with the dialogues between Job and three of his friends who are convinced that this series of tragedies is the result of Job's sin. In Job's responses are words and thoughts found often in the hearts and minds of those going through difficult times. Today's passage is echoed by many who look up from their pain and see the wicked living on, growing old and increasing in power. What are we to think when we see God's people in pain and the wicked prospering?

I believe that there are three things that we learn from this passage. First, life is not a snapshot but a video. While Job's suffering is unimaginable throughout most of the book, God's blessings return to him. Second, we only see what's happening with a person on the outside. The wicked may be prospering on the outside, but we don't see the emptiness, fears and doubts that fill their hearts and minds in the morning and continue throughout the day. On the other hand, the believer can experience peace even in the midst of the greatest trial. Finally, this life is short. The believer, regardless of earthly suffering, will spend eternity in heaven. The wicked, regardless of earthly "prosperity," will spend eternity in hell. The wicked may live on, grow old and increase in power, but time on earth pales in light of eternity.

Father, give us an eternal mindset so that we can live our time on this earth with a proper perspective. In Jesus' name. Amen.

reflection

_____

_____

_____

_____

_____

further suggested reading:

Job 20-21

Chosen

Job 22:1-3

Then Eliphaz the Temanite replied: "Can a man be of benefit to God? Can even a wise person benefit him? What pleasure would it give the Almighty if you were righteous? What would he gain if your ways were blameless?"

"Can a man be of benefit to God?" That's a great question, isn't it? God is the Creator of all things. He is sovereign over all. How can man possibly be of help to God? Let me offer some thoughts.

- Although God can do anything he wants to do, anytime he wants to do it, normally he chooses to work through men and women. He created Adam and Eve to populate the earth. He charged Noah to build the ark. He called Moses to lead Israel out of slavery and Joshua to take them into the Promised Land. He commissioned the disciples to take the Gospel to the ends of the earth.

- Although God can do anything he wants to do, anytime he wants to do it, he has chosen to bring praise to himself through men and women. He tells us that we should demonstrate his work in us in such a way that others will see our good works and give him the honor he deserves.

- Although God can do anything he wants to do, anytime he wants to do it, he has commanded you and me to share the Gospel. We are to be prepared to explain what it means to trust in Jesus Christ as Lord and Savior.

Think of it. The Sovereign Creator has chosen you and me to benefit him in eternal work! If that doesn't get you excited, check your pulse.

Father, it is an amazing truth that you would choose to use me in your eternal work. Thank you for that great and awesome privilege! In Jesus' name. Amen.

reflection

_____

_____

_____

_____

_____

_____

_____

further suggested reading:

Job 22-24

Godly Wisdom

 *May 25*

Job 28:28

And [God] said to the human race, "The fear of the Lord - that is wisdom, and to shun evil is understanding."

How does a person become wise? Where does one get wisdom? Some say wisdom comes from educational training. Put people in the right systems of learning, and they will become wise. Others say wisdom comes from experience. Textbook learning goes only so far. It's the boots-on-the-ground school of hard knocks that produces true knowledge. But God's answer takes us in a different direction.

God says that the essence of wisdom is "the fear of the Lord." To fear the Lord means "to submit to," "to venerate" and "to be in awe of." Wisdom is not acquisition, analysis, assimilation and application of knowledge. The wise man fears the Lord even when he cannot understand God's ways. Wisdom says, "You are God and I am not."

Maybe you are in a Job-like situation. Right now the things you are going through don't make sense. Remember, wisdom does not mean that I know all the answers; it means I know the One who does . . . and I submit myself to him. I didn't say it was easy. But Scripture says that's where godly wisdom begins.

Father, give us the courage and humility to submit ourselves to you. Remind us often that wisdom is not standing with all the facts; rather, it is standing in awe of you. In Jesus' name. Amen.

reflection

_____
_____
_____
_____
_____
_____
_____
_____
_____
_____

further suggested reading:

Job 25-28

Temptation

May 26

Job 31:1

I made a covenant with my eyes not to look lustfully at a young woman.

Long before *Playboy, Sex and the City*, adult programming and the Internet, there was lust - the uncontrolled or illicit sexual desire or appetite. Lust lives in the heart long before it is aroused through the gates of the mind. Job made an agreement with his "gate keepers."

Temptation isn't a sin. It's the giving in to the longing that causes the fall. Job made a pact with his eyes, to refrain from the second and third or even a fixed look at the opposite sex that might catch his attention. Job's statement, "I made a covenant" is not a casual, "I probably shouldn't do that." Rather, it was a serious commitment saying, "I won't do that!"

I encourage every man to read *Every Man's Battle* by Stephen Arterburn. The book reminds us how easy it is to fall in this area and gives practical helps on how to make the same commitment Job made. I have only had one man tell me he was not tempted in this area. Unfortunately, his denial led to a fall. Don't deny the temptation. Take steps, like Job, to live obediently.

Father, some reading this today have given in to the sin of lust. Give them the courage to admit their sin, confess it and get the help they need to make Job's covenant. In Jesus' name. Amen.

reflection

further suggested reading:

Job 29-30

Security

Job 31:24-25, 28

If I have put my trust in gold or said to pure gold, 'You are my security,' if I have rejoiced over my great wealth, the fortune my hands had gained . . . then these also would be sins to be judged, for I would have been unfaithful to God on high.

Jesse Livermore (1877-1940) was a Wall Street legend. Even after the market crashed in 1929, he was still worth more than $100 million. His trading techniques are still used in the stock market. Arthur Cutten (1870-1932) was one of the wealthiest Americans in the 1920s. He saw a grain shortage coming in 1924 and made several million dollars by buying up the grain futures. Ivar Krueger (1880-1932) was a Swedish hero for the money and business he brought to his country. He was called the "match king" for his European monopoly on the match industry.

However, Livermore was bankrupt. In his 1940 suicide note, he told his wife that he was a failure. Cutten was eventually prosecuted on fraud and tax evasion. He died of a heart attack. Before Kruegar took his own life, deception was discovered in his business holdings. His companies owed more than the Swedish national debt.

One writer says, "Like many others who never make the headlines, these men could make a living, but they never learned how to live." That's what happens when wealth is our security. We start believing in the god of money and begin the long slippery slide to the bottom of the slope.

Father, forgive us for thinking that security is found in anything other than you. Forgive us if we have been unfaithful to you in this area. Remind us, one more time, that we can't serve you and money. In Jesus' name. Amen.

reflection

_____

_____

_____

_____

_____

_____

_____

_____

further suggested reading:

Job 31

153

Be Still and Listen

Job 33:12-14

But I tell you, in this you are not right, for God is greater than any mortal. Why do you complain to him that he responds to no one's words? For God does speak - now one way, now another - though no one perceives it.

Job was spent. He was worn out from his suffering and worn down by the misplaced advice of his friends. In his despair, Job felt that God would not respond to him. He concluded that God was silent. Been there? There now?

A fourth person enters the story to address Job's situation. His name is Elihu, and after a short introduction, he refutes Job's thinking that God is silent. "For God does speak," Elihu asserts, "now one way, now another - though no one perceives it." The noise of life makes it hard to hear God speaking. But that doesn't mean he is hushed. In fact, he often speaks most clearly in the most challenging times. As C. S. Lewis wrote, "God whispers to us in our pleasures, speaks to us in our conscience, but shouts in our pains: It is His megaphone to rouse a deaf world" (C.S. Lewis, *The Problem of Pain*, Harper Collins. 2001).

Remember, God is not silent. He has not forgotten you. Be still and listen. Hear his whispers. Hear him speaking. Hear him shouting how much he loves you even in your pain. Hold on! Don't give up! He's coming to your rescue.

Father, I admit that there are times when it seems you are silent. Help me listen more closely. Help me get away from the noise. Calm my heart to hear your whispers. Encourage my heart with your shouts. In Jesus' name. Amen.

reflection

_____

_____

_____

_____

_____

_____

_____

_____

_____

_____

further suggested reading:

Job 32-34

How Great Is God

Job 36:26

How great is God - beyond our understanding! The number of his years is past finding out.

How can those trapped in an aging body understand the One who never changes?

How can those who measure life by birthdays comprehend the One who has never had one?

How can one who stumbles in sin understand the One who stands in perfection?

How can people who struggle with communication wrap their minds around the One who spoke the world into existence?

How can those who watch man's great creations collapse (think Twin Towers) understand the Creator of the universe whose creation continues to stand?

How can people who need stepladders to hang pictures on a wall comprehend the One who hung the stars in the sky?

How can those who don't know what they are going to eat for lunch understand the One who knows what you are going to have for lunch on May 29, 2099, or if you'll even be needing lunch that day?

How can one trapped in space understand the One who is everywhere at the same time in his full being?

How can one who is powerless understand the One who is omnipotent?

How can those who can't control their two-year-old understand the One who is in sovereign control over world leaders?

"How great is God - beyond our understanding!" How arrogant are those who won't believe until they can fully comprehend the Incomprehensible, describe the Indescribable and fathom the Unfathomable. The starting point of wisdom is standing in awe of God.

Father, we bow before you the incomprehensible God. Although we can't fully understand you, thank you for revealing all we need to know about you in your Word. In Jesus' name. Amen.

further suggested reading:

Job 35-37

He Can Be Trusted

Job 38:1-5

Then the LORD spoke to Job out of the storm. He said: "Who is this that obscures my plans with words without knowledge? Brace yourself like a man; I will question you, and you shall answer me. "Where were you when I laid the earth's foundation? Tell me, if you understand. Who marked off its dimensions? Surely you know! Who stretched a measuring line across it?"

Job had been through hell on earth. He lost his possessions, his children and his health. Discouragement set in like a winter blizzard, and he began to question God's love. Finally, God responds. Quite honestly, I want God to come with tenderness and comfort. I admit that after all Job has been through, God's "Brace yourself like a man; I will question you, and you shall answer me" sounds a little harsh. Remember that the anchor that we hold onto during the difficult times is God's character. He is all-loving even when he tells us to "brace" ourselves.

In our passage today, God reminds Job why he can be trusted. He is eternal. There was never a time when he was not; there will never be a time when he is not. He is independent. He depends on no one or no thing for his existence. He didn't need Job to hold one end of the tape measure when he marked off the dimensions of the earth. He is the Creator. Whatever exists is created by and sustained by his gracious hand.

You see, God knew that the answer to Job's questions was not "Why?" but "Who?" When we understand that the "Who?" behind all our life is God, that knowledge translates into trust.

Lord Jesus, our prayer today is this: let our knowledge of who you are allow us to trust you every step of the journey. In your name. Amen.

reflection

_____

_____

_____

_____

_____

_____

further suggested reading:

Job 38-39

Focus on God

Job 42:1-6

Then Job replied to the LORD: "I know that you can do all things; no purpose of yours can be thwarted. You asked, 'Who is this that obscures my plans without knowledge?' Surely I spoke of things I did not understand, things too wonderful for me to know. You said, 'Listen now, and I will speak; I will question you, and you shall answer me.' My ears had heard of you but now my eyes have seen you. Therefore I despise myself and repent in dust and ashes."

After tragedy struck, Job moved into the natural and normal period of questioning. But God abruptly confronted Job and refocused his vision. Job was looking at his situation; God said, "Look at me." With his focus on God, Job saw three things.

First, Job saw God's omnipotence. His power enables him to do anything he desires to do. Second, Job saw God's incomprehensibility. God acts in ways our puny human minds simply cannot grasp. Even in tragedy, there are things "too wonderful for [us] to know." Third, Job saw God at work. Job moved from knowledge about God to seeing and experiencing God. This overwhelming knowledge moved him to repentance.

If you are going through a difficult situation, let me remind you that this change of heart doesn't happen overnight. Through the healing process, God gives us time and space to ask our questions. Faith and doubt, courage and discouragement, strength and weakness weave in and out of our emotions like the on-again-off-again warmth of the sun on a partially cloudy day. Keep looking to him . . . even through your tears. Keep talking to him . . . even with your questions. Keep trusting him . . . even in your doubts. He loves you! He cares for you! You can trust him!

Father, please shine your comfort on the people going through a great challenge. Hold them close to you. Help them experience your presence. Help them to say with Job, "My ears had heard of you, but now my eyes have seen you." In Christ's name. Amen.

reflection

_____

_____

_____

further suggested reading:

Job 40-42

Ruler of All

Psalm 2:6-7

"I have installed my King on Zion, my mountain." I will proclaim the Lord's decree: He said to me, "You are my holy son; today I have become your father."

Written by David, 1000 years before Christ, this Messianic psalm proclaims that the Anointed One is on the way. The psalm describes a coronation ceremony where the Ruler is crowned. The psalm exhorts the pagan nations to abandon their rebellious plans and submit to the Son.

God sent his Son to earth in a way that caused many to miss him. Born to a poor young Jewish girl, Jesus grew up with the stigma of illegitimacy. His three years of ministry were seemingly cut short by a humiliating death on a Roman cross. His resume was hardly that of a King.

Yet it was because of his humility and obedience to death that "God exalted him to the highest place and gave him the name that is above every name." Jesus is the King installed on Zion, God's holy hill. One day every knee will bow and every tongue confess that he is Lord . . . Ruler of all! Don't wait until it's too late. Confess Jesus as your Savior, Lord and King today!

Father, may we surrender to the King each day. May we serve him with a full-out passion. May we demonstrate that he is indeed the Lord of our lives. In Jesus' name. Amen.

reflection

_____

_____

_____

_____

_____

_____

_____

_____

_____

_____

_____

further suggested reading:

Psalms 1-6

Birthmark

Psalm 11:1-2

In the LORD I take refuge. How then can you say to me: "Flee like a bird to your mountain. For look, the wicked bend their bows; they set their arrows against the strings to shoot from the shadows at the upright in heart."

I am sure you have seen the cartoon with two deer talking to each other. One deer has what looks like a big target with a bull's-eye in the middle positioned over his heart. The other deer says, "Bummer of a birthmark, Ralph."

If you are a believer, you have a "birthmark" in the shape of a cross right on your heart. It is a constant reminder that Jesus came and died an awful death so that you can have an abundant life . . . today and forever. However, be sure of this, that "birthmark" makes you a target of the enemy. Satan prowls around like a lion looking for an opportunity to spring out from the shadows.

We are no match for Satan and his sinister schemes. But remember your "birthmark!" You belong to the One who has already defeated the enemy and his most potent weapon . . . death. You can say confidently with the Psalmist, "In the Lord I take refuge." That's the beauty of our "birthmark."

Father, today, in the midst of the enemy's attack, we take refuge in you and you alone. In Jesus' name. Amen.

reflection

further suggested reading:

Psalms 7-11

The Lord Is on His Heavenly Throne

Psalm 11:4

The LORD is in his holy temple; the LORD is on his heavenly throne. He observes everyone on Earth; his eyes examine them.

When discouragement barges through the front door of your heart . . . *The LORD is in his holy temple; the LORD is on his heavenly throne.*

When you feel insignificant and alone . . . *The LORD is in his holy temple; the LORD is on his heavenly throne.*

When the stock market takes your financial future on a bungee cord jump . . . *The LORD is in his holy temple; the LORD is on his heavenly throne.*

When you feel like tomorrow's meeting is "do or die" for your career . . . *The LORD is in his holy temple; the LORD is on his heavenly throne.*

When your child jettisons the faith . . . *The LORD is in his holy temple; the LORD is on his heavenly throne.*

When you feel like your spiritual journey is moving backward instead of forward . . . *The LORD is in his holy temple; the LORD is on his heavenly throne.*

When you are waiting for the test results . . . *The LORD is in his holy temple; the LORD is on his heavenly throne.*

When you are grieving the death of a loved one . . . *The LORD is in his holy temple; the LORD is on his heavenly throne.*

When you are grieving the death of a dream . . . *The LORD is in his holy temple; the LORD is on his heavenly throne.*

God is always on his heavenly throne . . . ***and he never takes his eyes off you!***

Father, thank you for the reminder of your sovereign power and your intimate care. In Jesus' name. Amen.

reflection

_____

_____

_____

further suggested reading:

Psalm 12

My Rock, Fortress and Deliverer

Psalm 18:2

The LORD is my rock, my fortress and my deliverer; my God is my rock, in whom I take refuge, my shield and the horn of my salvation, my stronghold.

This verse is packed! Let's break it down.

My Rock: Here is the picture of a huge rock that a person could hide behind. God is our stable and secure hiding place.

My Fortress: A fortress was a high place of shelter and defense where a person could run for protection. What a beautiful picture of the heavenly Father!

My Deliverer: I am incapable of rescuing myself. God is the One who comes to find me and carries me out of harm's way.

My Refuge: God is a strong tower that I run into for safety.

My Shield: As the soldier uses his shield to stop flaming arrows or the enemy's weapon in hand-to-hand combat, so God protects me from the flaming darts of Satan.

My Horn of Salvation: Animal's horns were symbols of strength. It is God who will give me all I need to do whatever he calls me to do.

My Stronghold: When God is with me, I can stand my ground against the enemy. With God I never have to retreat.

Father, I am helpless and hopeless on my own. I thank you for being my Rock, fortress, deliverer, refuge, shield, horn of salvation and stronghold! Thank you in Jesus' name. Amen.

reflection

_____

_____

_____

_____

_____

_____

_____

further suggested reading:

Psalms 13-18

The Glory of God

Psalm 19:1-3

The heavens declare the glory of God; the skies proclaim the work of his hands. Day after day they pour forth speech; night after night they reveal knowledge. They have no speech, they use no words; no sound is heard from them.

For some reason, I am impressed with the magnificence of the heavens each summer when we visit our family in Oklahoma. Maybe my awareness is due to the big Oklahoma sky. Maybe it's because we are away from the city lights. Or maybe it's because during our time away, I slow down enough to look up (I hope that's not the case). Often Lori and I stand outside and gaze at the stars. We check out the Big and Little Dippers, the Seven Sisters, the North Star and a bunch of other constellations that we try to locate on our star locator app. But one thing's for sure, *the heavens declare the glory of God.*

C. H. Spurgeon wrote that "the book of nature has three leaves, heaven, earth, and sea, of which heaven is the first and the most glorious, and by its aid we are able to see the beauties of the other two" (C.H. Spurgeon, *The Treasure of David*, Unknown, 1984). True, isn't it? When we look up into the skies we see God's glory shining in the stars.

The same God, whose glory shines in the sky, desires to shine in you and through you. Paul says that he wants us to "shine like stars in the universe" (Philippians 2:15). Maybe you don't feel much like shining today. In fact, some circumstances in your life are making you feel rather dull. I encourage you to look up. God loves you so much that he sent his only Son to die on a cross just for you. Through Christ, you can let your light shine in such a way that people see God at work in your life. Ready? Time to shine!

Father, thank you for revealing yourself in the heavens. I pray that you would reveal yourself personally to all who are reading these words. Through Christ allow each of us to "shine like stars in the universe." In Jesus' name. Amen.

reflection

_____

_____

_____

_____

_____

_____

further suggested reading:

Psalms 19-24

Singular Endeavor

June 6

Psalm 27:4

One thing I ask from the LORD, this only do I seek: that I may dwell in the house of the LORD all the days of my life, to gaze upon the beauty of the LORD and to seek him in his temple.

My most dangerous times are unfocused times. Pursuits, activities and responsibilities - all good in and of themselves - pull me in many different directions, and, more often than I like to admit, I lose my focus. Spurgeon says it this way: "Divided aims tend to distraction, weakness, disappointment." I have experienced that to be true.

But King David, a man with much on his plate, focused his sights on "one thing." This singular endeavor was his heart's desire and active quest. David wanted a heart ignited with a burning passion to follow hard after God. He was not content to just read about God or think about God or talk about God. David desired to experience God's presence every day of his life.

An ignited heart is not cloistered in a commune. The fire burns in the normal activities of life. This focused fire burns with a passionate desire to follow God in the twists and turns, up the mountains and down the valleys of this journey we call life. And whether we are running at full speed or standing still to catch our breath, whether we are carefully positioning our feet for the climb or maneuvering the steep descent, we have this "one thing" . . . desire. Oh, God, let the fire burn!

Father, that is our prayer and desire. Please, by your Spirit, let your fire burn in our hearts. In Jesus' name. Amen.

reflection

_____

_____

_____

_____

_____

_____

_____

_____

_____

_____

further suggested reading:

Psalms 25-30

God Is Always Close

Psalm 34:18

The LORD is close to the brokenhearted and saves those who are crushed in spirit.

Broken hearts come in many forms. Some are crushed by a sixth grade break-up; others when he walks out after twenty-five years. Some come from the rejection of a dear friend; others by reckless words that pierce like a sword. Some hearts are broken when the job is lost; others when the retirement watch doesn't quite justify the years of sacrifice. Sometimes kids go astray or go away. Sometimes loneliness sits heavy on the heart. Sometimes discouragement settles in, and you're not sure when or why it came. Sometimes you come to the crushing realization that what you desperately wanted is just not going to happen. Anyone who lives this life will experience a broken heart, that's for sure.

And there is another thing that's for sure - the Lord will be right there with you. God is always close. If you are a follower of Jesus, he lives in you! But there is something about a broken heart that highlights his presence. There's something about a crushed spirit that amplifies his voice. Funny, isn't it? When our hearts hurt, we hear him more clearly. When our spirit is crushed, we see him more plainly.

It's not like we go out looking for a broken heart or excitedly anticipate a crushed spirit. But they will come - unforeseen, uninvited, unwelcomed. The Lord is close with comfort. The Lord is there with hope. He never lets go of his children. He saves those who are crushed in spirit.

Father, thank you for the promise of your word. Thank you for being close to the brokenhearted. We know that, Father, because you are close to us. Thank you in Jesus' name. Amen.

reflection

_____

_____

_____

_____

_____

_____

_____

further suggested reading:

Psalms 31-36

Help Is on the Way

June 8

Psalm 40:1-3

I waited patiently for the LORD; he turned to me and heard my cry. He lifted me out of the slimy pit, out of the mud and mire; he set my feet on a rock and gave me a firm place to stand. He put a new song in my mouth, a hymn of praise to our God. Many will see and fear and put their trust in the LORD.

What do you do when the results of your sin deliver you into a "slimy pit"? Where do you go for relief from "the mud and mire" of self-inflicted wounds? While the specifics of this Psalm are not known, we do know that David asked for rescue from a hole dug by his own sin (Psalm 40:12).

Sometimes our arrogance or ignorance causes us to conclude that God will not be around in difficult situations of our own making. We hear God saying, "You made your bed; now lie in it." But God is not the one who causes those words to rattle in our heads. Even when our backs are turned on him, he turns to us. Even when we distance ourselves, he still hears our cry for help. Our Father responds to the needs of his children.

He lifts us out of sin's slippery places and puts us on a rock of forgiveness and restoration so that we can stand firm. He replaces our cries for help with a new song, a "hymn of praise." We damage our reputation and witness. But God's work in our life causes onlookers to "see" what he has done, "fear" his mighty power and "put their trust in the Lord." Wait patiently for the Lord. Help is on the way!

Father, thank you for coming to our aid even when we cry out to you from the pit of sin-inflicted situations. Thank you for forgiveness and restoration. Thank you for firm footing that allows us to return to the journey of obedience. In Jesus' name. Amen.

reflection

_____
_____
_____
_____
_____
_____
_____

further suggested reading:

Psalms 37-41

Meet with God

June 9

Psalm 42:1-2

As the deer pants for streams of water, so my soul pants for you, my God. My soul thirsts for God, for the living God. When can I go and meet with God?

The deer is out of breath and out of strength. His running through the mountains has exhausted his body but focused his mind. There is one thing he can think about . . . one thing he needs. He yearns for a mountain stream, running with cold, refreshing water. He pants for water in his breath, thinks about where to find it in his mind and longs for it in his heart.

The psalmist likens the deer's search for water to his quest for God. As every part of the deer desires a drink, so every part of the psalmist craves God. His inward parts thirst for the living God. He wants to be near God, wants to enjoy God, wants to experience God and wants to be satisfied by God.

That's not only the desire of the psalmist, is it? You and I want the same thing. We have tried many things that left our soul dry. We have sampled the world's offerings without being satisfied. We have hiked the dead-end trails and scaled the wrong mountains. It's time to meet with God. Thankfully, we need not look for him; he has made himself known to us through Christ.

Father, allow all those who are thirsty to look up and see you. Allow all those who are hungry be filled by you alone. Thank you for coming to us, revealing yourself to us and satisfying our deepest longing. In Jesus' name. Amen.

reflection

_____
_____
_____
_____
_____
_____
_____
_____
_____

further suggested reading:

Psalms 42-45

Difficult Times

Psalm 42:5

Why, my soul, are you downcast? Why so disturbed within me? Put your hope in God, for I will yet praise him, my Savior and my God.

The Christian life is not free from challenges. In fact, this may not be the news you want to hear - a person following hard after Christ will experience some hard times. No one goes out seeking a dark valley. But, ready or not, here they come. Do you know anyone who hasn't experienced a deep disappointment, a relationship break-up, a loss, the death of a loved one, an undesired move, a wayward child, personal rejection, illness? The list goes on. In this life there will be trouble.

In his book, *The Faith,* Charles Colson has an excellent chapter dealing with the inevitable suffering of the Christian life. Based solidly in Scripture and illustrated with stories of real people, Colson says that "suffering belongs to our calling as Christians." Regarding the inevitability of tough times, Colson writes, "This is why easy-believism, the prosperity gospel, is so abominable: it sets a person up for a terrible fall when the first hardship comes, as it will. Whatever glimmer of faith the person might have had may well be snuffed out." Then Colson concludes, "So the real question is not whether we will suffer but how we will react to adversity when it comes. We can see it as a miserable experience to be endured, or we can offer it to God for his redemptive purposes" (*The Faith*, Charles Colson, Zondervan, 2008).

The man after God's own heart knew his share of difficult times. David experienced disappointment and discouragement firsthand. He wrote of his hard times openly and often in the Psalms. But David also knew that God never wastes our time. He uses every circumstance to build us, grow us and develop us. God uses them, as Colson says, "for his redemptive purposes."

Whatever you are going through today, even if your soul is "downcast" and "disturbed," I invite you to join David in his prayer:

Oh, God, my hope is in you. Oh, my God, I will praise you! [Then wait quietly and ask him to ignite your heart.] *In Jesus' name. Amen.*

reflection

_____

_____

_____

_____

further suggested reading:

Psalms 46-49

God Owns All Things

June 11

Psalm 50:9-12

I have no need of a bull from your stall or of goats from your pens, for every animal of the forest is mine, and the cattle on a thousand hills. I know every bird in the mountains, and the insects in the fields are mine. If I were hungry I would not tell you, for the world is mine, and all that is in it.

This passage reminds us of God's ownership of all things and sets the stage for the believer's theology of possessions. Check this out.

- **God owns all things.**
  The earth is the Lord's and everything in it (Psalm 24:1). From the raw material to everything made from it, God is the sole owner of all things. Do you believe that? . . . Really?

- **Everything we have is a gift from God.**
  We fool ourselves into thinking that our hard work and acumen here allowed us to have the things we have. But be sure, we have nothing that has not been given to us by God. Do you treat what you have as rightful possessions or gracious gifts?

- **Everything we have is to be used to honor God.**
  God has given me everything that I have for a purpose. I cannot spend his gifts on myself in the vacuum of a self-absorbed life. Are you honoring God with what he has given you?

- **As a manager of God's gifts, I must be faithful.**
  The requirement of a manager is to be faithful with what has been entrusted to you (1 Corinthians 4:2). Are you using God's gracious gifts according to his desires?

Father, it's easy to conclude that we are owners, not managers; consumers, not stewards. We fool ourselves into thinking that what we have is a result of our training, expertise and hard work. Remind us often of the truth in today's passage. Help us to manage your gifts in a way that honors you. In Jesus' name. Amen.

reflection

further suggested reading:

Psalms 50-54

Pole of Fear

June 12

Psalm 56:3-4

When I am afraid, I put my trust in you. In God, whose word I praise - in God I trust and am not afraid. What can mere mortals do to me?

Scott is a daredevil . . . to say the least. I have never seen him back down from anything. From his cycle riding to his traveling the world to his business ventures, the term "risk-taker" aptly describes him. That's why I was so surprised when he wouldn't climb the pole to the zipline platform. Granted, the zip-line platform was high. And, granted, the pole to the platform demanded a few maneuvers, but I never expected him to say, "I'm not climbing that pole!" No matter how much we encouraged and cajoled, his feet stayed planted on the ground. We had some serious (and not so serious) discussions about Scott's refusal to climb. But here's one thing that we concluded: **_Everybody has a "Pole of Fear."_** You may be described as a risk taker, but there is something you won't or can't do because of your fear.

What is your "Pole of Fear"? Does it have to do with your family? Is it found in relationships? Do you fear getting close to others? Maybe your "Pole of Fear" makes itself known in your job. Maybe your self-doubt is a subconscious paralyzer. Maybe you fear failure. You can't stand the thought of letting someone down or letting him or her see your vulnerability. Or maybe your "Pole of Fear" is getting close to God and letting others help you in the process.

Remember, everyone has a "Pole of Fear." The words "fear" and "afraid" are found 483 times in the Bible! But the remedy to fear is found in today's passage. The psalmist says, "When I am afraid, I put my trust in you . . . in God I trust and am not afraid." Turn your fear over to God. He is more than capable to turn your "Pole of Fear" into a pathway of faith.

Father, we are all afraid of something. As we stand before our poles of fear today, help us to trust in you. Thank you for giving us everything we need to climb. In Jesus' name. Amen.

reflection

further suggested reading:

Psalms 55-59

Calm Your Heart

Psalm 62:1-2

Truly my soul finds rest in God alone; my salvation comes from him. Truly he is my rock and my salvation; he is my fortress, I will never be shaken.

On a recent trip to Washington D.C. with my family, I could feel the vibration of each email, text and call as I carried my phone in my pocket. While checking out the sights in our nation's capital, I was tempted to see who was communicating with me and what he or she wanted. I know what I wanted . . . a respite from work. I wanted to focus on my family. But the temptation was there to check out each vibrating reminder that someone needed, or thought he needed, my attention. In today's multi-media world, we are always plugged in. But here's our problem . . . we are plugged into the wrong source.

I can only find the rest for my worn-out soul in one place - God alone. The first part of today's passage literally reads, "Only to God is my soul silent." Only to God did David look with complete calmness. He knew that God was his "rock" (source of safety) and "salvation" (deliverance). David said God "is my fortress" and like a soldier sitting inside the impenetrable walls of a great stronghold, David rested in the Lord.

How about you? Are you wearied from being plugged in to the wrong sources? Are the distracting calls of life turning your attention from the only One who can bring calmness to your frenetic heart? I challenge you to an experiment. For one day, unplug from Facebook, Twitter, email, texting, phone calls, radio, computer and television. Start that day by reading God's word, spending time in prayer and continuing to communicate with God throughout the day. Take a walk on a trail, or spend some time at a park enjoying God's great creation. God can calm your heart. You've just been too busy to let him.

Father, we can get wound tight over small things. Help us find rest in the midst of our responsibilities. And remind us often that real rest is found only in you. In Jesus' name. Amen.

reflection

_____

_____

_____

_____

_____

further suggested reading:

Psalms 60-66

170

Heavy Burdens

June 14

Psalm 68:19

Praise be to the Lord, to God our Savior, who daily bears our burdens.

In some stretches of life, the burdens are weighty. Sickness, diagnosis, treatments and recovery produce a tangible load on our souls. Death and grief cloud our hearts and minds with a thick fog. Job loss shocks, then discourages. If the new job doesn't come on our timeline, a wave of "what-if" panic sets in. Challenges with children, strained relationships, delayed dreams, death of dreams, failure, sin . . . the list of heavy burdens continues.

The weighty stretch becomes unbearable when we feel that the load must be carried alone. The situation is always present. We feel the weight with each step. Soon a once overflowing heart is depleted of joy, energy and desire to keep going.

But . . . "Praise be to the Lord, to God our Savior" . . . we don't have to carry the things that weigh down the soul! We don't even have to share the load! We have One who carries every weighty concern that we have stuffed in our backpacks. We have One who walks with us, lives with us, in fact, lives in us! We have One who relieves the pressure, takes away the guilt, gives courage in the face of death, gently blows away the fog of grief, provides us whatever we need to do whatever he calls us to do and restores a sense of real joy to the broken heart. He is asking you, right now, to stop and lay your burdens down. He desires to pick up the heavy pack and carry it for you. God our Savior is the One who "daily bears our burdens!"

Dear Father, thank you. Thank you for not letting me walk alone. Thank you for not letting me walk with the weight. Thank you for carrying my burdens today. Thank you, in advance, for carrying my burdens tomorrow. In Jesus' name. Amen.

reflection

further suggested reading:

Psalms 67-72

Take Me There

Psalm 73:23-24

Yet I am always with you; you hold me by my right hand. You guide me with your counsel, and afterward you will take me into glory.

Asaph was discouraged. Even though he was the leader of one of King David's three Levitical choirs, even though he was serving the Lord, Asaph "envied the arrogant when [he] saw the prosperity of the wicked." Asaph said, "When I tried to understand all this, it troubled me deeply." But then he gained an eternal perspective. In contrast to the temporary and ultimately meaningless gains of the "wicked," Asaph noted the godly advantages. Check out four benefits found in today's passage.

I am always with you. The personal relationship we have with the eternal God is more precious than any earthly possession. Check that - all earthly possessions! The Creator is always with us, living in us. Presence!

You hold me by my right hand. Asaph said, "My feet had almost slipped; I had nearly lost my foothold." But the Father is there, holding me steady by my right hand with his strong right hand. Security!

You guide me with your counsel. As we approach forks in the road, he warns us of the dangerous path and guides us along the right way. God's Word is light for the journey. Protection!

And afterward you will take me into glory. I just got back from a Starbucks run with my daughter. She plugged her iPhone into the auxiliary, and we crooned this song about heaven by Trip Lee called *Take Me There* (Okay, it's a rap, but the words are great). Check out the chorus (you can Google the verses).

> I just wanna go where
> I'm only breathing your air
> Father hear my prayer
> Take me there
> Take me there
> (I wanna see you)
> I just wanna see you
> Brighter than I'm used to you
> Finally see it clear see it
> Take me there
> Take me there
> Take me there

Father, thank you that death is only a transition into eternal life. Thank you that one day you will take me into glory where I'm only breathing your air. Thank you that one day I'll see you brighter than I'm used to. Thank you that one day you will take me there! In Jesus' name. Amen.

further suggested reading:

Psalms 73-77

The Sheep Pens

Psalm 78:70-71

He chose David his servant and took him from the sheep pens; from tending the sheep he brought him to be the shepherd of his people Jacob, of Israel his inheritance.

God normally ignites our hearts in natural ways. I believe a burning passion is kindled in the midst of the normal everyday "sheep pens" of life - carpooling kids to practice, making house payments, repairing leaky toilets, contemplating career changes, doing relationships, building a marriage, working through conflict and writing checks for car repairs. It's from the "sheep pens" that God calls us to higher levels of meaning and significance. That's what happened to King David.

God called David to the palace from the pens. It was in David's lonely, thankless, smelly shepherding work that God ignited the future leader's heart. David learned the art of shepherding sheep and then transferred the principles to people. David's heart of integrity that developed when no one was looking became the same heart of integrity that led a nation to greatness. The skill in nurturing, protecting and caring for sheep became the skill in leading a people to worship God. But remember, God developed David in the pens.

Maybe you feel like you are living and working in the "sheep pens." It stinks. It's not particularly pleasant. It's not where you want to be or thought you would be. You feel alone and maybe even abandoned. Let me remind you that God is not wasting your time. Today he is preparing you for tomorrow. Remember that he does his best work in the sheep pens.

Father, give us patience in the pens. Help us learn all you need us to learn so that we can be the servants you desire us to be. In Jesus' name. Amen.

reflection

_____
_____
_____
_____
_____
_____

further suggested reading:

Psalms 78-80

Godly Shepherds

June 17

Psalm 78:72

And David shepherded them with integrity of heart; with skillful hands he led them.

Today's passage is our staff's theme verse at The Bible Chapel. I chose it years ago while studying through the Psalms. It describes the three things that we are committed to do as church leaders . . . and three things that we should be committed to do as followers of Jesus.

Shepherd. Empty sheep pens never get messy. But where there are sheep, there are messes. Shepherding is the calling to be involved in the mess of people's lives. Adultery and addictions, divorce and depression, broken bodies and broken hearts - life is messy. But shepherds (imperfect and broken themselves) are willing to wade through the mess and tend the sheep.

Integrity of heart. Shepherds must tend their hearts. It won't take long for an unhealthy shepherd to have a pen full of unhealthy sheep. Leaders must lead themselves before they can lead others.

Skillful hands. Leaders are learners. We must constantly develop shepherding skills that benefit those God has placed in our charge. An unskilled, untrained and undisciplined shepherd will lead the sheep down dangerous and deadly paths.

This verse is not just for church leaders. From parents of children to presidents of companies, we must lead with tender shepherding, integrity of heart and skillful hands.

Father, makes us godly shepherds. Give us the desire to develop whole and obedient hearts. Give us the craving to continue to develop the skills of our calling. In Jesus' name. Amen.

reflection

further suggested reading:

Psalms 81-83

The Promise of Eternal Life

Psalm 89:48

Who can live and not see death, or who can escape the power of the grave?

On my desk to the left of my computer is a *Time* magazine with the cover story, *How To Die.* Describing the last days of his mom and dad, the story is written by Joe Klein, I have no problem with the topic. But I do find it strange that *Time* is explaining how to die without addressing what happens next. Okay, maybe I don't find that strange . . . just sad.

Scripture is clear that everyone is going to die. The writer of the Hebrews tells us that it is appointed unto men once to die (Hebrews 9:27). No one has the power over the day of his death (Ecclesiastes 8:8). Death is indeed the destiny of every man (Ecclesiastes 7:2). But Scripture is also clear that death is not final. Following death, judgment comes (Hebrews 9:27). And for the believer, the Judge is our Savior, who is there to welcome us home.

If you are walking through the last days with someone whom you love, I encourage you to talk openly and honestly about Jesus. Let him or her know how much he loves them. Let him or her know that he died for his or her sins on the cross. Use the time to explain how he or she can know him and be sure of what happens when he or she closes his or her eyes in death. Let's not leave it to *Time* to teach us how to die. God's word is the only place we find the promise of eternal life. Here are some passages to read and reflect upon.

John 5:24
Very truly I tell you, whoever hears my word and believes him who sent me has eternal life and will not be judged but has crossed over from death to life.

John 8:51
Very truly I tell you, whoever obeys my word will never see death.

John 11:25-26
Jesus said to her, "I am the resurrection and the life. The one who believes in me will live, even though they die; and whoever lives by believing in me will never die."

Father, thank you that even when we walk through the valley of the shadow of death, we don't have to fear. Thank you for being with us to give us the courage and comfort we need to cross over from death to life through Jesus. In his name we pray. Amen.

further suggested reading:

Psalms 84-89

Crashing Waves

Psalm 94:18-19

When I said, "My foot is slipping," your unfailing love, LORD, supported me.
When anxiety was great within me, your consolation brought me joy.

Sometimes we can feel it coming on. Like a person who loses his footing on a steep climb, we can feel our emotions slipping. The waves of anxiety build until they crash into our hearts and drench our souls.

- *Our teenager is late coming home on a stormy night.*
- *Our boss wants to see us first thing in the morning.*
- *The doctor wants to run some more tests.*
- *Our mind swirls in the waiting room for news from the surgery.*
- *The doctor says, "I'm sorry. There is nothing more we can do."*
- *She was supposed to call to tell me if I got the job an hour ago.*
- *The savings are gone.*
- *He walks out the door.*

Life is filled with things that cause our emotions to slip and fear to crowd in. The stuff of life is beyond our control. And it's the lack of control that causes our emotions to implode. What do we do standing in the midst of life when we feel the fear coming on? The psalmist instructs us to turn hard toward God.

It is our loving Father who comes to our aid. As we take on the crashing waves, he keeps us standing. When our feet begin to slip, he grabs us and holds on tight. His peace passes human understanding. His comfort brings joy even in the midst of howling winds of trials. When we know God, help is not on the way; our Helper is always present with us.

Father, some people are reading this with a heart saturated by anxiety. Allow them right now to feel the calming comfort of your Spirit. Give them a certainty of your presence that always comes with a deep peace. Let them know that since you are for us, nothing can stand against us. In Jesus' name. Amen.

reflection

_____

_____

_____

_____

_____

further suggested reading:

Psalms 90-97

Sing a New Song

Psalm 98:1

Sing to the LORD a new song, for he has done marvelous things; his right hand and his holy arm have worked salvation for him.

Many years ago, we had Sunday evening services at The Bible Chapel where people could stand up and share a short devotion. Every year, the parents of a longtime member would visit and his father would share. The first time that I heard the father speak, it was amazing. He took an obscure passage of the Old Testament and made it come alive. When he visited the next year, he shared from the same passage. It was still pretty good. Then the next year . . . same passage. And the next year . . . same passage. The first year I heard the guy, I likened him to a Bible-teaching John Wayne. By year five I saw him as Barney Fife. The guy only had one teaching bullet!

I have seen more than a few people get stuck in a spiritual rut. Every time you talk with them, God is "teaching them" from the same passage. They praise God for the same things, struggle with the same sin and ask the same questions. Like the high school athlete still talking about that touchdown run to win the championship 40 years ago, some believers are stuck in time. But look at today's passage. It is time to "sing to the Lord a new song."

God's past faithfulness gives me confidence. God's future promises give me hope. But it is God's work in my life today that refreshes my relationship with him. Look around you. He is doing marvelous things in your life. He is moving you forward with spiritual victories. He is stretching you with challenging times. He is causing you to depend on him. Today he is forming you into what he needs you to be tomorrow. His mercies are new every morning. It's time to sing a new song!

Father, please don't let us get stuck in a spiritual rut. Refresh us for the journey today, and put a new song in our heart! In Jesus' name. Amen.

reflection

_____

_____

_____

_____

_____

further suggested reading:

Psalms 98-103

Enduring Love

Psalm 106:1

Praise the LORD. Give thanks to the LORD, for he is good; his love endures forever.

Psalm 106 describes the "mighty acts" that God performed for his people and the long history of their rebellion against him. The psalm reminds us that Israel "made a calf and worshiped an idol," "exchanged their Glory for an image of a bull" and "forgot the God who saved them." Yet God never stopped loving them. Amazing, isn't it? Our heavenly Father's love "endures forever."

We live in a "what have you done for me lately" world. Our interaction with most people is conditional. For you, this conditional acceptance may have started in your home. You may have had a mother or father who demonstrated love only when you performed. They expressed great pride over "A's" and "touchdowns" and "homeruns" and "first chairs" and "lead roles." But you felt disappointments over "B's or C's" or "fumbles" or "strikeouts" or "mediocre performances" or when you were simply a member of the "supporting cast." But the love of the heavenly Father is different. His love endures forever. And since it is a perfect love, it is always expressed in a perfect unconditional way.

Think about it. When I trust in God and become a child of God, there is nothing I can do to make God love me more. And there is nothing I can do to make God love me less. God's love for me doesn't waver. He will love me as much tomorrow as he does today. That does not give me a license to sin; rather, it inspires me to obey such a good and loving God.

Thank you, Father, for your enduring love. Thank you for taking away my worries that you might withdraw your love based on my performance. Thank you for your perfect, unconditional, lasting love that is mine through Jesus. In his name. Amen.

reflection

further suggested reading:

Psalms 104-106

God's Love

Psalm 108:4

For great is your love, higher than the heavens; your faithfulness reaches to the skies.

God's love is something believers need to understand, accept and apply. A. W. Tozer explains this characteristic of God in his book, *The Knowledge of the Holy.*

Love is an essential attribute of God. All of God's attributes, Tozer explains, are expressed fully and together. He never suspends one in order to express another. Since he is self-existent, his love has no beginning. Since he is eternal, his love has no end. Since he is infinite, his love has no limits. Since he is holy, his love is pure.

God's love shows us that he is friendly, and his Word assures us that he is our friend and wants us to be his friends. Tozer says, "No man with a trace of humility would first think that he is a friend of God; but the idea did not originate with men." God himself said that Abraham was his friend, and he desires the same friendship with us.

Love is an emotional identification. Tozer writes, "It is a strange and beautiful eccentricity of the free God that He has allowed His heart to be emotionally identified with men. Self-sufficient as He is, He wants our love and will not be satisfied till he gets it. Free as He is, He has let His heart be bound to us forever."

Love takes pleasure in its object. "The Lord," Tozer says, "takes peculiar pleasure in His saints . . . Christ in His atonement has removed the bar to the divine fellowship. Now in Christ all believing souls are objects of God's delight."

Heavenly Father, thank you for loving me. Thank you for a relationship with you through Jesus. Thank you for calling me your friend. In Jesus' name. Amen.

reflection

further suggested reading:

Psalms 107-110

Ponder That!

Psalm 111:2

Great are the works of the LORD; they are pondered by all who delight in them.

The word "ponder" means to "seek with care, consider something deeply and thoroughly, meditate upon." There are many of God's great works we could ponder, but for today let's consider one aspect of God's great creation - the stars.

Our sun, powerful enough to burn our skin and draw oxygen from every plant on earth, is a mere wimp among the stars in the sky. If the giant star Antares were positioned at the same location as the sun - 93 million miles away - Earth would be inside it! And our sun and Antares represent just two of 500 billion stars that swim around the vast galaxy of the Milky Way. A dime held out at arm's length would block 15 million stars from view if our eyes could see with that power. One other galaxy, Andromeda, lies close enough (a mere 2 million light-years away) to see with the naked eye. It showed up on star charts long before the invention of the telescope. It is twice the size of the Milky Way and home to a trillion stars. Get this - the Milky Way and Andromeda are only two of a hundred billion galaxies all swimming with stars.

Take some time to go outside tonight and look at the stars. And remember, the same God who created the stars loves you so much that he sent his Son to die on the cross so that you could be his friend forever. Ponder that!

Father, all your works are great. We are in awe of your power and the power of your love that allows us to know you, love you and live for you. Slow us down to ponder your great works in the universe and in our lives. In Jesus' name. Amen.

reflection

_____

_____

_____

_____

_____

_____

_____

further suggested reading:

Psalms 111-114

Surrender

Psalm 115:3

Our God is in heaven; he does whatever pleases him.

At some point, the prayer that comes from trembling lips and a shaken life is short and to the point - "I surrender." Jesus prayed fervently for the desires of his heart, yet submitted himself willingly to the sovereign plan of God. And so must we surrender ourselves to God's plan for us. God "does whatever pleases him." But know this - everything that pleases him is good and right.

Back in 1676, a hymn writer named Samuel Rodigast had a dear friend who became seriously ill. In his fervent prayer for the friend's healing, Rodigast wrote the following words in his hymn *Whatever My God Ordains Is Right:*

Whate'er my God ordains is right:
Holy his will abideth;
I will be still whate'er he doth,
And follow where he guideth:
He is my God;
Though dark my road,
He holds me that I shall not fall:
Wherefore to him I leave it all.
Whate'er my God ordains is right:
He is my Friend and Father;
He suffers naught to do me harm,
Though many storms may gather,
Now I may know both joy and woe,
Someday I shall see clearly
That he hath loved me dearly.
Whate'er my God ordains is right:
He never will deceive me;
He leads me by the proper path,
I know he will not leave me:
I take, content,
What he hath sent;
His hand can turn my griefs away,
And patiently I wait his day.
Whate'er my God ordains is right:
Here shall my stand be taken;
Though sorrow, need, or death be mine,
Yet I am not forsaken.
My Father's care is round me there;
He holds me that I shall not fall:
And so to him I leave it all.

Father, to you I leave it all, knowing that someday I will see through all of life's challenges that you have "loved me dearly." In Jesus' name. Amen.

further suggested reading:

Psalms 115-118

God's Word

June 25

Psalm 119:18

Open my eyes that I may see wonderful things in your law.

Quoting Isaiah, the Apostle Paul wrote, "'No eye has seen, no ear has heard, no mind has conceived what God has prepared for those who love him' – but God has revealed it to us by his Spirit" (1 Corinthians 2:9). God's Spirit knows God's thoughts. When the believer reads God's Word, it is the Spirit of God, living within us, who reveals God's words and thoughts to us.

Today's passage, then, is a pre-Bible reading prayer. Our minds can be distracted. We can simply read the Bible to check off that day's reading. Prior to reading God's Word, here is a prayer we should pray.

Dear heavenly Father,
Thank you for giving me your Word. Thank you for the privilege of opening it and reading it today. I admit to you that I am in a hurry. I am busy and distracted. So please slow me down. Help me focus. Keep distractions away. Help me listen to things in your Word that I need to hear. Use your Word to point out areas of sin that I need to confess. Open my eyes to blind spots that I keep missing. Show me where I am off track. Open my eyes to a biblical perspective of where I am and where I should be. Instruct me regarding business interactions. Help me understand and apply your instructions that will guide my morning meetings. Instruct me regarding relationships. Open my eyes to hear from you regarding the person I am dating (if single) or my spouse (if married). I desire to be a godly parent. Open my eyes to your Word that will help me raise my children according to your instruction. Lord, I desire to know you more fully and deeply. Speak to me in a new and fresh way through your Word. Father, please open my eyes to see the wonderful truths in your instructions. In Jesus' name. Amen.

reflection

further suggested reading:

Psalm 119

Building Our Family

Psalm 127:1

Unless the LORD builds the house, the builders labor in vain.

- Too many parents are convinced that they must provide all their children's wants, so they build and fill houses instead of building and filling lives.
- They are convinced that little Bobby is Division I material, so they make sure he's on every team, gets every lesson and goes to every camp regardless of the sacrifices of money and time for the rest of the family.
- They are still complaining that there is no prayer in school but seldom pray with their own kids at home, other than before meals.
- They leave it to Christian schools to instill Christian values.
- They want their teens connected to church without having them attend youth group.
- They work and save so that little Susie has an all-expenses-paid four years to the college of her choice.
- It's the teacher's fault if their child doesn't make the grade.
- It's the coach's fault if their child doesn't make the play.
- They play the "I work hard to provide for my family" card instead of the "I work long and hard to fill an inner need of satisfaction and meaning" reality.
- They still believe the "Oh, it's not 'quantity time' but 'quality time'" lie.
- They "fear" social media, but still provide their children with smartphones and Facebook accounts.
- They decry the "nanny state" but build "nanny families."
- They work harder to keep their bodies fit than they do to keep their marriages strong.

As parents, we need to be more concerned with the spiritual than we are with the athletics, academics, arts, awards and appearance. Unless we are serious and intentional about building our family according to the Lord's instruction, we will get stuck with a big house filled with small, self-absorbed and self-saturated people.

Father, we acknowledge that unless you are the architect and builder of our family, we labor in vain. Don't let us labor in vain. Help us see what we need to change and give us the courage to change it. Give us the strength to be godly leaders of our children. In Jesus' name. Amen.

reflection

_____

_____

further suggested reading:

Psalms 120-127

Forgiveness

Psalm 130:3-4

If you, LORD, kept a record of sins, Lord, who could stand? But with you there is forgiveness, so that we can, with reverence, serve you.

Forgiveness. The word is powerful and calming, refreshing and cleansing, renewing and burden-lifting. "I forgive you." Those words tell guilt to go away and invite peace to take its place. If God kept a record of all our evil thoughts, reckless words and aberrant actions, our spiritual legs would buckle under the weight. We would be buried under the pile of our wickedness. And the pile would forever stand as a monument to our depravity.

But God does not keep a record of our sins. He nailed them to the cross, where our Lord paid the penalty for every morsel of juicy gossip, every white lie, every murder and every despicable action of man, on the cross. And when we trust in Jesus' death as our own, he throws our sin into the depth of the sea. He puts it behind his back. The God with perfect memory chooses to remember our sin no more.

How should we respond to God's great forgiveness? Should we take it for granted? Should we use it as a license to sin? Should we use it as an excuse for spiritual lethargy? No! It allows us to stand and follow with thanksgiving. It is a part of God's love and acceptance that should make us want to worship and honor him with our lives. Forgiveness allows us to serve God with the reverence he alone deserves.

Father, thank you for your great forgiveness. Thank you for not keeping a record of my sin. Thank you for allowing me to stand before you clean because of Jesus. Help me to live free from my sinful past and walk with you in the freedom of forgiveness today. In Jesus' name. Amen.

reflection

_____
_____
_____
_____
_____
_____

further suggested reading:

Psalms 128-134

Fearfully and Wonderfully Made

Psalm 139:13-16

For you created my inmost being; you knit me together in my mother's womb. I praise you because I am fearfully and wonderfully made; your works are wonderful, I know that full well. My frame was not hidden from you when I was made in the secret place, when I was woven together in the depths of the earth. Your eyes saw my unformed body; all the days ordained for me were written in your book before one of them came to be.

What do you think of your body? Yeah, I know . . . a pretty personal question. But self-image is huge today, and so many people don't like what they see when they look in the mirror. And the results? Anorexia. Bulimia. Acceptance gained by promiscuity. Addictions. Recently, a young girl sitting in front of me on a flight had scars all over her legs and arms from cutting. What do you think of the body God made just for you?

In her book *Real Sex*, Lauren Winner writes the following:

> *Bodies are not simply pieces of furniture to decorate or display; they are not trappings about which we have conflicted feelings . . . they are not objects to be dieted away, made to conform to popular standards, or made to perform unthinkable athletic feats with the help of drugs; they are neither tools for scoring points nor burdens to be overcome (Real Sex,* Lauren Winner, Ink Books, 2005, p. 33-34).*

Winner goes on to explain that God has given us the great gift of our bodies to honor him. It is through our bodies that we worship and serve and sing his praises and carry out his instructions. We need to thank God for the physical gifts he has given us and teach our children to do the same.

In the New Testament, Paul reminds us that our bodies are the dwelling place of God, and we should take care of them not harm them. God has given us meaning and purpose to carry out. He has ordained all our days. We have been fearfully and wonderfully made. That is a reason for great praise.

Father, thank you for forming us, knitting us together, giving us purpose and ordaining our days. May we use our bodies as vehicles of obedience. May we honor you with our bodies. In Jesus' name. Amen.

reflection

further suggested reading:

Psalms 135-139

The Passion of Real Life Experience

Psalm 145:3-4

Great is the LORD and most worthy of praise; his greatness no one can fathom. One generation commends your works to another; they tell of your mighty acts.

The story of God is settled in Scripture. Yet he uses people to pass it on. One generation tells the story of God's greatness to another. Of course, that means that each generation has a story to tell. Certainly we should know and retell the stories of the Bible. But along with the accounts of Scripture, we need stories of our own. Stories based on knowledge need to be combined with stories based on personal experience. This allows for truth to be passed on with passion.

How do you experience the mighty acts of God so that you can pass them on with passion? Here are a few ideas.

- **Share the Gospel with a friend or family member.** You will never get over the joy of experiencing someone trusting in Christ. Don't live on the stories of other people. Write your own story of God's power to save.

- **Serve at a local mission or shelter.** I am convinced that serving those in need does much more for me than the people I serve. While you are serving, find some time to hear the stories of those in the mission or shelter. When you take the time to serve, God works in your heart in powerful ways.

- **Serve in your local church.** Don't confuse attending a small group or Bible Study with actually serving. Attending a small group and serving is the difference between having a meal and exercising. Those who are only spiritually fed are going to have a spiritual weight problem.

- **Go on a short-term mission trip.** Away from your personal comfort zone, you see God at work in new and exciting ways. Every mission trip I take, I see God in refreshing ways and am personally stretched.

- **Step out on faith.** Follow God with such radical obedience that if he doesn't show up, you'll fall flat on your face. Anyone can live with probabilities. Probabilities seek to alleviate risk. Faith demands living with possibilities. But a certain amount of risk is involved when you step out in faith.

Father, we don't want to pass on impassionate stories to our children. Help us to combine the truth of your Word with the passion of real life experience. Give us stories to tell of the times when you were powerfully at work in our lives. In Jesus' name. Amen.

further suggested reading:

Psalms 140-145

Confidence

June 30

Psalm 146:3-6

Do not put your trust in princes, in human beings, who cannot save. When their spirit departs, they return to the ground; on that very day their plans come to nothing. Blessed are those whose help is the God of Jacob, whose hope is in the LORD their God. He is the Maker of heaven and earth, the sea, and everything in them - he remains faithful forever.

What provides you with confidence? What brings a calmness and peace to your heart? What gives you hope? A thriving economy? A stable job? Your person in the White House? A hefty retirement account? A strong military?

Check out today's passage. Human beings - even the most powerful of them . . . even the best of them - cannot save. Man cannot give us what we need. Besides, death puts to rest any semblance of confidence in the powerful. On the day the dominant dies, his ability to enact plans dies with him.

In whom or in what do you gain your confidence? If your hope is not found in the Lord, sooner or later your teetering tower of trust will come crashing down. Without God it's just a matter of time before your faux calm turns to feverish chaos. But there is One who is eternal. He is the Maker of heaven, Earth, sea and everything in them. He "remains faithful forever." Blessed is the one whose confidence is in him.

Father, it is tempting to put our trust in the stuff and people around us. Give us great leaders, but never let us forget that you are the only One who will stand for eternity. Help us to follow hard after you. In Jesus' name. Amen.

reflection

further suggested reading:

Psalms 146-150

Wholehearted Trust

July 1

Proverbs 3:5-6

Trust in the LORD with all your heart and lean not on your own understanding; in all your ways admit to him, and he will make your paths straight.

Wholehearted trust. That's where a life sold out to God begins. The life of faith is not based on probabilities (the desire to eliminate risk) but possibilities (the desire to see God do amazing things). Trust is believing that through Jesus, God has done for me what I can't do for myself, and through the Holy Spirit, God does for me what I can't do by myself. Wholehearted trust does not have all the answers but knows the One who does. When I trust in the Lord, I no longer have to depend on my limited knowledge.

Wholehearted trust is the confidence that God knows best in all situations. He will always lead me in the right direction. He will always supply all I need to do what he wants me to do. Trust does not mean I disengage my brain or throw reason out the proverbial window. But there are times when I just can't figure it out, when things don't make sense and when the directional signs are not well marked. That's when wholehearted trust must kick in.

Wholehearted trust gives me the courage to move forward when I am fearful; the strength to keep going when I am worn out; and the boldness to follow God's "Charge!" when my heart is crying, "Retreat!" When I recognize God as the leader in everything, he will remove the obstacles so I can follow the straight paths that lead to his intended destination. And when I arrive, there is a true sense of satisfaction knowing that I have taken a journey with God. Wholehearted trust is not easy, but it is right. It honors God and it always produces the best for me.

Father, turn my halfhearted attempts at obedience into wholehearted trust. Turn my wavering into unshakeable faith. Show me the futility of trusting in myself. Show me the spiritual success of trusting in you alone. In Jesus' name. Amen.

reflection

_____

_____

_____

_____

_____

_____

further suggested reading:

Proverbs 1-4

Sexual Sin

Proverbs 5:11-14

At the end of your life you will groan, when your flesh and body are spent. You will say, "How I hated discipline! How my heart spurned correction! I would not obey my teachers or turn my ear to my instructors. And I was soon in serious trouble in the assembly of God's people."

God is not silent about sexual sin. He doesn't cover his mouth and whisper needed truth. He doesn't spell out the words to protect our "innocent" ears. In this section of Proverbs, he slams the hammer down with a series of admonitions. I see four important warnings in today's passage.

- **Sexual sin ends in regret.** Far too many people begin to evaluate their actions at the end of their life when all they can do is groan over consequences. While it's never too late for forgiveness, it can be too late to repair relationships. Our kids don't enter a growth freeze while we get our act together. Think of the legacy you want to leave and live today to that end.

- **Sexual sin results from a lapse in discipline.** No two ways about it. Sexual sin is more than getting caught with your pants down; it's living with your guard down. A sinful lapse of discipline is costly . . . in one moment of unbridled passion, a marriage can be destroyed, a family lost and a reputation ruined.

- **Sexual sin produces arrogance.** The most arrogant people I have ever spoken with are those engaged in sexual sin. Their hearts spurn instruction. When you jettison God's instruction and follow your sinful nature, you become self-absorbed and self-centered.

- **Sexual sin is never a private matter.** The apostle Paul wrote, "Do not be deceived: God cannot be mocked. A man reaps what he sows. The one who sows to please his sinful nature, from that nature will reap destruction; the one who sows to please the Spirit, from the Spirit will reap eternal life" (Galatians 6:7-8). Sooner or later, those who continue in sin will come to ruin in the midst of the assembly.

Father, protect us from ourselves. Keep us humble before you. May we live our lives following hard after you . . . with no regrets. In Jesus' name. Amen.

reflection

further suggested reading:

Proverbs 5-9

When Words Are Many

July 3

Proverbs 10:19

Sin is not ended by multiplying words, but the prudent hold their tongues.

Today's verse is a warning to the person who talks too much. Like Old Man River, his mouth just keeps on flowing along. The talker never met a silent moment he couldn't fill, a life experience he couldn't share, a story he couldn't top. Never mind if you've heard the story before; he'll tell it again. Never mind if the repeated story changes; he's gotta keep it interesting. Never mind if he has to add some assumptions or presumptions; he's on a roll. Grab a cup of coffee. Get comfortable. You won't have to add anything to the conversation . . . um, sorry, monologue. Just pretend that you're listening. Just nod every once in a while. Smile. Appropriately furrow your brow. It's like throwing gasoline on a fire! Watch the talker go!!

The problem with the talker? Sooner or later, he tells a story that he shouldn't. He drops a name that never wanted to go public. He takes a "just between you and me" and makes it headline news. Leaving people scratching their heads, he con-tradicts himself, he exaggerates or just embellishes the facts a bit. He says some things that he regrets and many things that he can't remember. You see, "when words are many, sin is not absent." The more you talk, the more the potential for sin.

The remedy? Zip it! Weigh your words. Hold your tongue. Think before you speak. That simple exercise is going to keep you from a lot of sin and regret.

Father, please help us to hold our tongues today. Keep gossip far from us. Help us not to share the things we should keep to ourselves. In Jesus' name. Amen.

reflection

_____

_____

_____

_____

_____

_____

_____

_____

further suggested reading:

Proverbs 10-13

A Friend Loves at All Times

July 4

Proverbs 17:17

A friend loves at all times, and a brother is born for a time of adversity.

Real friendship is not conditional. It is not based on give and take but give and give. There are times when love is difficult. There are times when actions make acceptance hard. But a friend loves at all times. A true friend is a safe harbor, a comforting hiding place.

When your words are short and sharp . . . *a friend loves at all times.*

When you are exhausted and want to just veg . . . *a friend loves at all times.*

When you are excited and want to emote . . . *a friend loves at all times.*

When you need to blow off some steam . . . *a friend loves at all times.*

When your actions hurt . . . *a friend loves at all times.*

When you are selfish . . . *a friend loves at all times.*

When you are insensitive . . . *a friend loves at all times.*

When you forget . . . *a friend loves at all times.*

When you keep remembering . . . *a friend loves at all times.*

When you are standing tall on the mountain of success . . . *a friend loves at all times.*

When you are face down in the valley of failure . . . *a friend loves at all times.*

Thank God for good friends!

Father, thank you for good friends you place in our lives. Thank you for people who see beyond our actions and know our heart. Thank you for people we don't have to be on our best behavior around. Thank you for the people with whom we can be real. In Jesus' name. Amen.

reflection

further suggested reading:
Proverbs 14-17

Lasting Relationship

Proverbs 18:24

One who has unreliable friends may come to ruin, but there is a friend who sticks closer than a brother.

Companions are a dime a dozen. Just provide the external hooks of wings, beer, cigars and football, and you have all kinds of companions hanging around. Add the social externals of position, status and wealth, and the room is crowded. Even Christians like the "many companions" thing. All the externals mentioned above mixed in with a little "Jesus" or "church" or "Bible" and, all of a sudden, you have a Cool Guy Christian Club. Evangelical name droppers love to be in the CGCC!

A friend, on the other hand, is rare. He hangs around without the external hooks. When the food is gone and football season is over, a friend still shows up. When you are no longer the CEO, a friend still loves to be seen with you. When you downsize from the deck and pool to just the deck, a friend still helps flip the burgers. When things go belly up and you have to trade in the Porsche for a Pinto, a friend still calls "Shotgun!"

Look around. Be discerning. One of these days the wings and beer will be gone. One of these days the money will be spent. One of these days a Cool Guy Christian Bible Study will not be enough. One of these days people who just hang around will not be enough; you're going to need someone to stick close. That day is coming. Better find that friend now.

Father, help us understand the difference between a companion and a friend. Help us develop lasting relationships today so that we will not be alone tomorrow. In Jesus' name. Amen.

reflection

further suggested reading:

Proverbs 18-21

Times of Trouble

Proverbs 24:10

If you falter in a time of trouble, how small is your strength!

The test of strength is adversity. When things get tough, you quickly find out how strong you really are. Anybody can guide a boat over smooth waters. But when the storm hits and the winds blow and the boat is rocked, only the strong can maneuver through the waves. The weak and fearful bail out. They take their empty professions of faith and go home. But the strong move forward with resolve.

The test of adversity is preparation. The reality is that you are either getting ready to go through a time of trouble; you are in a time of trouble; or you are just coming out of a time of trouble. We have to be prepared. We have to be in the Word gaining strength and wisdom. We have to be in worship - preparing our hearts. We have to be connected with other believers - no one is strong enough to go it alone. We have to be using our gifts - a lot of food and no exercise make for a flabby Christian. We have to be telling others about Jesus. Adversity is the training camp of the soul.

The test of preparation is discipline. Becoming a Christian is a free gift. Growing as a Christian is hard work. It calls for sacrifice. Your time, talents and treasures belong to God, not you. It calls for engaged minds and ignited hearts. It calls for rekindling the fire in your soul. Spiritual discipline is not self-sufficiency. It is the wisdom to latch on to the Source, be filled with his strength, and be controlled by his Spirit.

Father, don't let us falter in times of trouble. Hold us up and carry us through the hard times. Keep us strong. Help us to be prepared. Keep us disciplined. In Jesus' name. Amen.

reflection

_____
_____
_____
_____
_____
_____
_____
_____

further suggested reading:

Proverbs 22-24

The Real Test of the Heart

July 7

Proverbs 27:21

The crucible for silver and the furnace for gold, but people are tested by their praise.

With adversity comes the test. The fires of trial drive us to God. The battering storms cause us to cry out in desperation. Hardship drops us to our knees. But there is one test much greater than adversity. It is the test of success . . . the sweet smell, taste and experience of success . . . that's the real test of a man's character.

Promotions. Awards. Higher positions. More money. Those are the things that test a man's character. The danger of reading your own press is that you start actually believing it. Success tempts us to think that we are good without God. That we really do deserve the accolades. That our genius produced such a rewarding outcome. That our gutsy move saved the company. Success turns many hearts inward instead of upward. Success is the real test of the heart.

How are you doing? You up there on the mountaintop of career. You up there with the trophies of accomplishment. Be careful up there in the heights. The peak of success is surrounded by a slippery slope. It's a long, hard, painful slide to the bottom. If you are not careful, success will produce pride, and pride always comes before the fall.

Father, may we never forget that you are the Mover behind all our advancement. The Giver behind all that we have. The Shepherd of our careers. And the Creator we must bow before in love and awe. Don't let selfish pride infest our hearts. Keep them turned to you. In Jesus' name. Amen.

reflection

further suggested reading:

Proverbs 25-27

Secret Sin

July 8

Proverbs 28:13

Whoever conceals thier sins does not prosper, but the one who confesses and renounces them finds mercy.

Living with secret sin may not impact your wallet. In fact, the money may keep rolling in and piling up. Living with secret sin may not impact your career. In fact, the ladder may keep on extending as you make the climb. Living with secret sin may not impact your golf game. In fact, your handicap may go lower and lower. Living with secret sin may not impact your friendships. In fact, no one may ever know.

But living with secret sin does real damage to your heart. Sin will cause your soul to shrivel. Your love for God will shrink. Your heart will become hardened. Your spiritual thinking will be dulled. Your spiritual emotions will become cold. And you can be sure that sooner or later, your sin will find you out, and you will be neck deep in consequences. Sin always produces consequences.

It's time to change course. God's great mercy is just a step away from secret sin. When you admit your sin and walk away from it, you will find the relief of forgiveness. Instead of the stress of secret sin, restoration will come to your contrite soul. Instead of hiding in secret, you can walk openly in the freedom of obedience. It's time to stop the secret games and make the journey home to God's welcoming arms of mercy.

Father, thank you for the promise of forgiveness. Give us the courage to confess our sins and the desire to come back home. In Jesus' name. Amen.

reflection

further suggested reading:

Proverbs 28-29

The Prayer of Agur

Proverbs 30:7-9

"Two things I ask of you, LORD; do not refuse me before I die: Keep falsehood and lies far from me; give me neither poverty nor riches, but give me only my daily bread. Otherwise, I may have too much and disown you and say, 'Who is the LORD?' Or I may become poor and steal, and so dishonor the name of my God."

I'm sure you've heard of the bestselling *Prayer of Jabez*. It's a book about an honorable man in the Old Testament who cried out to God, "Oh, that you would bless me and enlarge my territory! Let your hand be with me, and keep me from harm so that I will be free from pain" (1 Chronicles 4:10). We like prayers that ask for more influence, impact and opportunity, don't we? But I doubt you've heard the prayer of Agur. I have thought about writing a book about it, but I'm doubtful that publishers would touch it. Agur was a simple man with two simple, yet powerful, requests.

First, Agur prayed for integrity. He did not want to live a life of duplicity. Notice he didn't pray, "God, please help me to tell the truth." He prays that God will keep opportunities for falsehood far away, out of his reach. He prayed that God would keep him from the temptation and the sin. Second, Agur prayed for just enough - not too much lest pride and self-sufficiency overtake him, not too little lest he be tempted to steal food for his family. Agur prayed for that balance between dependence and desperation. He didn't want a full barn so he could eat, drink and be merry. He prayed for "daily bread." Daily bread kept Agur thankful to God for today's provision and dependent on God for tomorrow's.

I have nothing against Jabez's prayer (heck, it sold a lot of books!). But I love the prayer of Agur. His desire for integrity and dependence is the crying need of a culture bent on doing whatever it takes to get ahead and saturated in self dependence. Thankfully, we Christians do not have to be influenced by our culture.

Heavenly Father, we wonder why we have such trouble with sin when we keep it so close. We wonder why we are not closer to you as we view our materialistic, overflowing lives. Wake us up! In Jesus' name. Amen.

reflection

further suggested reading:

Proverbs 30-31

Gladness of Heart

Ecclesiastes 5:18-20

This is what I have observed to be good: that it is appropriate for a person to eat, to drink and to find satisfaction in their toilsome labor under the sun during the few days of life God has given them - for this is their lot. Moreover, when God gives someone wealth and possessions, and the ability to enjoy them, to accept their lot and be happy in their toil - this is a gift of God. They seldom reflect on the days of their life, because God keeps them occupied with gladness of heart.

The book of Ecclesiastes is a life journal written by King Solomon - a man who had it all and tried it all. He had money, and he spent it on every pleasure he could find. He denied himself nothing his eyes desired. He had power, and he used it to do whatever he thought would make him happy. He had all the "toys," and he played with each one until they were rusted and worn. At the end of his journal, he finally concluded that fearing God and keeping his commandments was the "whole duty of man."

As Solomon takes us on his journey to find meaning, he pulls off the road every once in a while for a teaching moment. This passage is one of those moments. First, Solomon says, when a person stops living for himself and starts living for God - when he finds his true purpose and passion - there is genuine satisfaction. Work is still work involving "toilsome labor" and challenges. But when you're doing what God has made you to do there is deep satisfaction.

Second, when a person understands that wealth and possessions are a gift from God and should be used for God, he can finally enjoy them. When we have God's perspective on our stuff, he "enables" us to enjoy the stuff. A change in mindset from "my stuff to own" to "God's stuff on loan" turns the frenzied pursuit into a satisfied journey. And check out Ecclesiastes 5:20. When we find our calling and have a biblical understanding of "stuff," our days are not about groaning and griping, complaining and carping, fear and fret, apprehension and anxiety. "God keeps him occupied with gladness of heart." Is that cool or what?

Father, please teach us the biblical perspective of possessions. Help us understand that all we have comes from you and is to be used for you. And . . . help us to appropriately apply that knowledge. In Jesus' name. Amen.

reflection

further suggested reading:

Ecclesiastes 1-6

Meaningless

Ecclesiastes 12:13-14

Now all has been heard; here is the conclusion of the matter: Fear God and keep his commandments, for this is the duty of all mankind. For God will bring every deed into judgment, including every hidden thing, whether it is good or evil.

Solomon, the writer of these words, had everything . . . and nothing at the same time. The book of Ecclesiastes is a reflective journal of his personal search for meaning. Like many before and after him, Solomon's search led him on a search for all the wrong things in all the wrong places.

Solomon's journey was paved with gold. He was the wealthiest man who ever lived. Yet all his money could not fill the hole in his heart. Solomon was born a king. Yet his personal power left an empty taste in his mouth. Solomon's pursuit led him down the path of unbridled sexual pleasure. Yet the warm bodies of the most beautiful women left his soul cold. After exploring all the dead-end trails, he could only conclude the following: "Meaningless! Meaningless! Utterly meaningless! Everything is meaningless." Solomon's life seemed to be overflowing, but his soul was bone dry. Thirty-five times in his reflective journal, he describes his life efforts as "meaningless."

After living an ostentatious life, Solomon comes to a simple conclusion: Fear God (live a life of worship), keep his commandments (he knows what he's talking about) and don't forget the judgment (one day we will give an account before God). It's a shame Solomon did not start with that conclusion. Thank God, we can.

Father, your Word is given for our instruction. Help us learn from Solomon. May we fear you, follow you and live with an eternal perspective. Remind us that we will give an account. Help us live with that in mind. In Jesus' name. Amen.

reflection

further suggested reading:

Ecclesiastes 7-12

God's Gift

July 12

Song of Solomon 8:8-9

We have a little sister, and her breasts are not yet grown. What shall we do for our sister on the day she is spoken for? If she is a wall, we will build towers of silver on her. If she is a door, we will enclose her with panels of cedar.

The Song of Solomon pulls no punches regarding sex. But it is in no way crude or vulgar. Through exquisite poetry, the book vividly describes this beautiful gift from God in the context of marriage. Today's passage explains that the training for biblical sexuality begins at home. The family asks, "How can we prepare our sister for God's gift?"

If she is like a wall, we will build towers of silver on her.
The city wall was strong and protected those who lived within from enemies. The tower was where the battle gear was hung. The battle ornaments gave a sense of strength and encouragement. If the young girl remained strong like a wall - refusing to give in to sexual temptations - the family would encourage and honor her virtue.

If she is a door, we will enclose her with panels of cedar.
If the young woman was promiscuous - open to the advancement of men -then the family would place restrictions on her in order to protect her from hurting herself prior to marriage.

As the young person (this instruction applies to young men as well) matures and becomes sexually aware, it is the parents' responsibility to encourage proper behavior and restrict improper behavior. This type of interaction is not easy. It takes time and energy that only those who love a person are willing to give. This is not the description of an overly strict family but one that cares enough to do their job in teaching sexual responsibility.

Father, I pray that you will give moms and dads the courage they need to teach and train their children in the area of sexuality. Our children will learn about sex. I pray that learning takes place in a healthy way in the healthy environment of the home. In Jesus' name. Amen.

reflection

---

further suggested reading:

Song of Solomon 1-8

Settle the Matter

Isaiah 1:18

"Come now, let us settle the matter," says the LORD. "Though your sins are like scarlet, they shall be as white as snow; though they are red as crimson, they shall be like wool."

When it's all said and done, there is only one matter to settle. That is the issue between sinful man and a holy God. Left to ourselves, we can't have a relationship with God. Left to ourselves, we fall far short. Our baptism, confirmation, generous giving and regular church attendance are not enough to make us right with God. We are in a helpless and hopeless situation. Because of our sin, we deserve to die - spiritually, physically and eternally.

But God did for us what we could not do for ourselves. He demonstrated his great love by sending his Son to pay the penalty for our sins. Jesus - fully God and fully Man - died as our substitute. He alone paid the penalty for our sins. Trusting in Jesus is simply this: I believe that Jesus died for me. I believe that the death of Jesus paid the penalty for my sin. I trust in Jesus alone to place me into an eternal relationship with the living God.

Our sins, once red and vibrant, through Jesus are as white as fresh snow and pure white wool. God wants to settle the matter with you. God loves you and desires to know you intimately and deeply. Today I urge you to trust in Jesus as the only way the stain of your sin can be washed away and forgiven. The following prayer is a guide to help you settle the matter with God.

Dear heavenly Father, I know that I am a sinner and cannot earn my way to you. My best efforts on my best day fall short. Right now, I trust in Jesus alone as the only way I can have a relationship with you. I trust in Jesus as the One who paid the penalty of sin by his death on the cross, one-time-for-all-time. Thank you for hearing my prayer, forgiving my sins and placing me in your family. In Jesus' name. Amen.

reflection

_____

_____

_____

_____

_____

_____

further suggested reading:

Isaiah 1-4

Holy, Holy, Holy

July 14

Isaiah 6:1-3

In the year that King Uzziah died, I saw the Lord, high and exalted, seated on a throne; and the train of his robe filled the temple. Above him were seraphim, each with six wings: With two wings they covered their faces, with two they covered their feet, and with two they were flying. And they were calling to one another: "Holy, holy, holy is the LORD Almighty; the whole earth is full of his glory."

Can you imagine seeing the things that Isaiah described in this passage? The great prophet saw the Lord! He was seated on his throne as king over all. He was high and exalted in position over all the nations. His long robe filled the temple as a sign of his royalty and majesty.

Above the Lord were angelic six-winged beings. In humility, the angelic beings used two wings to cover their faces as they hovered before God. With two wings, they, showing their service to the Most High, covered their feet. And with two wings they flew in continued activity. As they flew, they called out to one another, "Holy, holy, holy is the Lord Almighty; the whole earth is full of his glory." Isaiah's response to such a vision was to cry out, "Woe to me! I am ruined!"

We thank God that he is our heavenly Father. And we can approach him with the endearing "Abba, Father." Jesus, our Savior, calls us his friend. While our relationship is an intimate one, he is still the omniscient, omnipotent, omnipresent, eternal Creator. Thank God for our personal relationship with him. But let's not forget that he is holy and the "whole earth is full of his glory!" When we, like Isaiah, get a real picture of who God is, we can only fall on our knees and worship him.

Father, forgive us for taking your greatness for granted. Help us to be those who live in awe of your Person and actions. As we draw near to you as our Father, may we never forget that you are holy, holy, holy. In Jesus' name. Amen.

reflection

_____

_____

_____

_____

_____

further suggested reading:

Isaiah 5-6

His Word Stands Firm

Isaiah 7:14

Therefore the Lord himself will give you a sign: The virgin will conceive and give birth to a son, and will call him Immanuel.

Quoting from today's passage, the Gospel writer Matthew states the birth of Jesus as a matter of fact: *This is how the birth of Jesus Christ came about . . .* But imagine explaining that you were "with child" absent the physical act. Imagine trying to explain the pregnancy to your fiancé. Joseph couldn't accept it. His plan for a quiet divorce was the act of a godly man with a broken heart. He would move on . . . she would have the baby alone. That was the plan until the angel came and explained the situation to Joseph.

Now zoom back 400 years . . . keep zooming . . . 600 years . . . a little more . . . 700 years! Here the prophet Isaiah gives the information that moves the virgin birth from "unbelievable" to "expected." When God makes a promise, it is going to come true. His Word stands firm. He never goes back on his Word.

Works that way today, doesn't it? The promises God makes will come to be. He never renegotiates. He never changes his mind. He never bases his promises on our actions. We may have to wait, but the waiting allows us to develop our trust. When God makes a promise, it is a matter of fact, even before it happens.

Father, I thank you for always being able to trust your Word. Thank you for always bringing about your promises. Help us to keep depending on you as we wait for your promises. In Jesus' name. Amen.

reflection

_____

_____

_____

_____

_____

_____

_____

_____

_____

_____

further suggested reading:

Isaiah 7-8

Enter the King!

Isaiah 9:6-7

For to us a child is born, to us a son is given, and the government will be on his shoulders. And he will be called Wonderful Counselor, Mighty God, Everlasting Father, Prince of Peace. Of the greatness of his government and peace there will be no end. He will reign on David's throne and over his kingdom, establishing and upholding it with justice and righteousness from that time on and forever. The zeal of the LORD Almighty will accomplish this.

Jesus is the Wonderful Counselor. I can go to him anytime for anything. He is never too busy. No appointment needed. He understands. He sympathizes with my weaknesses. He has been tempted and yet never gave in. His perfect counsel corrects my selfish thinking and gives guidance to my foolish heart.

Jesus is the Mighty God. All things were created by and for him. Apart from him, nothing was made that has been made. He touched blind eyes, and they saw. He touched withered limbs, and they were normal and healthy. He calmed the raging storm with his Word. He raised the dead. He arose from the dead! He is fully God and fully Man.

Jesus is the Everlasting Father. From everlasting to everlasting he is God. The Word became flesh in the manger, but there has never been a time when Jesus was not nor will there ever be a time when he is not.

Jesus is the Prince of Peace. He reigns as King, and one day will bring peace to the earth. But now he brings peace to the heart. He said, "Peace I leave with you; my peace I give you. I do not give to you as the world gives. Do not let your hearts be troubled and do not be afraid" (John 14:27).

For unto us a child is born! Enter the King! Exit the darkness! The Light of the world has come!

Father, thank you for demonstrating your love to me by sending your Son - the Wonderful Counselor, the Mighty God, the Everlasting Father, the Prince of Peace - to die in my place on the cross. Help me to respond appropriately to such unfathomable love. In Jesus' name. Amen.

reflection

_____

_____

_____

further suggested reading:

Isaiah 9-12

Omnipotence

Isaiah 14:24, 27

The LORD Almighty has sworn, "Surely, as I have planned, so it will be, and as I have purposed, so it will happen. . . . For the LORD Almighty has purposed, and who can thwart him? His hand is stretched out, and who can turn it back?

God's attribute of *omnipotence* means that God is able to do all that he desires to do. When he plans something, it will come to be. If he purposes something, it will happen. Nothing can prevent his plan. When his hand is stretched out to do something, no one can turn it back. *Omnipotence* comes from two Latin words. *Omni* means "all," and *potens* means "powerful." God's decisions are always in line with his character, and he has all the power to do whatever he decides to do.

Scripture is clear that God is strong and mighty (Psalm 24:8). Nothing is too hard for him to accomplish (Genesis 18:14; Jeremiah 32:17, 27; Luke 1:37). Often God is called "Almighty," describing him as the One who possesses all power and authority (2 Corinthians 6:18; Revelation 1:8; et. al.). In fact, Paul says that God is "able to do far more abundantly than all we ask or think" (Ephesians 3:20).

Reflect on this attribute of God. When God plans something for your life, he is not dependent on circumstances, your strength, your network or the economy. He is not wringing his hands hoping that you are in the right place at the right time. God's will is not reliant on whom you know. God has great plans for you, and he'll get them done. Watch and see . . . and enjoy watching God at work!

Father, I praise you that you are all-powerful. Nothing can derail your plans or thwart your purposes. Help me trust that you - the Omniscient One - are working all things out for my good. In Jesus' name. Amen.

reflection

_____

_____

_____

_____

_____

_____

further suggested reading:

Isaiah 13-16

In That Day

Isaiah 17:7-8

In that day people will look to their Maker and turn their eyes to the Holy One of Israel. They will not look to the altars, the work of their hands, and they will have no regard for the Asherah poles and the incense altars their fingers have made.

The phrase "in that day" refers to a time of God's judgment, followed by a time of blessing for his people, on those who oppose him. In some passages this phrase refers to the end times; in others it refers to the current situation. Here the phrase refers to a time when Israel, because of disobedience, would be invaded by the Assyrian army.

In the day of the invasion, God's people finally turn to him for help and deliverance. The altars they had built to foreign gods would be of no assistance. Asherah poles were wooden symbols of Asherah, the Canaanite fertility goddess and partner of Baal. But the lifeless Asherah poles would offer no aid when the enemy swarmed down upon the people.

If you are trusting in anything but God, one day the circumstances of life will clearly show you the utter futility of your "gods." The altars of career and possessions will offer no relief from your predicament. The "Asherah" poles of position and power will not take up arms to defend you against life's merciless enemies. One day you will look to your Maker. Please don't wait until "that day." Turn your eyes to the Holy One today!

Father, open our eyes to see the gods we serve. Give us the strength to destroy altars and tear down the poles. Help us to acknowledge you as our Maker as the Holy One . . . and turn our eyes to you. In Jesus' name. Amen.

reflection

_____

_____

_____

_____

_____

_____

_____

further suggested reading:

Isaiah 17-20

Eternal Life

Isaiah 22:12-13

The Lord, the LORD Almighty, called you on that day to weep and to wail, to tear out your hair and put on sackcloth. But see, there is joy and revelry, slaughtering of cattle and killing of sheep, eating of meat and drinking of wine! "Let us eat and drink," you say, "for tomorrow we die!"

God loves his children too much to let them wallow in their sin. He gets our attention one way or another. When Israel lived in blatant disobedience, God disciplined them to get their attention and turn their hearts back to him. With the enemy on the way, God called on his people to repent of their sin. Instead, they lived it up with food and drink. They neither turned to God for deliverance nor feared their eternal destiny.

"Let us eat and drink, for tomorrow we die" describes a philosophy that leaves God entirely out of the picture and faces death without a belief in eternal life. Paul quotes this passage in 1 Corinthians 15:32 to show the futility of life - present and future - without God. This belief that death is the end of existence produces a self-absorbed existence bent on immediate pleasure.

The Bible, however, presents a different belief system. Believers know that man is an eternal being headed for an eternity with or without God - heaven or hell. Believers understand that only through Christ can we know God now and enjoy him forever. But do we live like we truly believe that truth? Do we believe that we will one day stand before Christ and give an explanation of our life? Do we really believe that the life we live today will determine the account we give tomorrow?

Father, it's too easy for us to focus on the here and now and forget the hereafter. It's too easy for us to aim at pleasure and possessions, leave you out of the picture and think that we will never have to give an account. Shake us out of such unbiblical thinking. Help us make each day on this earth count for you. Remind us that what we do today will need an explanation tomorrow. In Jesus' name. Amen.

reflection

_____

_____

_____

_____

_____

further suggested reading:

Isaiah 21-23

Fear

Isaiah 26:3-4

You will keep in perfect peace those whose minds are steadfast, because they trust in you. Trust in the LORD forever, for the LORD, the LORD himself, is the Rock eternal.

Fear shows up at the most inconvenient times. Like the winds of a tornado, it swirls through our heart destroying the places where calm dwells. Fear usually comes with a partner - a call from the doctor with a report of bad news, an appointment with our supervisor who may be telling us that the company is downsizing, the upheaval of the stock market playing havoc with what we thought would be our retirement, a child out late who was supposed to have been home an hour ago.

But our passage today reminds us that fear can be dulled, even driven away, when we keep our mind on the Lord, rather than our circumstances. This focus results in "perfect peace," a deep settled calmness. Why? Because the mind stayed on God trusts him. Life still happens. But in the midst of our storms he is the immovable anchor. And we can trust in him forever. He is the "Rock eternal."

I don't know what you are going through today. But God does. If you are reading this with a fearful heart, he is inviting you to trust him even as the winds of fear howl around you. He is inviting you to a place of rest and peace. The following prayer is for you. Use it as a guide, make it your own, and trust in the Rock eternal.

Dear Father, I am fearful. (Name the circumstance) is causing anxiety to fill my heart. I am scared of what may happen or what may not happen. Please help me let go of the fear and turn it over to you. Please fill my heart with the perfect peace that you promise. Help me to keep my mind focused on you. You are the eternal Rock. I cling to you as the anchor for my fearful soul. In Jesus' name. Amen.

reflection

_____

_____

_____

_____

_____

_____

further suggested reading:

Isaiah 24-27

Heart Far from God

Isaiah 29:13

The Lord says: "These people come near to me with their mouth and honor me with their lips, but their hearts are far from me. Their worship of me is based on merely human rules they have been taught."

- We can sing beautiful worship songs with beautiful harmony . . . *with hearts far from God.*
- We can stand attentively during the reading of Scripture . . . *with hearts far from God.*
- We can say the Lord's Prayer in beautiful unison . . . *with hearts far from God.*
- We can recite the amazing truth of the Apostles' Creed . . . *with only our mouth and lips.*
- We can give our money to the church . . .even lots of it . . . *with hearts far from God.*
- We can take the bread and the cup . . . *with our minds on something other than the great sacrifice of Jesus.*
- We can attend church every weekend . . . *motivated by guilt instead of worship.*
- We can serve the poor . . . *with hearts far from God.*
- We can take care of widows and orphans . . . *out of obligation instead of spiritual service.*
- We can read the Bible every day . . . *only to check off our daily reading assignment.*
- We can say prayers . . . *while our mind is wandering.*

God is never impressed with people who come near him only to impress others with their spirituality. God is not impressed with impressive recitation of mindless liturgy. God is not impressed when our worship is based on a set of traditions and rules that allow words to come from our mouth while nothing comes out of our heart.

Saying prayers, singing songs, reciting creeds is not worship if our heart is disengaged. Jesus said that true worshipers worship God in Spirit and in truth "for they are the kind of worshipers the Father seeks" (John 4:23). Are you the kind of worshiper God is looking for?

Father, help us to be the kind of worshipers you seek. Don't allow us to say words disconnected from our heart. Don't allow us to go through religious motions. Please keep our worship fresh and our hearts engaged. In Jesus' name. Amen.

further suggested reading:

Isaiah 28-29

Wait for Him

Isaiah 30:18

Yet the LORD longs to be gracious to you; therefore he will rise up to show you compassion. For the LORD is a God of justice. Blessed are all who wait for him!

God's people were not acting like God's people. They were "heaping sin upon sin." They were rebellious, deceitful and unwilling to listen to God's instructions. They formed an alliance with Egypt, looking to Pharaoh, instead of God, for help. They rejected the prophets and told them, "Give us no more visions of what is right . . . and stop confronting us with the Holy One of Israel!"

Yet look at today's passage. God desires to pour out his grace. God can't wait to demonstrate his great compassion. Certainly, he is a God of justice and there are consequences for sin. But like a loving father who disciplines his child for playing in a dangerous street, God holds us tightly and reminds us how much he loves us and cares for us.

Too often our sin occurs because things aren't happening the way we think they should or as fast as we think they should. Our impatience moves us to take matters into our own hands. We like it when we are in control . . . or at least feel like we are in control. But God blesses those who wait for his will to be shown, his way to be revealed and his path to be illuminated. "Blessed are all who wait for him!"

Father, thank you for your great grace and compassion. Thank you for desiring to pour out your grace and love on us. Thank you even for your discipline when we play on the dangerous road of sin. Give us patience to wait on your will in your time. In Jesus' name. Amen.

reflection

further suggested reading:

Isaiah 30

We Long for You

July 23

Isaiah 33:2

Lord, be gracious to us; we long for you. Be our strength every morning, our salvation in time of distress.

The true believer longs for God. He desires a relationship that grows more personal and intimate as the years go by. She desires to experience God more fully and walk with him more closely. And in this developing relationship, there are three things we desire.

We desire God's grace. Like a person who looks at his face in a lighted magnifying mirror, the closer we get to God, the more we see more our blemishes. The developing believer understands the great need for God's great grace. We long for spiritual blessings we need but don't deserve. We desire, in the words of the old hymn, grace that exceeds our sin and our guilt.

We desire God's strength. Like Christian in *Pilgrim's Progress*, we know the journey has many obstacles along the way. Circumstances slow us down and wear us out. Some people can help carry our load; others add to it. The growing believer understands his weaknesses and limitations. He longs for God's strength every morning.

We desire God's deliverance. Trouble hits us from all directions. Stress weighs down our heart. Sickness, job loss, separation, divorce . . . no one is immune from living in a sin-ridden world. But right there in the midst of our distress, God comes and delivers us. The situation doesn't always go away, but his peace passes all human understanding.

Father, we long for you. We are incapable of making this journey on our own. We long for your grace, strength and salvation. Thank you for hearing and answering our prayer. In Jesus' name. Amen.

reflection

further suggested reading:

Isaiah 31-35

A Legacy of Spiritual Blessings

Isaiah 39:8

"The word of the Lord you have spoken is good," Hezekiah replied. For he thought, "There will be peace and security in my lifetime."

Hezekiah was in the prime of his life when the illness hit. Isaiah told him to get things in order before he died. Lying on his bed close to death, Hezekiah pleaded with God to save him. God heard his prayer and promised the leader another fifteen years. Hezekiah was overjoyed! Unfortunately, pride overtook his heart. When envoys came from Babylon to give condolences, the recovered king showed them everything in his kingdom!

What was Hezekiah thinking? Why would a leader give away guarded secrets? God was not pleased with Hezekiah and let him know that the consequences of his actions would be placed on his sons after him. That's when Hezekiah spoke the words in today's passage. In essence he says, "Well, at least I don't have to worry about it."

Sin always has consequences, and sometimes they fall on the generation after us. The result of our sin is a terrible legacy to leave to our sons and daughters. It has been well said that no man is an island. What we do today does matter - today and tomorrow. Let's not follow the example of Hezekiah. Let's leave God's blessings to our children, not the mess of our sin.

Father, please remind us that what we do today counts for tomorrow. Help us to leave a legacy of spiritual blessing to those who follow us. In Jesus' name. Amen.

reflection

_____

_____

_____

_____

_____

_____

_____

_____

further suggested reading:

Isaiah 36-39

Forgiveness

Isaiah 43:25

I, even I, am he who blots out your transgressions, for my own sake, and remembers your sins no more.

Forgiveness is an issue for many believers. Far too many of us find it hard to forgive others and even harder to forgive ourselves. It's hard to forgive when the hurt is deep. Pain is an emotion that begs for a source, and when the source is another person, it's hard to release it . . . even to God. But an unwillingness to forgive is like holding a ball of fire; you will end up burning yourself.

Forgiving others may not be your biggest issue. You may struggle with forgiving yourself. All of us have disappointed and hurt those we love. Maybe it was a reckless word that pierced a friend like a sword. Maybe you abandoned your marriage. Maybe you disappointed your children. Maybe a rash decision led you to financial ruin. All of us wish we would have done things differently. But again, unforgiveness is that ball of fire that just keeps the pain coming.

Look at today's passage. These are the words of the eternal God. When we come to him with a repentant heart and ask him to forgive us, notice what he does with our sins. First, he blots out our transgressions. Think of your greatest sin written in big, bold letters and highlighted on a piece of paper. God dips a brush in a jar of ink and applies it to the sin. The indictment is covered over; it can no longer be read. Second, God chooses to remember our sin no more. This has nothing to do with the capacity of his memory; it has everything to do with the depth of his grace. Through Christ, God forgives us completely. Let's follow his example by forgiving others and ourselves.

Father, thank you for full and complete forgiveness. Thank you for blotting out our sin and choosing to remember it no more. Please help us forgive others - regardless of the pain they have caused - and help us forgive ourselves in order to live in the freedom of your great grace. In Jesus' name. Amen.

reflection

further suggested reading:

Isaiah 40-43

My Purpose Will Stand

Isaiah 46:9-11

Remember the former things, those of long ago; I am God, and there is no other; I am God, and there is none like me. I make known the end from the beginning, from ancient times, what is still to come. I say, 'My purpose will stand, and I will do all that I please.' From the east I summon a bird of prey; from a far-off land, a man to fulfill my purpose. What I have said, that I will bring about; what I have planned, that I will do.

Regardless of the economic forecast . . . *I am God and there is no other . . . My purpose will stand.*
Regardless of congressional votes or Supreme Court decisions . . . *I am God and there is no other . . . My purpose will stand.*
Regardless of who wins the next election . . . *I am God and there is no other . . . My purpose will stand.*
Regardless of the governments that come to power in the Middle East . . . *I am God and there is no other . . . My purpose will stand.*
Regardless of the rogue rulers who make great claims . . . *I am God and there is no other . . . My purpose will stand.*
Regardless of those who threaten nuclear buildup . . . *I am God and there is no other . . . My purpose will stand.*
Regardless of terrorists' threats . . . *I am God and there is no other . . . My purpose will stand.*

Even when the doctor's report was not what I wanted to hear . . . even when he walks away . . . even when my heart is broken . . . even when I wait for God to answer . . . even when my dream dies . . . even when I don't get the job . . . even when my child is estranged . . . even when I am discouraged . . . even when I am depressed . . . even when I don't feel like pushing forward . . . even when grief hits me like a vicious upper cut . . . even when things don't make sense. REMEMBER. *I am God and there is no other . . . My purpose will stand.*

Father, wherever we stand today . . . whether it is in joy, sadness, disappointment, discouragement, confusion, fear, impatience or anxiety . . . we proclaim that you are God and there is no other. We thank you that your purpose will always stand. In Jesus' name. Amen.

reflection

_____

_____

_____

further suggested reading:

Isaiah 44-48

Can You Trust Me?

Isaiah 50:10

Who among you fears the LORD and obeys the word of his servant? Let the one who walks in the dark, who has no light, trust in the name of the LORD and rely on their God.

Discovering God's will is often one of the most challenging things a believer faces. God's revealed will in Scripture is clear - "Do this," "Don't do that." But God's individual will is not always so straightforward. Many believers who desire to follow hard after God struggle with questions such as the following:

- Is this the person God wants me to marry?
- Is this the college God wants me to attend?
- Is this the calling God has placed on my life?
- Is this the job God wants me to take?
- Is this the place where God wants me to live?
- Is this the home God wants us to buy or rent?

Now granted, some believers make life-altering decisions without ever asking, "Is this God's will?" But for those who are intent on following hard after God, these questions, and many more, are ones for which we seek God's specific direction. And sometimes, as we seek God's will, we feel like the person who "walks in the dark, who has no light."

Today's passage reminds us that God does not intend for the "dark path" to be confusing or permanent. He uses dark stretches to develop and deepen our faith. He calls us to follow hard after him, even with our questions, and trust him to open and close the appropriate doors. He calls us to rely on him for wisdom and discernment, for strength and peace. There will be times when the path seems dark. But these are the times God uses to ask us a question, "Can you trust Me?" Can you?

Father, for all those walking through a stretch of path where there seems to be no light, remind them today that you will never leave or forsake them. Remind us all that dark paths cause us to trust you and rely on you. And remind us that when we trust you in the darkness, we see you more clearly in the light. In Jesus' name. Amen.

reflection

_____

_____

further suggested reading:

Isaiah 49-51

Bring Good News

Isaiah 52:7

How beautiful on the mountains are the feet of those who bring good news, who proclaim peace, who bring good tidings, who proclaim salvation, who say to Zion, "Your God reigns!"

I just returned from a mission trip to Panama with about forty teens, nine leaders and a dozen missionaries who met us and ministered with us during an impactful week. In order to present the gospel most effectively, our team was divided into three groups - dancers, puppets and drama. The dancers and puppets performed in elementary schools while the drama group took the message to high schools (Amazingly these presentations were done in the public schools!). During the week we shared the Gospel with over 3,500 students!

After the presentations, a clear Gospel message was given by one of the missionaries. The Panamanian students were invited to respond to the Good News of Jesus. Afterwards our teens passed out tracts and spoke to the students about Jesus. Through interpreters, our teens shared their love for Jesus and commitment to serve him.

As I read today's passage, I couldn't help but think about our teens who went to Panama and the hundreds of others who go out from our church to share Christ in another culture. First, our preparation to go on mission trips is an intense process. Our trips are not purposed for those who like to travel and see the world. Our focus is clear - we go to tell people about Jesus. Second, how encouraging it is to see people, young and old, take time out of their busy lives to proclaim salvation! How beautiful are the feet of those who go across the ocean (or across the street) to bring good news and proclaim the peace with God that can only come through Jesus!

Father, thank you for people, young and old, who are willing to take the time and risk to go into a new culture to share the message of Jesus. Thank you for your hand of protection on all who go. Bless them and stretch them and remind them that what they do is beautiful in your sight. Lord, encourage those who can go to go. And encourage those who can't travel to pray and give. In Jesus' name. Amen.

reflection

further suggested reading:

Isaiah 52

The Back of the Line

July 29

Isaiah 53:5-6

But he was pierced for our transgressions, he was crushed for our iniquities; the punishment that brought us peace was upon him, and by his wounds we are healed. We all, like sheep, have gone astray, each of us has turned to his own way; and the LORD has laid on him the iniquity of us all.

Jesus was given no advantages. The Father sent him to the back of the line and made him experience all the pain of humanity. He was not strikingly handsome or a head taller than the rest of the crowd - *he had no beauty of majesty to attract us to him* . . . He was not a person readily accepted by virtue of personality - *he was despised and rejected by men* . . . Although fully God, he was not born with a silver spoon in his mouth - *a man of sorrows and familiar with suffering.*

Jesus came from heaven to earth . . . and was sent to the back of the line - *stricken, smitten, afflicted, pierced, crushed, oppressed, a lamb to the slaughter, cut off from the land of the living.* The King of Kings lived life as the king of suffering. He was not a victim of circumstance. He was not in the wrong place at the wrong time. He was sent to the back of the line by the Father - *it was the Lord's will to crush him and cause him to suffer.*

Jesus was given no advantages in life and died a brutal death. That's what it took to pay the penalty of sin. Nothing less would do. Jesus left heaven and went to the back of the line for you and me. I was the one who went astray. I was the one who turned to my own way. God laid my sin on Jesus. There is only one way to respond to such love - fall down and worship him! Every day! With your whole life!

Lord Jesus, thank you for willingly going to the back of the line for me. In your precious name. Amen.

reflection

further suggested reading:

Isaiah 53-57

The Fellowship of the Living God

July 30

Isaiah 61:10

I delight greatly in the LORD; my soul rejoices in my God. For he has clothed me with garments of salvation and arrayed me in a robe of his righteousness.

The Good News begins with bad news: We are separated from God and can do nothing about it. Our best effort on our best day cannot bridge the great divide between sinful man and the holy God. Our only option, not one option or one of many options, our **one and only option** is to turn to Christ and trust in him as the One who paid the penalty of my sin on the cross. When I stand before the Judge having trusted in Christ, two things happen.

- **God clothes me with the garments of salvation.** Not on the basis of what I have done but fully on the merits of Christ's work on the cross, God rescues me from an eternity separated from him. He declares me "not guilty" (justification). He takes off my old worn out clothes and gives me a beautiful clean wardrobe - garments of salvation.

- **God gives me a robe of his righteousness.** Not only does God declare me "not guilty," he declares me "righteous." When he looks on me, dressed in the garments of salvation and the robe of his righteousness, he views me as blameless because of the work of Jesus on the cross.

The Good News begins with bad news. All have sinned and fall short of the glory of God. And our sin deserves death (physical, emotional, spiritual). But the Good News is that Jesus came and did for us what we could not do for ourselves. When we trust in Jesus as the only way to know God, we are set free from our old clothes and our old way, and finally can enjoy the fellowship of the living God. That, by the way, is what we have wanted all along.

Lord Jesus, thank you for your work on the cross to make my salvation possible. Thank you for a new set of clothes and a beautiful robe of righteousness. Amen.

reflection

_____

_____

_____

_____

further suggested reading:

Isaiah 58-62

God Acts on Our Behalf

Isaiah 64:4

Since ancient times no one has heard, no ear has perceived, no eye has seen any God besides you, who acts on behalf of those who wait for him.

God acts on our behalf. He saves, delivers and rescues. His arm is not too short to reach down to help us. He is never stingy with his forgiveness. His grace is a constant flow. His mercy never ceases. There is no end to his love. He acts on our behalf. And notice that he acts on behalf of those who "wait for him."

I am convinced that many people never see God act on their behalf because they are too busy acting on their own behalf. Why wait on God when you can get it done yourself? They barge ahead on their own. They make their deals, cut their path and build their stuff. And then when their deals fall through, their path leads to the edge of a cliff and their buildings crumble, they wonder why God didn't act.

Slow down and wait on God. He is seldom early, but he is never late. His right-on-time presence will provide all we need, to do what he has called us to do at just the right moment. He is not silent or ignoring your need. He is waiting for his perfect time. Waiting on God is always worth the wait.

Father, we are in a hurry . . . slow us down. We are impatient . . . help us wait on you. Thank you for being a God who acts on our behalf. In Jesus' name. Amen.

reflection

further suggested reading:

Isaiah 63-66

Set Apart

August 1

Jeremiah 1:4-5

The word of the LORD came to me, saying, "Before I formed you in the womb I knew you, before you were born I set you apart; I appointed you as a prophet to the nations."

God's selection of Jeremiah was made before the prophet was even formed. The word "knew" means more than intellectual knowledge. It describes a personal relationship. God knows those he calls intimately. Jeremiah was not set apart for a general use. Rather God had something very specific in mind. He "appointed" Jeremiah "as a prophet to the nations."

Is this verse just for Jeremiah? I don't think so. Speaking to believers, Paul wrote, "For he chose us in him before the creation of the world to be holy and blameless in his sight" (Ephesians 1:4). Think of that amazing truth! Before time began, God chose you to be holy and blameless in his sight. Like Jeremiah, God knew you intimately before you took your first breath.

And like Jeremiah, he set you apart. He has something very specific in mind for you to do. He has appointed you to a specific assignment. He has placed a significant calling on your life. We cannot waste what God has graciously given us. Such love on the part of God demands love, worship and action on the part of man. Determine what God has called you to do; then, go about getting it done.

Father, give us the wisdom to know what you have called us to do. Give us the courage to do it. And give us the perseverance to get it done. In Jesus' name. Amen.

reflection

further suggested reading:

Jeremiah 1-3

Crossroads

Jeremiah 6:16

This is what the LORD says: "Stand at the crossroads and look; ask for the ancient paths, ask where the good way is, and walk in it, and you will find rest for your souls. But you said, 'We will not walk in it.'"

Sooner or later every person stands at a crossroad. It may be a mental crossroad, and you will have to determine which direction to let your mind go. It may be an emotional crossroad, and you'll have to determine where your heart will travel. At some point, every person will stand before a crossroad and must determine which path he will take.

At each crossroad, there is a decision between two paths. One path appears most inviting. It offers quick fixes, instant gratification and downhill terrain. It also offers much fellowship along the way. But around the bend, out of sight from the point of the crossroad, there is disaster. The inviting path is strewn with brokenness - broken lives, broken families and broken hearts.

The other path, the right path, is often the hardest. It involves a disciplined journey with adventuresome challenges. There are swift rivers to cross and hills to climb. There are some dark clouds and powerful storms. But all along, there is One who walks with you. He lightens the load and gives a constant helping hand. He assures you that you'll reach the destination, even when you feel like calling it quits. And when you are out of strength, he'll carry you. This path is the good way. Walk in it and find rest for your soul.

Father, for all those standing at a crossroad today, open their minds to think clearly, their eyes to see far and their hearts to make the right decision. Help them to walk in the good way and find the rest that only comes from you. In Jesus' name. Amen.

reflection

further suggested reading:

Jeremiah 4-6

Pride

August 3

Jeremiah 9:23-24

This is what the LORD says: "Let not the wise boast of their wisdom or the strong boast of their strength or the rich boast of their riches, but let the one who boasts boast about this: that they have the understanding to know me, that I am the LORD, who exercises kindness, justice and righteousness on earth, for in these I delight," declares the LORD.

Pride comes in a variety of packages. We all have things we are proud of. Maybe your pride stems from the elite college you attended or the prized job you have landed. Maybe your pride comes from the car you drive or the house where you park it. Maybe your pride is generated by important relationships or the success your children. "Best T-ball player on the team!" Maybe your vast intellect swells your head. Isn't it amazing how some people are experts on every subject, even when they are not really experts on any subject?

Pride comes in a variety of deliverables. Some people are open boasters. Two minutes into a conversation, they are expelling the hot air that puffs them up. Others are more private in their pride. Their "aw-shucks" demeanor hides the pride well, but it secretly drives them and provides a sense of worth. It is amazing how we can, at the same time, deflect a compliment while absorbing the pride it produces.

Our passage today gives us some clear instruction regarding pride. Surely God gives some people great intelligence. Others he provides with a spiritual, emotional and/or physical strength. Still others he blesses with wealth. Some get the triple dip waffle cone of wisdom, strength and riches (I'm not fond of triple dippers either). But our boasting is not to be generated from what we have but from whom we have. The only basis for our boasting is that we have the understanding to know the living God. What a difference it would make in our lives and the lives of those around us if we stopped boasting about our stuff and started boasting about our Savior.

Lord, when we boast - openly or secretly - point it out to us. Remind us that all the things that produce pride come from your hand. May our only boasting be in you. In Jesus' name. Amen.

reflection

_____

_____

_____

further suggested reading:

Jeremiah 7-10

Cry Out to God

Jeremiah 14:7

Although our sins testify against us, do something, LORD, for the sake of your name. For we have often rebelled; we have sinned against you.

How should believers communicate with God when they are experiencing the consequences of their sin? Should we just suck it up and endure the results? Does God listen to our prayers for help when we are standing in the penalty of our own rebellion? Today's passage helps us answer these questions.

Israel had rejected God. They had turned to other gods and worshipped created things rather than the Creator. As always, sin has consequences. In order to get the attention of his rebellious children, God sent a drought and famine. Earlier in the passage, we read that servants are sent for water but return with empty jars; the ground was cracked; the doe deserted her newborn fawn; wild donkeys "stand on the barren heights and pant like jackals." But here's one of the important lessons we learn from today's passage: Even in our self-inflicted circumstances, we can and should cry out to God for his help.

No doubt some of you reading this are experiencing the pain of self-inflicted wounds. You have lost the things you love, and you have no one to blame but yourself. You feel empty and alone. And you are doing your best to suck it up and endure. You feel that God does not want you to ask for his help. Read Israel's prayer: "Although our sins testify against us, do something, Lord, for the sake of your name." God wants to help you! Even when we "shoot ourselves in the foot," the Father comes to help us on the journey. He gives us what we don't deserve. That's called grace. And he doesn't give us what we do deserve. That's called mercy.

Father, thank you for your grace and mercy in our lives. We are unworthy of your love, yet you love us. We are unworthy of your help, yet you come to our aid in your timing and will. We are unworthy of your forgiveness, yet you sent Jesus to pay the penalty for all of our sins on the cross. Help us never to hold back from calling on you for help. In Jesus' name. Amen.

reflection

further suggested reading:

Jeremiah 11-13

Where Do You Place Your Hope?

August 5

Jeremiah 14:22

Do any of the worthless idols of the nations bring rain? Do the skies themselves send down showers? No, it is you, LORD our God. Therefore our hope is in you, for you are the one who does all this.

Let's be honest: Idols are pretty cool until we need something from them. Idols, of course, can be categorized under one of the three "P's": Possessions, Power, and Position. They are the things we spend our time and energy thinking about and working for.

We love possessions . . . love to drive them, live in them and play with them. We love position . . . love to have the right job with the right title and the right salary. We love power . . . love to be in control and call the shots. But . . . have you ever seen a father praying to the god of "job" when his little child is sick? Have you ever seen a mother bowing in the front yard before the god of "house" when her marriage started to crumble? We love our idols . . . until we need something from them and learn they are powerless.

The Israelites learned that lesson the hard way. They had turned from God and turned to idols. But when drought and famine hit their lives, they found the idols unable to provide the needed rain. They found out that the idols were not so cool after all. They finally realized that God was the only One who could provide what was needed, so they put their hope in him. Here's the question: Where do you place your hope? Really? Your idols may be cool for now, but wait until you need something from them.

Father, show us the worthless idols in our lives. Help us to identify them and destroy them. Help us to place our hope in you and you alone. In Jesus' name. Amen.

reflection

_____

_____

_____

_____

_____

_____

further suggested reading:

Jeremiah 14-15

223

Trust in God

August 6

Jeremiah 17:7-8

But blessed is the one who trusts in the LORD, whose confidence is in him. They will be like a tree planted by the water that sends out its roots by the stream. It does not fear when heat comes; its leaves are always green. It has no worries in a year of drought and never fails to bear fruit.

Don't place your faith in nouns. Sooner or later every *person* will disappoint, every *place* will lose its luster and every *thing* will wear out, become outdated or lost. But there is One who will never disappoint. That's why the person who puts his trust in God will be blessed. Today's verse gives three benefits of trusting in the Lord.

Constant Nourishment. The person who trusts in the Lord is like a tree planted by a stream. The roots make their way to the fresh and nutritious flow. The tree will never lack for food. Thus, the believer, whose confidence is in the Lord, will have no lack of spiritual sustenance.

Constant Protection. The heat comes, but the tree by the stream is appropriately shielded. There is enough sun to make it grow but not too much to burn its leaves. Thus, the believer will experience some heat through various circumstances and challenges. We need some heat to make us grow. But God will always be there to protect us. He will not give us more than we can bear.

Constant Fruit. Dry times come. But the tree planted by the stream has everything it needs to bear fruit. Thus, the believer will experience some dry spiritual times . . . but connected to the source of nourishment and protection, we will continue to produce the good works that God prepared in advance for us to do (Ephesians 2:10).

Two questions arise to challenge you: In whom or what do you trust? In whom or what do you place your confidence? The answer to those questions will determine whether or not you are receiving the nourishment, protection and fruit that come from dependence on the heavenly Father.

Father, make us like trees planted by streams of water. Please nourish and protect us. Allow us to accomplish the good works you prepared for us. In Jesus' name. Amen.

reflection

further suggested reading:

Jeremiah 16-20

Run to Him

Jeremiah 23:23-24

Am I only a God nearby," declares the LORD, "and not a God far away? Who can hide in secret places so that I cannot see them?" declares the LORD. "Do not I fill heaven and earth?" declares the LORD.

The message of Israel's false prophets was a made up message crafted to satisfy people rather than God. In response to Israel's sin, they assured peace, but they did not get this assurance from God. False teachers from every generation bring messages that their hearers desire instead of a true word from God. To every false teacher and prophet God says, in essence, "You've got to be kidding!"

In today's passage, God responds to the prophets by explaining two of his attributes. He is both omnipresent and omniscient. God's omnipresence means that he is everywhere at the same time in his full being. He is both nearby and far away. God's omniscience means that he knows everything there is to know about everything there is to know. His knowledge and presence fills the heaven and earth.

How can we apply these truths? First, his omnipresence reminds us that we cannot hide from God. If you think you are doing something that God cannot see . . . think again. And he is the One to whom we must give our final account. Second, God knows us inside and out. You can fool others . . . even those who are close to you . . . but you cannot fool God. The characteristics of God prevent us from playing games with him. Wherever we are, he is there. Whoever we are, he knows us fully. And . . . here's the good part . . . knowing us fully, he still welcomes us with open arms. In him there is forgiveness and restoration. Don't run from him (You can't!). Run to him. He is waiting with open arms.

Father, remind the person trying to hide from you of the truths found in today's passage. Help that person come clean and come home. In Jesus' name. Amen.

reflection

_____

_____

_____

_____

further suggested reading:

Jeremiah 21-25

Great Plans

Jeremiah 29:11-13

"For I know the plans I have for you," declares the LORD, "plans to prosper you and not to harm you, plans to give you hope and a future. Then you will call on me and come and pray to me, and I will listen to you. You will seek me and find me when you seek me with all your heart."

This familiar passage provides great confidence. Think of it! God has great plans for our life. He wants to prosper us and not to harm us. God is working to give us hope and a certain future. But do you know the context of this passage?

This promise was written to God's people in exile. Because of their sin, God had allowed Nebuchadnezzar to take them from Jerusalem to Babylon. They were living in an unfamiliar land under the authority of a pagan king. The people of Israel were experiencing the results of rejecting God and following other gods. They were living out the consequences of their sin. Yet right in the middle of their exile, God reminds them that he is not through with them. The discipline is not for harm but for restoration. In exile the people would finally turn back to God. And when they did, God heard their prayers. When they sought him, they found him.

Maybe you are living in the results of your sins today. You are experiencing the self-inflicted wounds of rebellion. You feel alone and forgotten. You feel that God is done with you. But he isn't done with you! Today's passage teaches us that God never gives up on us. Right in the middle of sin's consequences, he has plans for us. His intent is never to harm but to bring us back to the land of spiritual prosperity. He wants us to turn back to him, call on him and pray to him. He promises to hear our cries. And he promises that when we seek him with a sincere heart, we will find him waiting for us with open arms. God is not finished with you!

Father, thank you for not giving up on me. Thank you for discipline that turns my heart back to you. Thank you for hearing my cries. Thank you for open arms of forgiveness and restoration. In Jesus' name. Amen.

reflection

_____

_____

_____

_____

further suggested reading:

Jeremiah 26-29

Confession

Jeremiah 31:19

After I strayed, I repented; after I came to understand, I beat my breast. I was ashamed and humiliated because I bore the disgrace of my youth.

When we trust in Christ as the only way to have a relationship with the living God, we are unplugged from our sinful nature and plugged into the power of Christ; however, the sinful nature is not deleted from our life. The old master calls out to us and his voice is familiar and inviting. And there are times when we stray to the land of sin. The Apostle John wrote, "If we claim to be without sin, we deceive ourselves and the truth is not in us." But when "we confess our sins, he is faithful and just and will forgive our sins and purify us from all unrighteousness" (1 John 1:8-9).

What does confession look like? Our passage today gives us great insight into this important spiritual discipline.

After I strayed, I repented. A flippant "I'm sorry" or "I'm sorry I got caught" does not cut it with God. Confession involves repentance. In repentance, I understand that I am heading the wrong direction. I stop. Turn around. And head back home. Repentance involves turning from the wrong direction and turning to the right direction.

After I came to understand, I beat my breast. To beat one's breast was a figurative expression of mourning and grief. True confession involves sorrow for sinning against God. God does not take sin lightly; neither should we.

I was ashamed and humiliated. When some share their salvation story, it is more about their sin than being saved from it. But we should never glory in our sin. We should be ashamed and humiliated by what we have done. Sin, and being proud of it, shows the immaturity of youth.

All of us sin. All of us stray. And all of us must understand and practice true confession.

Father, help us turn from our sin, grieve our rebellion and be ashamed of what we have done. May we be those who never glory in our sin but glory only in the Savior who continues to deliver us from it. In Jesus' name. Amen.

further suggested reading:

Jeremiah 30-33

Ignoring God's Word

Jeremiah 37:1-2

Zedekiah son of Josiah was made king of Judah by Nebuchadnezzar king of Babylon; he reigned in place of Jehoiachin son of Jehoiakim. Neither he nor his attendants nor the people of the land paid any attention to the words the LORD had spoken through Jeremiah the prophet.

Josiah was a great ruler; his son was not. Zedekiah was a puppet king operated by Nebuchadnezzar. But that wasn't his biggest problem. As today's passage states, neither he nor his leaders paid any attention to the words of the Lord. And the people of the land followed their lead. They ignored what God said through Jeremiah the prophet.

Ignorance of God's Word is one thing. But ignoring God's Word is something entirely different. Not knowing an instruction of Scripture does not nullify our sin, but it means we acted unaware. However, knowing God's instruction and choosing to ignore it demonstrates a rebellious spirit and a disregard for the Author.

How are you doing with the Scripture that you know? Are you obeying it or choosing to ignore it? Are you striving to follow the instruction or electing to pay no attention to it? The consequence of ignorance is sad. The consequence of ignoring God's Word is tragic.

Father, may we not be simply hearers but doers of your Word. We have no excuse for ignorance. We certainly have no excuse for not paying attention to Scripture. Forgive us for our ignorance and our ignoring spirit. In Jesus' name. Amen.

reflection

_____

_____

_____

_____

_____

_____

_____

_____

further suggested reading:

Jeremiah 34-39

God Disciplines Those He Loves

August 11

Jeremiah 44:2-5

This is what the LORD Almighty, the God of Israel, says: "You saw the great disaster I brought on Jerusalem and on all the towns of Judah. Today they lie deserted and in ruins because of the evil they have done. They aroused my anger by burning incense to and worshiping other gods that neither they nor you nor your ancestors ever knew. Again and again I sent my servants the prophets, who said, 'Do not do this detestable thing that I hate!' But they did not listen or pay attention; they did not turn from their wickedness or stop burning incense to other gods."

Some people conclude from passages like today's that God is unloving. How could he bring disaster on his people? How could he leave their towns deserted? How could a loving God be aroused by anger? How could he allow them to be taken into captivity? The answer is found in God's love and mercy.

Like a loving father, God disciplines those he loves. What loving father would let his toddler play by a busy road? The father teaches the child the danger by instruction. If the child continues to waddle toward the danger, discipline is applied. The discipline does not show a lack of love. The father loves his child too much to allow him to be hurt or killed by a car.

God loves us too much to allow us to play by the spiritual life's equivalent of a busy highway. He loves us too much to allow us to continue living in spiritual danger. When we ignore his instruction, he applies discipline. The writer to the Hebrews said it this way: "God disciplines us for our good, in order that we may share in his holiness. No discipline seems pleasant at the time, but painful. Later on, however, it produces a harvest of righteousness and peace for those who have been trained by it" (Hebrews 12:10-11).

Father, none of us like the consequences of our sin. No discipline seems pleasant at the time. But thank you for loving us so much that you never give up on us. Thank you for applying the discipline that produces a harvest of righteousness and peace. Help us to be willing to be trained by it. In Jesus' name. Amen.

reflection

further suggested reading:

Jeremiah 40-44

229

Ambition

August 12

Jeremiah 45:5

Should you then seek great things for yourself? Do not seek them. For I will bring disaster on all people, declares the LORD, but wherever you go I will let you escape with your life.

Jeremiah 45 is a short message to Baruch, Jeremiah's faithful secretary. Baruch "had written on a scroll the words that Jeremiah was . . . dictating." Baruch's brother, Seraiah, was given an important position by King Zedekiah, and it would have been tempting for Baruch to seek a royal position like his brother. But Jeremiah reminded him not to seek great things for himself.

Ambition is a double-edged sword. We want to succeed in our work and provide for our family. We want our children to be ambitious. We want them to study hard and make good grades. We want them to attend a challenging college or training school that will prepare them well. We teach them not to settle for second best. But the double-edged sword of ambition must have a clear purpose or it cuts the wrong way.

As believers, our purpose is to do great things for God. Our ambition should be to follow hard after him. God doesn't want us to slide through life with a "whatever" attitude. We are his work of art, created in Christ Jesus to do the things that he prepared in advance for us to do (Ephesians 2:10). The Apostle Paul said, "It has always been my ambition to preach the gospel where Christ was not known." (Romans 15:20). What is your ambition? How would you complete the sentence, "It has always been my ambition to _____ _____."

Father, place a drive and passion and ambition in our hearts. Teach us the difference between selfish ambition and godly ambition. Help us to do great things for you. In Jesus' name. Amen.

reflection

_____

_____

_____

_____

_____

_____

further suggested reading:

Jeremiah 45

Seemingly Secure

August 13

Jeremiah 49:16

"The terror you inspire and the pride of your heart have deceived you, you who live in the clefts of the rocks, who occupy the heights of the hill. Though you build your nest as high as the eagle's, from there I will bring you down," declares the LORD.

The godless nations thought that they were in charge. They inspired terror. Their hearts grew proud. They thought their strategic strongholds were impenetrable. They seemed to be in complete control. They had taken God's people into captivity. But their pride deceived them. Even from their "nest as high as the eagle's," God said, "from there I will bring you down."

Like these godless nations, we are tempted to build strongholds. We work to make sure that we can acquire all we want. We invest to make sure that our money is making money. We structure our life so that we are secure in retirement. We build our nest as high as the eagle's. But the pride of our hearts deceives us. We learn, sometimes tragically, that we are not in control after all.

Jesus once told a story about a man whose ground produced a good crop. The man was already wealthy; his barns were full. But instead of generosity, he practiced greed. He tore down his barns and built bigger ones. He was satisfied in his security. But God told him, "You fool! This very night your life will be demanded of you." Sometimes we can deceive ourselves in our seeming security. At the end of the day, the only safety is found in God alone.

Father, help us not put our security in possessions, power or position. Help us not be deceived by the world's offering of confidence. May our trust be in you and you alone throughout this life and as you take us home. In Jesus' name. Amen.

reflection

_____

_____

_____

_____

_____

_____

further suggested reading:

Jeremiah 46-49

231

Experience God's Great Forgiveness

August 14

Jeremiah 50:20

"In those days, at that time," declares the LORD, "search will be made for Israel's guilt, but there will be none, and for the sins of Judah, but none will be found, for I will forgive the remnant I spare."

Israel sinned against God. They rejected him and served lifeless idols. They ignored his instructions and even the warnings sent through Jeremiah. Their hearts were hardened; they jettisoned their faith. And as a result of their sin, God disciplined them. Israel was taken into captivity. Jerusalem and its important buildings were destroyed. Sin always has consequences.

But God does not give up on his people. The discipline was not to destroy but to restore. In his timing, he stepped in to bring Israel back home. And he provided complete and clear forgiveness. A search for Israel's guilt would be fruitless. None of Israel's sins could be found. God said, "I will forgive the remnant I spare."

Maybe today the scars of your life show that you have lived far from God. You know the consequence of walking away. You know the inward pain and regret. You know the pain that you have caused others. But please hear this - there is no sin that God cannot and will not forgive. When we come in true repentance, he forgives and chooses to forget. You can make a search for your guilt, but it will not be found. It's time to come home and experience God's great forgiveness and grace.

Father, help all those who have wandered away find the path back to you. Let them experience your forgiveness. Let them live restored. And may they show the same grace to others that you have shown to them. In Jesus' name. Amen.

reflection

_____

_____

_____

_____

_____

further suggested reading:

Jeremiah 50-52

The Goodness of God

August 15

Lamentations 3:21-26

Yet this I call to mind and therefore I have hope: Because of the LORD's great love we are not consumed, for his compassions never fail. They are new every morning; great is your faithfulness. I say to myself, "The LORD is my portion; therefore I will wait for him." The LORD is good to those whose hope is in him, to the one who seeks him; it is good to wait quietly for the salvation of the LORD.

Words cannot describe the horror that faced God's people when Babylon marched into Jerusalem to destroy the walls of the city and the hearts of the people. No king, prince, priest, prophet or commoner was exempt from devastation and slaughter. Starving mothers resorted to cannibalism. The ceremony of worship ended. People were dragged off into slavery. The author, probably Jeremiah, understands that Babylon was used merely as a human instrument of God's judgment. Yet through his laments, he wrestles with the ways of God.

In the middle of the laments, Jeremiah stops for a moment to focus on the goodness of God. These are the things that Jeremiah calls to mind, and it gives him hope.

God's great love. Jeremiah reminds himself and his readers that they are alive only because of God's love. Even in the most desperate times, God's great compassion never fails. You may be in a difficult situation today. Remember how much God loves you.

God's great faithfulness. Even when we are faithless, God is faithful. We can always depend on him to bring a fresh pouring out of his love and compassion every morning. God will give us everything we need . . . one day at a time.

God's great salvation. Deliverance for Israel would not come the next day or the day after that. But they knew that God was their "portion" (their only hope), and they chose to wait on him. Can you "wait quietly for the salvation of the Lord"? He will come . . . in his way and in his timing.

Father, thank you for your great love, faithfulness and salvation that comes even in the most difficult times. Help us wait on you . . . even when waiting and trusting are really hard. In Jesus' name. Amen.

reflection

further suggested reading:

Lamentations 1-5

Watchmen

Ezekiel 3:16-17

At the end of seven days the word of the LORD came to me: "Son of man, I have made you a watchman for the people of Israel; so hear the word I speak and give them warning from me."

Ezekiel was in the group exiled to Babylon by Nebuchadnezzar in 597 B.C. He was married, lived in his own house and, though confined in Babylon, had a relatively free existence. It was there in exile that Ezekiel was called by God, in a very vivid way, to become a prophet. God told Ezekiel, "I have made you a watchman for the people of Israel."

Ezekiel's job was no small task. First, he had to stay in tune with God. God spoke through him so he had to make sure he heard clearly. Second, Ezekiel had to deliver God's warnings to rebels, and many of the messages were not well received. But God told the prophet, "When I say to a wicked man, 'You will surely die,' and you do not warn him or speak out to dissuade him from his evil ways in order to save his life, that wicked man will die for his sin, and I will hold you accountable for his blood." Think of it! If Ezekiel failed to pass along God's word to those under his care, he was held responsible.

While you may not have received the vision from God that Ezekiel did, many of you reading this are watchmen. Mothers, fathers and grandparents are watchmen as they pass along God's word to their children and grandchildren. Pastors are watchmen as they teach Scripture to their congregations. Leaders are watchmen as they guide those whom God has placed in their office or school or region. Will we be held accountable like Ezekiel? Hmm . . . I believe so.

Father, remind us of the weight of the assignments that you give to us. Help us be a faithful watchman passing on your Word - with its warnings and encouragement - to those under our charge. In Jesus' name. Amen.

reflection

further suggested reading:

Ezekiel 1-6

Undivided Focus

Ezekiel 11:19-20

I will give them an undivided heart and put a new spirit in them; I will remove from them their heart of stone and give them a heart of flesh. Then they will follow my decrees and be careful to keep my laws. They will be my people, and I will be their God.

This passage appears on the pages of Ezekiel like an oasis in the desert. In this section of the book, God has been describing his judgment on the leaders of Israel. They gave in to idolatry and rebelliousness. They had forsaken the God who chose them to be his own. The glory of God left the temple in Chapter 10. But here, God reminds the people that he is far from finished with them.

God will bring his people back home. He will take their divided hearts and give them one focused solely on him. He will put a new passion in them to follow hard after him. Removing the hardened heart bent on sin and inserting a heart that is pumping spiritual vitality throughout their bodies, he will give them a heart transplant. When God works in his people, they follow and obey.

God will bring you back home, too, if you let him. He desires that you follow his decrees and keep his laws. He wants you to be his son or daughter. He desires to be your God. He will take the heart that he shares with the other stuff in your life and make it fully his. He will take your spirit that has been running from him and replace it with a desire to follow him. He will remove the heart calloused from years of sin and give you one that beats for him. Do you want this kind of change? The following prayer will help you get started.

Father, I am tired of running and tired of this life separated from you. I have been doing my thing, living my own way, and it has worn me out. I want to be changed by you . . . a new spirit, new heart, new passion to follow hard after you. I don't want to share my loyalties. Give me an undivided focus to obey your Word. In Jesus' name. Amen.

reflection

_____

_____

_____

_____

_____

_____

further suggested reading:

Ezekiel 7-11

False Teachers

August 18

Ezekiel 13:22-23

Because you disheartened the righteous with your lies, when I had brought them no grief, and because you encouraged the wicked not to turn from their evil ways and so save their lives, therefore you will no longer see false visions or practice divination. I will save my people from your hands. And then you will know that I am the LORD.

Even when God's people were living in exile, false prophets filled the land. They "disheartened the righteous" and "encouraged the wicked." They led the unsuspecting away from God. False prophets and teachers will be around until the end of time. Therefore, we need to know how to spot them. Ezekiel 13 gives us three important things to look for.

1. **False teachers follow their own spirit** (Ezekiel 13:3). A false teacher speaks more about himself or herself than about God. He or she is a self-promoter. In essence, people follow him or her instead of God.

2. **False teachers speak their own words.** They say, "The Lord declares," when the Lord has not sent them (Ezekiel 13:6). Evaluate how a false teacher misuses Scripture. He will ignore it or twist it out of context. This is why it is so important for us to be grounded in Scripture. The best way to spot a counterfeit is to be intimately familiar with the real thing.

3. **False teachers provide a flimsy foundation.** "They lead people astray, saying, 'Peace,' when there is no peace, and because, when a flimsy wall is built, they cover it with whitewash" (Ezekiel 13:10). Believers must be able to discern content from presentation. The false teacher's presentation and performance appears good from the outside, but the content is like a flimsy wall. Sooner or later, it will fall.

Father, we live in a world full of false teachers. Give us discernment. Ground us in your truth. Help us spot and stay away from those who whitewash flimsy walls. Don't let us be deceived by false teachers. In Jesus' name. Amen.

reflection

---

further suggested reading:

Ezekiel 12-13

Idols

Ezekiel 14:6

Therefore say to the people of Israel, 'This is what the Sovereign LORD says: Repent! Turn from your idols and renounce all your detestable practices!'

Even in exile, Israel still had challenges. Even after being disciplined for their rebellion, they continued to worship idols. As a result, God addressed the sin. He always does.

The insidious issue of idols is not so much the object. After all, the object is an inanimate piece of wood, stone or metal. It cannot see, hear or respond. But God explained that when we bow before anything other than him, we set up idols in our hearts (Ezekiel14:3). The heart, the center of our mind, emotion and will, becomes divided. We internalize our idols, and it (or they) becomes the focus of our heart. Our idols normally don't show up in the form of a statue. Rather they are the heart emotions of lust, greed, avarice, pride, self-absorption, self-promotion, jealousy, appearance. The insidious issue of idols is not the "thing" but what the thing represents.

Here's today's question: Do you have anything, besides God, set up in your heart? If so, "This is what the Sovereign LORD says: 'Repent! Turn from your idols and renounce all your detestable practices!'"

Father, we pause now to evaluate our hearts. Examine us. Show us what is inside. Give us a good look at our sin. Then give us the strength and commitment to turn from that thing that turns us from you. In Jesus' name. Amen.

reflection

_____

_____

_____

_____

_____

_____

_____

_____

further suggested reading:

Ezekiel 14-15

My Sin

Ezekiel 18:20

The one who sins is the one who will die. The child will not share the guilt of the parent, nor will the parent share the guilt of the child. The righteousness of the righteous will be credited to them, and the wickedness of the wicked will be charged against them.

"No man is an island, entire to itself," the poet John Donne wrote, "Each is a piece of the continent, a part of the main." That's certainly true. No person lives untouched by others. In large part we are shaped by family and friends. And the influence of significant people in our lives is real and strong.

But family members and friends are not perfect. Some of you may still be reeling from an unloving or even abusive parent. Some of you may still have the scars of divorce. Some of you may still be climbing out of the hole you followed close "friends" into. And many (too many) use their past experience to rationalize their present action. Today's passage makes this truth clear: You cannot blame your present sin on the sin of others. You are personally held responsible for your actions.

Three important questions to honestly ask, answer and act upon are the following:

1. Am I blaming my sin on the sins of others?
2. Am I willing to take personal ownership of my sin?
3. Am I willing to turn from my sin and turn to God?

Father, it is easy to blame my sin on the actions of others. Remind me that I own my sin. Remind me that I will be held accountable for my sin. Help me quit blaming others. Help me turn from my sin and turn to you. In Jesus' name. Amen.

reflection

_____

_____

_____

_____

_____

_____

further suggested reading:

Ezekiel 16-19

Stand in the Gap

Ezekiel 22:30

I looked for someone among them who would build up the wall and stand before me in the gap on behalf of the land so I would not have to destroy it, but I found no one.

Israel was far from God. The leaders were abusing their God-given power. The people turned their God-given desire to worship towards worthless idols. God's chosen people were making choices against him. And God looked for someone . . . anyone . . . to build up the spiritual walls and stand in the gap. But he found no one.

God is still looking for people to build spiritual walls and stand in the gap. He is looking for moms more concerned about their daughter's walk with God than her circle of popular friends. He is looking for fathers more concerned about their son's heart than his batting averages. He is looking for leaders unwilling to compromise regardless of the pressure. He is looking for men and women to stand strong in the face of culture. He is looking for people who will demonstrate to family and friends what it looks like in real life to follow hard after God.

Here's the question. As God looks for someone to build up the wall and stand before him in the gap, whom will he find? Here's the bigger question - will he find you?

Father, give us strong spiritual hands so that we can build strong spiritual walls. Give us strong spiritual feet to stand in the gap. Let me be the person you find to build and stand strong for you. In Jesus' name. Amen.

reflection

further suggested reading:

Ezekiel 20-23

The Message

August 22

Ezekiel 24:27

At that time your mouth will be opened; you will speak with him and will no longer be silent. So you will be a sign to them, and they will know that I am the LORD.

The phrase "They will know that I am the LORD" occurs fifty-four times in the book of Ezekiel. God works to get the attention of his people. Sometimes through tender encouragement, sometimes through discipline, God acts to show those he loves how much he loves them. When believers stray, God will not stand passively by and watch them walk away. He will get the attention of his children.

The Old Testament prophet was a vital part of the process. More often than not, the prophet spoke words of warning and impending doom. Many times prophets were rejected for speaking God's message. Often they were persecuted. But they did not retreat from their mission.

The sovereign God can do anything he wants to do anytime he wants to do it. But most of the time, he uses people in the process. Like the prophets, God gives us a message to share on his behalf. Sometimes it is a message of encouragement, sometimes warning. Sometime we are called to comfort; other times we are sent to confront. Sometimes we are sent to speak to unbelievers about how to have a relationship with God. Other times we are sent to believers to give them words of spiritual instruction. When God opens our mouths with his message, we cannot be silent. We must share the message God gives us so that people will know that he alone is the LORD.

Father, thank you for not standing passively by as your children walk away. Thank you for entrusting us with the message of eternal life. When you open our mouths, may we be earnest to speak clearly and boldly. In Jesus' name. Amen.

reflection

_____

_____

_____

_____

_____

further suggested reading:

Ezekiel 24-28

Pride

Ezekiel 31:10-11

Therefore this is what the Sovereign LORD says: Because the great cedar towered over the thick foliage, and because it was proud of its height, I gave it into the hands of the ruler of the nations, for him to deal with according to its wickedness. I cast it aside.

Through the prophet Ezekiel, God let the nations know that he was in charge. Their vast armies were no match for his power. Their economies could not out resource his resources. He used countries for his sovereign purposes. But he never let them get by with their wickedness.

The great Empire of Egypt "towered over" other nations . . . for a time. They were proud of their attainments and accomplishments. They felt indestructible. They boasted of their great height. However, when God had had enough of their conceit, he cast them aside.

We need to remember, "Pride goes before destruction, a haughty spirit before a fall" (Proverbs 16:18). The things that puff us up drag us down. When we become proud of our "height," God will trim us back. He will not leave his children, but he will humble us. Living in the highlands of pride we have a tendency to look down on God. He will keep us in a place where we must look up to him. That's the position of dependence, service and worship. The spiritual journey is not a path for those with proud, self-satisfied swagger.

Father, help us not to think too highly of ourselves. May our confidence come from you alone. Help us deal with our pride before a devastating fall. In Jesus' name. Amen.

reflection

further suggested reading:

Ezekiel 29-32

Spiritual Exercise

August 24

Ezekiel 33:31-32

My people come to you, as they usually do, and sit before you to hear your words, but they do not put them into practice. Their mouths speak of love, but their hearts are greedy for unjust gain. Indeed, to them you are nothing more than one who sings love songs with a beautiful voice and plays an instrument well, for they hear your words but do not put them into practice.

Some people collect knowledge like others collect coins. They are addicted to new tidbits of information. They are seminar junkies. They cannot turn down a new study bible or Bible study. But like too much food and too little exercise does damage to the waistline, too much knowledge never put into practice does damage to the soul.

In today's passage, God told Ezekiel that the people loved to hear him teach. He likened Ezekiel's messages to "one who sings love songs with a beautiful voice and plays an instrument well." But after listening to the message, although "their mouths speak of love . . . their hearts are greedy for unjust gain." They hear the words but don't put them into practice.

How about you? Are you eating too much and exercising too little? Do you appreciate the "love songs," beautiful voices and well-played instruments of a worship service but neglect practicing the message of the songs? Do you enjoy a good sermon like a good steak but never use the spiritual food for spiritual exercise? Do you speak love with your mouth but continue greed in your heart? Convicting, isn't it? Today is the day to put knowledge into practice.

Father, convict us if we are all head and no heart. Point out where we are enjoying the love songs but not sharing the love. Forgive us for speaking truth with our mouth but not living out the truth we proclaim. Show us where our words and actions don't match up. Give us the desire and courage to change. In Jesus' name. Amen.

reflection

further suggested reading:

Ezekiel 33-36

Restoration

August 25

Ezekiel 37:11-14

Then he said to me: "Son of man, these bones are the people of Israel. They say, 'Our bones are dried up and our hope is gone; we are cut off.' Therefore prophesy and say to them: 'This is what the Sovereign LORD says: My people, I am going to open your graves and bring you up from them; I will bring you back to the land of Israel. Then you, my people, will know that I am the LORD, when I open your graves and bring you up from them. I will put my Spirit in you and you will live, and I will settle you in your own land. Then you will know that I the LORD have spoken, and I have done it, declares the LORD.'"

The people of Israel expressed their feelings of utter despair, "Our bones are dried up and our hope is gone; we are cut off." They had lost all sense of spiritual life. Their relationship with God felt like nothing more than dry bones. Their confidence and courage were long gone. They saw themselves as cut off and abandoned.

Maybe you can relate. Bones dried up? Hope gone? Cut off? Like Israel, you are living in the exile of self-inflicted pain. The path you cut has led to the dead end. Hope of restoration seems impossible. Your spiritual GPS has run out of power and is showing a blank screen.

I have great news for you! The God, who resurrects dry bones, resuscitates lost hope and recaptures the abandoned, stands before you with open arms. Feel his embrace and get ready to live again. Thank God for his power to open spiritual graves and breathe life back into the soul. Thank God for his grace to forgive and mercy to restore. Thank God for his willingness to help you leave your past behind and build you a new future. Nothing is impossible with him.

Father, thank you for meeting us in our sin, despair and hopelessness. Thank you for making our dry bones rattle back to life. Thank you for forgiveness and restoration. Help us live out our thanks. In Jesus' name. Amen.

reflection

_____

_____

_____

_____

_____

further suggested reading:

Ezekiel 37-38

Watch for God

August 26

Ezekiel 39:22

From that day forward the people of Israel will know that I am the LORD their God.

As I write this, there is a blue band on my left wrist. I got it while working at our church's Vacation Bible School. On one part of the band it says, "The Bible Chapel." But I have kept wearing the band because on another part are the words, "Watch for God."

Those words are a reminder to me that God is at work all around me. From the striking sunrise to the soothing sunset . . . God is there. From the cloudless blue sky to the dark clouds filled with booming thunder and sheets of rain . . . God is there. God was even there in the 110 degree heat I experienced while visiting family in Oklahoma. He is there laughing in my joys and soothing me in my pain. He is there in every accomplishment and disappointment. He is there in those times when I feel I "pulled it off." And he is there when I fall hard. My problem is that I forget to watch for God and acknowledge his constant presence.

One day soon, I'll take off the wrist band. In fact, even now the letters are starting to wear away. But I don't want to forget its reminder. I want to spend my life watching for God. I want to see his endless activity in my life. And I want to celebrate his work with him. I want to be reminded throughout my distracted day that he is the LORD my God.

Father, your activity in us and around us never ceases. Help us see you, acknowledge you and celebrate life with you. May we be those who are always watching for you. In Jesus' name. Amen.

reflection

further suggested reading:

Ezekiel 39

Details of Our Lives

Ezekiel 40:3-4

He took me there, and I saw a man whose appearance was like bronze; he was standing in the gateway with a linen cord and a measuring rod in his hand. The man said to me, "Son of man, look carefully and listen closely and pay attention to everything I am going to show you, for that is why you have been brought here. Tell the people of Israel everything you see."

Ezekiel saw the restoration of the temple. The vision was given to him in detail. The man God introduced to Ezekiel "was standing in the gateway with a linen cord and measuring rod in his hand." The rest of the prophesy details the width and length of the walls, gates, courts, rooms and even the ovens and kitchens of the temple. When I read these chapters, I am always amazed at how specific God gets.

God is a God of immensity! He sees all the earth and everything on it. At the same time, God is a God of great detail. He cares that the jambs of the portico gateway are two cubits thick (Ezekiel 40:8). And . . . he cares about the details of our lives.

- He cares that you are having a good day . . . or a bad one.
- He cares about your disappointments . . . even the ones brought on by trivia stuff.
- He knows that you got soaked in his downpour (as I did a few minutes ago).
- He is concerned about your present spiritual drought.
- He cares about the things that make you sad . . . and enters your pain.
- He cares about the things that cause you to laugh . . . and laughs with you.
- He is involved in the minutes and seconds of your life. He uses them in his sovereign plan for you.
- He is not absent as your heart is breaking.
- He smiles as it beats for joy.

Someone has said that the devil is in the details. Not true . . . God is. And when he is present, the devil gets out of the way.

Father, thank you for caring about the details of my life. Thank you for using the details for my spiritual formation. In Jesus' name. Amen.

reflection

_____

_____

further suggested reading:

Ezekiel 40-43

The Lord Is There

Ezekiel 48:35

And the name of the city from that time on will be: THE LORD IS THERE.

Israel delivered from exile. The temple restored. Worship resumed. The glory of the Lord returns. The city renamed - THE LORD IS THERE! What a great day that was for the nation of Israel. "Dry bones" aptly described the time of their hopelessness. But God resurrected them from the spiritual grave. Now a thankful people bow before their powerful and personal God. He is with them. The Lord is there!

But the temple was destroyed again . . . after the time of Ezekiel. This time, however, it served as a physical reminder that God did not set up shop within carefully measured walls or holy rooms. Now, because of Immanuel, God is with us and will always be with us. The inscription written on our hearts is THE LORD IS THERE.

Think of it. Through the Holy Spirit, God lives within us! He resides in our hearts. He never leaves us. His presence is 24/7. If a person is looking to find God, he or she need look no farther than us! Write the words - THE LORD IS THERE - on a sign and "hang it on your heart." Display the sign through your words and actions. May all who look for God find him . . . right where you are.

Father, you live within me. Help me never to forget or get over that awesome truth. In Jesus' name. Amen.

reflection

_____
_____
_____
_____
_____
_____
_____
_____
_____

further suggested reading:

Ezekiel 44-48

Life of Obedience

Daniel 3:16-18

Shadrach, Meshach and Abednego replied to him, "King Nebuchadnezzar, we do not need to defend ourselves before you in this matter. If we are thrown into the blazing furnace, the God we serve is able to deliver us from it, and he will deliver us from Your Majesty's hand. But even if he does not, we want you to know, Your Majesty, that we will not serve your gods or worship the image of gold you have set up."

The profession of Shadrach, Meshach and Abednego is one of the most amazing in all of Scripture. Faced with death for not bowing before the king's gods, they felt no compulsion to defend themselves. They knew that God could save them if he chose. But "even if he does not, we want you to know, Your Majesty, that we will not serve your gods."

The furious king ordered the furnace heated seven times hotter than usual. The soldiers who threw the three Hebrew boys into the fire were killed by the heat. But King Nebuchadnezzar was amazed as he saw not three, but four men "walking around in the fire . . . unharmed." The fourth man, Nebuchadnezzar exclaimed, "looks like a son of the gods." God had sent an angel to deliver the young men.

For me, the deliverance, while crazy amazing, is not the coolest part of this story. I am struck by Shadrach, Meshach and Abednego's undeterred commitment to obedience. They knew that God was more than powerful enough to save them, but they didn't know if it was his will. But whether he saved them or not, they would not bow to anyone or anything other than God. That's the life of obedience God calls us to. Is that the life of obedience that we are committed to?

Father, prepare us today for tough decisions tomorrow. Help us not to obey you only when it is in our best interest. Help us to be willing to obey you even if you choose not to deliver us from the fire. In Jesus' name. Amen.

reflection

further suggested reading:

Daniel 1-3

Resolved Obedience

August 30

Daniel 6:21-22

Daniel answered, "May the king live forever! My God sent his angel and he shut the mouths of the lions. They have not hurt me, because I was found innocent in his sight. Nor have I ever done any wrong before you, Your Majesty."

When you follow God, you'll have some enemies. Daniel did. Their jealousy led to a scheme to get rid of Daniel once and for all. They wrote an edict that prohibited the worship of God. The king signed the edict into law. I love what happens next.

When Daniel heard about the new law, you know what he did? He went to his home. Went straight upstairs to a room where the windows opened to Jerusalem. He got down on his knees and prayed to his God "just as he had done before." The rest of the story is a Sunday School favorite. Daniel was thrown into a lions' den. But God shut the mouth of the hungry lions, and Daniel was lifted from the den without a scratch or wound "because he had trusted in his God."

This well-known story teaches us about resolved obedience. Daniel was not willing to give in, regardless of the pressure, regardless of the danger. Daniel was resolved to obey God no matter what. But lest you think Daniel was born a man of steel, check out what he was doing when the officials came to arrest him. Daniel was "praying and asking God for help." It is always God who gives us the strength we need to do what he has called us to do. He gave that strength to Daniel; he will give the same strength to you.

Father, Daniel was human like us. Give us that same strength you gave Daniel. We want to live with the resolve that comes from trusting in you. In Jesus' name. Amen.

reflection

---

further suggested reading:

Daniel 4-6

Worship Him

Daniel 9:4

I prayed to the LORD my God and confessed: "Lord, the great and awesome God, who keeps his covenant of love with those who love him and keep his commandments . . . "

In today's passage, there are three important things we learn about God. Let's check them out.

- *He is a personal God.* God is not to be held at arm's length. He is a God who desires a relationship with us and provides the way to himself through Jesus. Daniel uses the personal pronoun to describe his relationship with God. Can you, like Daniel, pray to "the LORD my God"?

- *He is unique.* There is no God like our God. He is unique in his greatness. He is omnipotent, omnipresent and omniscient. He inspires the wonder, admiration . . . the amazement of those who worship him.

- *He always keeps his covenant of love.* God will never go back on his promise. He will never renegotiate his commitment to love us through eternity. His love is not based on our performance. His commitment to us is based on his grace and mercy. Our relationship with God is all on him.

How do you respond to a God like our God? Only one way. Worship him with your entire life!

Father, you are the all-powerful God! Yet we can speak with you right now. Thank you for sending Jesus to enable us to have a relationship with you. Thank you for the certain promise that you will never remove your love from us. In Jesus' name. Amen.

reflection

_____

_____

_____

_____

_____

_____

_____

further suggested reading:

Daniel 7-12

Unconditional Love

 *September 1*

Hosea 1:10

Yet the Israelites will be like the sand on the seashore, which cannot be measured or counted. In the place where it was said to them, 'You are not my people,' they will be called 'children of the living God.'

Crazy! Absolutely crazy! But God goes to great lengths to demonstrate his great love. He gave the prophet Hosea an unenviable assignment. In order to demonstrate his love for Israel, even though she was acting like an unfaithful wife, God had Hosea marry one . . . an unfaithful wife, that is.

God told Hosea, "Go, take to yourself an adulterous wife and children of unfaithfulness, because the land is guilty of the vilest adultery in departing from the Lord." So he married Gomer. Then after her adultery, Hosea was directed to take her back. God said, "Love her as the Lord loves the Israelites though they turn to other gods." God wanted Hosea to experience the message and the Israelites to see unconditional love firsthand.

That's really what the book of Hosea is about . . . unconditional love. Even though the Israelites abandoned God, he did not abandon them. Even though they strayed, he restored and blessed them. Even though they did not act like it, he assured them that "they will be called children of the living God." Because of Jesus, God loves his children with the same unconditional love. Even when we wander, he will not leave us.

Father, thank you for your amazing love! Thank you for never leaving me even when I choose to leave you. In Jesus' name. Amen.

reflection

further suggested reading:

Hosea 1-2

The Heart of God

Hosea 3:1

> The LORD said to me, "Go, show your love to your wife again, though she is loved by another man and is an adulteress. Love her as the LORD loves the Israelites, though they turn to other gods and love the sacred raisin cakes."

Hosea's wife, Gomer, committed adultery. Some of you know the emotional and physical pain that act brings upon a marriage partner. Hosea felt the pain. He could have washed his hands and walked away from the relationship. He could have put the past behind and started fresh. But God gave him a different path to follow.

God instructed the prophet to go back to the woman who had defiled the marriage covenant and was, at the time, "loved by another man." Hosea worked through his pain as he worked his way back to Gomer. Even though she left, Hosea returned. He showed his love to the one who had shunned it before. He loved her just as God loved the Israelites even though they turned to other gods and offered raisin cakes to Baal in thanksgiving for harvest.

God showed Israel, through Hosea's pain, that his love was unconditional. Israel left God, but God never left them. What a lesson for us! Unconditional love does not give us a license to sin. It shows us the heart of God. It gives us a desire to demonstrate our love for him.

Father, help us respond to your great love. Thank you for loving us unconditionally through Jesus. Help us demonstrate our love for you. In Jesus' name. Amen.

reflection

_____
_____
_____
_____
_____
_____
_____
_____

further suggested reading:

Hosea 3

No Pretenders Allowed

September 3

Hosea 6:6

For I desire mercy, not sacrifice, and acknowledgment of God rather than burnt offerings.

The church building was constructed on an Indian reservation. Years later, it was rolled on logs to a prime corner lot in the nearest town. But by the time I filled the pulpit, the congregation had dwindled to twenty-five attenders. The people were faithful and very steeped in denominational ritual.

Every Sunday we said the Lord's Prayer and the Apostles' Creed. Every Sunday we sang the Gloria Patri and the Doxology. I preached out of the New International Version but was asked to switch to the King James. As one leader told me, "If the King James Version was good enough for the Apostle Paul, it's good enough for us." I'm not sure he was joking. Today the church building that was an historical landmark has been torn down. The people are gone as well. I have been told a funeral home now sits on the prime corner lot.

For sure, the Lord's Prayer needs to be recited. The Apostles' Creed sums up our core beliefs. I love the Doxology and Gloria Patri. But when good things become meaningless rituals, God says, "Time out!" He is not into words without meaning and hearts without emotion. He doesn't want people who simply go through the motions with a "check box" religion. He is the living God! He desires a fresh and vibrant relationship with those who follow him. The "acknowledgement of God" comes from a heart in tune and on fire. God has put up a sign for true worship that reads, "No Pretenders Allowed."

Father, search our hearts and knock down any walls of meaningless rituals. Keep us close to where your worship fires are burning. In Jesus' name. Amen.

reflection

---

further suggested reading:

Hosea 4-6

Whirlwind of Consequences

Hosea 8:7

They sow the wind and reap the whirlwind.

I heard someone say the other day, "Well, since God is sovereign, it really doesn't matter what I do. I am his child, and he will make everything I do work out for good." My response to that statement is, "What have you been smoking?" Today's passage is clear that if you sow the winds of sin, you will reap the whirlwind of consequences. In case you need to be convinced, check out these passages.

But if you fail to do this, you will be sinning against the LORD; and you may be sure that your sin will find you out.
Numbers 32:23

As I have observed, those who plow evil and those who sow trouble reap it.
Job 4:8

Whoever sows injustice reaps calamity.
Proverbs 22:8

Do not be deceived: God cannot be mocked. A man reaps what he sows. Whoever sows to please their flesh, from the flesh will reap destruction; whoever sows to please the Spirit, from the Spirit will reap eternal life.
Galatians 6:7-8

The sins of some are obvious, reaching the place of judgment ahead of them; the sins of others trail behind them.
1Timothy 5:24

Lord, you are a gracious God abounding in love and forgiveness. Please do not let us presume on your grace, love or forgiveness. In Jesus' name. Amen.

reflection

_____

_____

_____

_____

further suggested reading:

Hosea 7-8

The Fruit of Unfailing Love

September 5

Hosea 10:12

Sow righteousness for yourselves, reap the fruit of unfailing love, and break up your unplowed ground; for it is time to seek the LORD, until he comes and showers his righteousness on you.

Yesterday's passage reminded us that if we sow the winds of sin, we will reap the whirlwind of consequences. Today's passage tells us that the opposite is true. If we plant thoughts, words and actions that are in line with God's instruction, we will reap the fruit of unfailing love.

The fruit of unfailing love is sweet. It is a deep affection that says, "You are my child!" Then adds, "And you will be my child forever!" It brings us into an intimate relationship with God. It is meaningful and satisfying. The fruit of unfailing love explodes with flavor and sends juice running down our faces at every bite.

There are consequences to sin, but, thank God, there are results of righteousness. God's way leads us where we always want to go. The right path is not always smooth and downhill. There are some steep climbs and rough terrain. But the destination is one of great reward. Stay on the right path and enjoy the fruit of unfailing love. Look! Up ahead! There he waits with open arms!

Father, we like to wander. Keep us on your path and let us enjoy the fruit now and throughout eternity. In Jesus' name. Amen.

reflection

---

further suggested reading:

Hosea 9-11

Power over the Grave

September 6

Hosea 13:14

I will deliver this people from the power of the grave; I will redeem them from death. Where, O death, are your plagues? Where, O grave, is your destruction?

There is nothing glamorous about death . . . not one thing. Death comes to rip from our clutching hands that thing that we hold onto for dear life. Whether the process is quick and unexpected or wins the day after a long battle - death is the final enemy. It takes away futures and dreams and leaves loved ones walking numbly from a freshly dug grave.

But things are different for the believer. For sure we grieve but not like those who have no eternal hope. The God whom we serve holds power over the grave. He has bought us back from the strong claws of death to live forever with him. With Jesus, death never wins. It never takes a victory lap. Death is a transition from the life we've lived to the life we've been longing to live.

Writing about the resurrection from the dead in 1 Corinthians 15, the Apostle Paul used today's passage to remind his readers that death never stands on the winner's platform to receive a medal. Jesus holds absolute power over the grave. For all who trust in him, death is pushed aside as we transition to eternal life. If you would like to trust in Jesus, I invite you to pray the following prayer.

Lord Jesus, I admit that I am a sinner. I know that the penalty of my sin is physical, spiritual and eternal death. I acknowledge that I can't do anything about my situation. But I know that you came to pay the penalty for my sin. I trust in you alone as the One who died in my place. I trust in you alone as the only One who can place me in an eternal relationship with the living God. I desire to be your child. I desire to live as your child. Amen.

reflection

_____

_____

_____

_____

_____

_____

_____

further suggested reading:

Hosea 12-14

Regret

Joel 2:25

I will repay you for the years the locusts have eaten.

Regret is a painful emotion, a worse reality. There are so many past words we wish could be taken back. So many decisions we would like to undo. So many actions that brought unwanted and lasting consequences. For many people, sin has eaten away prime years of their lives. Maybe you are one of those people.

The prophet Joel described a day of punishment on God's people. Joel saw a large locust plague and drought that would devastate the land. He described the locusts - which should be taken literally - as God's army. The army of locusts came in massive numbers to devastate the land. They destroyed crops that not only eliminated that year's harvest but others to follow. Many have a similar thing happen in their lives. Addictions, bad decisions, divorce, abuse and many other sins bring a hoard of consequences that come in like locusts, devastating people in our lives. These "locusts" rob us and those we love of everything from a parent's affection to the physical needs of food, clothing and shelter. Sometimes we wonder if we can ever recover from the days of spiritual ruin.

Maybe you feel that your past sins have robbed you of many good years. God promises to "repay" his people "for the years the locusts have eaten." Remember the locusts came as a result of their sin. But in God's grace he desires to bring restoration. The following prayer will guide you in the process of redeeming the years the "locusts" devoured.

Father, I am sorry for my sin against you. I am sorry for the pain my sin has caused others in my life. I desire to turn from my sin and turn to you. I desire to follow hard after you from this day forward. I have wasted some precious years of my life. But please redeem the years the locusts have eaten. I wait on you to do your work in my life. In Jesus' name. Amen.

reflection

---

further suggested reading:

Joel 1-3

Forgiven Sins

September 8

Amos 1:11

This is what the LORD says: "For three sins of Edom, even for four, I will not relent. Because he pursued his brother with a sword and slaughtered the women of the land, because his anger raged continually and his fury flamed unchecked."

We love to hear about God's love, grace, mercy and forgiveness. Certainly, these are deep truths that form the bedrock of God's character. But there are other characteristics of God that are just as important . . . even though we may not enjoy thinking about them as much as the ones I've mentioned.

The prophet Amos was an adamant proclaimer of God's justice and righteousness. Amos did not back down on his declaration that God was going to judge unfaithful and disobedient people. Amos would have given a hearty "Amen" to Paul's warning, "Do not be deceived. God cannot be mocked. A man reaps what he sows" (Galatians 6:7).

We don't like to hear that, do we? We like to focus on forgiveness. But what we cannot forget is that even forgiven sins still carry consequences. For example, God can forgive the murderer, but the murderer still must go to prison for his deed. God can forgive the adulterer, but his spouse will carry the pain to the grave. We need to listen to Amos' warning. Remember it is better to be obedient on the front end than to deal with the consequence of sin - even forgiven sin - on the back end.

Father, may we never presume on your grace. Remind us that sin carries serious consequences. By your grace, keep us from sin. Just as by your grace, you forgive us when we sin. In Jesus' name. Amen.

reflection

_____

_____

_____

_____

_____

_____

_____

further suggested reading:

Amos 1

Passion to Action

Amos 2:7

They trample on the heads of the poor as on the dust of the ground and deny justice to the oppressed.

You have to stop at the gate. Only the guards can let you into Metro Amigo, a state-run orphanage located outside of Panama City. When you pull up to the building, many of the orphans will run to greet you. They long for the attention that has been stolen from them. Death has taken some parents from these children. Others have been abandoned by their moms and dads. These children - ranging in age from one to eighteen - have been denied justice. As a result, we decided to do something about it.

Through the generosity of many committed believers from The Bible Chapel in Pittsburgh and Panama, ANA Panama was birthed. This ministry provides transition homes where orphaned and/or abandoned children can experience the love of Christ and the acceptance of family. They also get needed education and learn a skill that will provide an income when they are on their own.

I have to tell you that I am wearied by "all talk and no action" people. They wax eloquently about the sad state of things. They get all worked up over how things ought to be. They think they have all the solutions. But actual involvement? Oh, no. That's for someone else. What good is talk without involvement? It's time to put passion to action!

Father, help us not be just hearers of your Word who can win Bible trivia contests but never actually do anything substantive for Christ. Shake us out of our all talk mode. Put urgency and action into our hearts. In Jesus' name. Amen.

reflection

_____

_____

_____

_____

_____

_____

_____

further suggested reading:

Amos 2

Bridge the Gap

September 10

Amos 4:13

He who forms the mountains, who creates the wind, and who reveals his thoughts to mankind, who turns dawn to darkness, and treads on the heights of the earth - the LORD God Almighty is his name.

The LORD God Almighty is his name. He formed the magnificent mountains like a child would mold a figure from a lump of clay. He creates the wind - the motion of air molecules and the air pressure that moves it along the earth's surface. He rotates the earth causing the sun to seemingly rise and set, ushering in the dawn and darkness. And he inhabits the heavens treading "on the heights of the earth." But you know what stuns me most? The eternal God chooses to reveal his thoughts to mankind. Astounding!

The God of heaven and earth reveals what he is thinking. Through the forty different authors of Scripture, the Creator explains himself to his creation. The One who has always been and always will be explains how he works in time. The all-knowing God tells his story so limited minds can understand. The God, who exists everywhere at the same time in his fullness, talks to man who can be only one place at one time. And God does not stop with the written word; he sent his Son to tell his story.

The Word became flesh and lived among us. Jesus came to explain the thoughts of the Father. Jesus demonstrated God's love and justice to us all the way to the cross. God tells us that we are separated from him and cannot bridge the gap. He did for us what we could not do for ourselves. He sent his Son to bridge the gap for us. The eternal God came to man, explained his plan, invites us to have a personal relationship with him and speak with him in prayer. Now that is amazing!

Father, you are the Lord God Almighty! You are the maker of heaven and earth! We love you and worship you for who you are! Thank you for being our Father. Thank you for inviting us to be your children. In Jesus' name. Amen.

reflection

further suggested reading:

Amos 3-5

God Listens

September 11

Amos 7:5-6

Then I cried out, "Sovereign LORD, I beg you, stop! How can Jacob survive? He is so small!" So the LORD relented. "This will not happen either," the Sovereign LORD said.

Recently I heard someone say, "It really doesn't matter if we pray or not. God is sovereign. He will accomplish whatever he wants to accomplish." Well, God is sovereign. I certainly agree with that. But God's sovereignty should never paralyze our prayer. Check out today's passage.

In Amos 7, God was getting ready to bring judgment on Israel for her disobedience. Then Amos cried out to the Lord and begged him to stop. Notice he cried out to the sovereign LORD and "the LORD relented." Yes, I understand that God is immutable. Yet repeatedly in Scripture, God listens to the prayers of his children.

In his classic work that addresses God's sovereignty and man's responsibility, J. I. Packer argues that sovereignty does not stop our prayers; rather, it is the reason we pray. Packer writes the following:

> If you are a Christian, you pray; and the recognition of God's sovereignty is the basis of your prayers. In prayer, you ask for things and give thanks for things. Why? Because you recognize that God is the author and source of all the good that you have had already, and all the good that you hope for in the future. This is the fundamental philosophy of Christian prayer. The prayer of the Christian is not an attempt to force God's hand, but a humble acknowledgement of helplessness and dependence. When we are on our knees, we know that it is not we who control the world; it is not in our power, therefore, to supply our needs by our own independent efforts; every good thing that we desire for ourselves and for others must be sought from God, and will come, if it comes at all, as a gift from his hands (*Evangelism and the Sovereignty of God*, IUP Academic, 1991, p. 15).

Oh, Father, we acknowledge you as our sovereign Lord. Please teach us to pray. In Jesus' name. Amen.

reflection

further suggested reading:

Amos 6-7

Restoration

Amos 9:14

And I will bring my people back from exile. They will rebuild the ruined cities and live in them. They will plant vineyards and drink their wine; they will make gardens and eat their fruit.

What is the purpose of discipline? Certainly it is unpleasant, even painful. It is never something we look forward to. It's something we try to avoid at all cost. Even when we know there is discipline at the end of a certain act, we may still carry out the act and still try to avoid the punishment. But what is discipline's purpose?

The book of Amos has focused on justice and righteousness. The nation of Israel had not been doing well at either. Because of their disobedience, God corrected them. This is a pattern throughout the Old Testament - disobedience followed by discipline. But there is another part of the pattern, and that part is the purpose of discipline. After punishment there is always restoration.

God loves us so much that he will not allow us to live far from him in a land of spiritual danger. He will get our attention but always with the purpose of restoring us to himself. He loves us too much to passively allow us to continue down a perilous path. His discipline is purposed to bring us back, rebuild our broken down walls and plant spiritual vineyards. God loves us enough to restore us.

Father, your word is clear that discipline is unpleasant. But thank you that you care enough to keep us from continued spiritual danger. Thank you for getting our attention, bringing us back home and rebuilding the walls that sin has destroyed. In Jesus' name. Amen.

reflection

further suggested reading:

Amos 8-9

Pride Goes Before a Fall

September 13

Obadiah 1:1-4

The vision of Obadiah. This is what the Sovereign LORD says about Edom - We have heard a message from the LORD: An envoy was sent to the nations to say, "Rise, let us go against her for battle" - "See, I will make you small among the nations; you will be utterly despised. The pride of your heart has deceived you, you who live in the clefts of the rocks and make your home on the heights, you who say to yourself, 'Who can bring me down to the ground?' Though you soar like the eagle and make your nest among the stars, from there I will bring you down," declares the LORD.

If you ever have trouble locating the book of Obadiah, don't worry. It's the shortest book in the Old Testament. The book is named after an obscure prophet whose name means, "Servant of the Lord." But the message is hard-hitting and straight to the point.

God declares that Edom is going to be destroyed because of the way she has treated his people. The tension between the two nations actually began in the womb. The Edomites were descendants of Esau, Jacob's twin brother. Esau was born first with Jacob grasping his heel. Later on, Esau sold his firstborn rights to Jacob for some red stew. Because of that unthinkable transaction, Esau was given the name Edom - the Hebrew word meaning "red." The Edomites and the Israelites (Jacob's descendants) continued the struggle until God, fed up with Edom's actions against Israel, said, "No more!" As one writer says, "Obadiah is Edom's day in court, complete with Edom's arraignment, indictment and sentence."

What do we learn from Obadiah? Pride goes before a fall! Edom's arrogance and cruelty against God's people led to their doom. Obadiah teaches us that even when it seems our enemy is winning, in the end, God will always deliver his people. Now that's a promise to hold on to!

Father, you are in control. You promise to protect your children. Your ways are not our ways, and your timing is not always our timing. But thank you for the certainty that in the end you will bring us safely home. In Christ's name. Amen.

reflection

Obadiah

Circumstantial Christian

Jonah 1:17-2:1

Now the LORD provided a huge fish to swallow Jonah, and Jonah was in the belly of the fish three days and three nights. From inside the fish Jonah prayed to the LORD his God.

Jonah had been running from God, ignoring God, wanting nothing to do with God . . .until . . . he woke up in the belly of a great fish. Amazing how our circumstance changes our attitude. Amazing, isn't it, how people, who are running from God, get "religion" when they find themselves in a difficult situation? I have met with men who wanted nothing to do with God until they lost their job, their marriage blew up or their child rebelled. Then they got serious about God until they found another job, their wife came back or the situation with teenage Tommy settled down. Then they were back to the same ole, same ole.

How about you? Are you a "Circumstantial Christian"? When things are going well, you pretty much leave Jesus out of the picture. But when things go south, when you get swallowed by the big fish, you're all about wanting Jesus to bail you out. Jonah had been ignoring God, flat-out turning his back on God, but now, "from inside the fish Jonah prayed."

Following Jesus should not be dependent on our circumstances. We should trust him just as much in our success as in our failure. When we have a job or when we don't, our dependence on him should be the same. When our marriage is going great, just as many prayers of thanksgiving should be on our lips as prayers for help are when things are challenging. Why is it that we get really serious about prayer right before the big exam? Why is it that we keep so busy running and only stop to pray "from inside the fish"?

Father, I don't want to be a circumstantial Christian. I don't want to get "religion" when things are challenging. I want to serve you full-out every day, in good times and bad times. Help me move from circumstantial to consistent. In Jesus' name. Amen.

reflection

_____

_____

_____

_____

further suggested reading:

Jonah 1-4

He Waits

Micah 1:2

Hear, you peoples, all of you, listen, earth and all who live in it, that the Sovereign LORD may bear witness against you, the Lord from his holy temple.

The name "Micah" means "Who is like the Lord?" And the prophet Micah writes a message to explain that there is no one like our God. He dwells in his holy temple, heaven itself. When he comes, the "earth and all who live in it" will know that God is the Sovereign LORD.

One commentator has written that Micah's message "alternates between oracles of doom and oracles of hope." He shows compassion in declaring God's coming judgment and promises of justice. Some may have trouble with that last sentence. How can God show compassion in judgment? The answer is straightforward. Sometimes the greatest demonstration of compassion is judgment. God's love moves him to discipline us when we move away from him and into the dangers of sin.

Maybe that's where you find yourself today. Like the prodigal son, you have moved to a distant country far from your loving Father. You know what it's like to lose the things you loved, to squander resources, to be alone, to be covered with the pig slop of sin. But the loving Father waits. He waits for you to tire of the consequences of living away from him. He waits for you to come to your senses. He waits for you with open arms. Time for you to make that journey back home, isn't it?

Father, I am tired of living away from you. I am tired of all the self-inflicted consequences of my sin. I am sorry for sinning against you and others whom I love. I want to come back home. Give me the strength to get up and return. I long for your forgiveness and loving embrace. In Jesus' name. Amen.

reflection

_____

_____

_____

_____

_____

_____

further suggested reading:

Micah 1

A Personal God

September 16

Micah 1:3-4

Look! The LORD is coming from his dwelling place; he comes down and treads on the heights of the earth. The mountains melt beneath him and the valleys split apart, like wax before the fire, like water rushing down a slope.

Deism is the view that God is the Creator but is not directly involved with his creation. In this view, God is like one who spins a top but does not interact with its spinning. He is viewed as a divine clockmaker who wound up the "clock" of creation and then left it to run on its own. The god of deism is passive and impersonal. Thankfully, he is not the God of Scripture.

The prophet Micah had no doubt that God got involved in the lives of his people. The phrase "The Lord is coming" is an expression used in the Old Testament to describe God's intervention in history. He does not stand idly by watching the top spin or the clock run down. God works in history. He moves in the lives of world leaders to accomplish his will. And he works in my life. He comforts, encourages, confronts, instructs and disciplines his children. Through his Word he speaks. Through his work he demonstrates his character.

Thus, there are deists (those who hold to deism), and then there are practical deists (those who say they believe in a personal God but don't think, feel or act like they do). How about you? I doubt that you are a deist. But do a quick assessment. Do you practically act like one?

Father, thank you for being a personal God who intervenes in history and is active in my life. Help me not to live like a practical deist. Help me acknowledge and feel your presence in my life through my days. I love you. In Jesus' name. Amen.

reflection

_____
_____
_____
_____
_____
_____
_____

further suggested reading:

Micah 2

Peace with God

Micah 5:2, 4-5a

But you, Bethlehem Ephrathah, though you are small among the clans of Judah, out of you will come for me one who will be ruler over Israel, whose origins are from of old, from ancient times . . . He will stand and shepherd his flock in the strength of the LORD, in the majesty of the name of the LORD his God. And they will live securely, for then his greatness will reach to the ends of the earth. And he will be our peace.

Seven hundred years before the birth of Jesus, the prophet Micah told about his coming. Micah was clear about the place of his birth and the clan from which he would come. Micah also pointed out the eternality of Jesus; his beginnings were before his birth. The Messiah would come to shepherd his people. He would lead with strength and majesty. Jesus "will be our peace."

The Apostle Paul says that no man stands righteous before God. All have turned away from him, and, in fact, no one seeks after him. People do not fear God. "The way of peace they do not know." But Jesus comes to change all that. It is through Jesus alone that we can finally have peace with God.

Do you have that peace? Have you trusted in Christ as the only way you can know God and finally enter into a relationship with him? Are you certain that you are at peace with God for eternity? If not, I invite you to pray this prayer.

Dear heavenly Father, I know that I am a sinner and am separated from you because of my sin. I know that I cannot earn my way to you or somehow be good enough for you. I know that I don't have peace with you. But I want to. Right now I trust in Jesus as the only way I can have that peace I long for. I trust in Jesus as the only way I can have a relationship with you. I am sorry for my sin. I long for your forgiveness. I long for peace with you through Jesus. I pray in his name. Amen.

reflection

_____

_____

_____

_____

_____

further suggested reading:

Micah 3-5

Knocked Down

Micah 7:8-9

Do not gloat over me, my enemy! Though I have fallen, I will rise. Though I sit in darkness, the LORD will be my light. Because I have sinned against him, I will bear the LORD's wrath, until he pleads my case and upholds my cause. He will bring me out into the light; I will see his righteousness.

Okay, maybe sin has knocked you for a loop. Maybe it has wrestled you to the ground and pinned your back to the mat. But you don't have to stay down. Today's passage is a bold reminder that it's time to get up, stand straight and, by God's grace, move forward.

For all who have been knocked down, read the passage again and then make these courageous statements with Micah.

- So, enemy, you rejoice over my failure? You think I will stay down on the mat? You think that my future is rendered ineffective by the sins of my past? Think again!

- No, I am not proud of my sin. I hate what I have done. I have dishonored God. But I will not stay down on the mat. By his grace, I will rise.

- I know my sin makes me sit in darkness. I feel guilty. I am guilty. But I will not stay in the darkened state of unforgiveness. The Lord is my light!

- Yes, I have sinned, and God disciplines those whom he loves. And I know this - the very One who disciplines me is my Advocate who will plead my case . . . and win!

- I know that I don't deserve God's grace. And yet he offers it to me. I accept it. He will pick me up off the mat. He will restore me!

- I have sinned. But my God will enable me to live in righteousness again!

Father, thank you for not giving up on me. Thank you for picking me up when I fall. Thank you for forgiveness. Thank you for restoration. Thank you for Jesus who paid the penalty for all my sin. Help me live in righteousness. In Jesus' name. Amen.

reflection

_____

_____

further suggested reading:

Micah 6-7

God Is on Your Side *September 19*

Nahum 1:3-5

The LORD is slow to anger but great in power; the LORD will not leave the guilty unpunished. His way is in the whirlwind and the storm, and clouds are the dust of his feet. He rebukes the sea and dries it up; he makes all the rivers run dry. Bashan and Carmel wither and the blossoms of Lebanon fade. The mountains quake before him and the hills melt away. The earth trembles at his presence, the world and all who live in it.

A century after Nineveh repented under Jonah's reluctant preaching, they were back at it. Since they were characterized by idolatry, violence and arrogance, God would not let his people suffer any longer under their cruel rule. While Jonah tells the story of God holding back his judgment, in Nahum God lets it fly. Nineveh was proud of its wall standing between 80 and 100 feet high and its moat 150 feet wide and 60 feet deep. But against God, human defenses are useless.

According to his plan, God raised up the Babylonians to conquer Nineveh. In fact, God arranged for the Tigris River to overflow and destroy a part of the wall so the Babylonians could get through. Under the Babylonian king Nabopolassar and his son Nebuchadnezzar, Assyria was wiped off the map. After their destruction in 612 BC, the site was not rediscovered until 1842 AD.

Nahum teaches us that God is on our side. Trust him. Challenges will come. Illness may knock the props from underneath us. Relationships may break our heart. Death of loved ones will bring overpowering waves of grief. But God is always preparing for our deliverance. For the believer the best is always yet to come. In the end WE WIN!

Father, in the trials of our day, remind us of the eternal victory guaranteed through Jesus. Thank you for always being on our side! In Jesus' name. Amen.

reflection

further suggested reading:

Nahum 1-3

Depend on God

*September 20*

Habakkuk 3:17-18

Though the fig tree does not bud and there are no grapes on the vines, though the olive crop fails and the fields produce no food, though there are no sheep in the pen and no cattle in the stalls, yet I will rejoice in the LORD, I will be joyful in God my Savior.

Can you trust God apart from tangible blessings? Can you keep believing when the answer doesn't come . . . at least in your timing? Can you continue to place your confidence in God when the answer is "No" to something that you've yearned for? Can your faith withstand disappointment and loss? Will you depend on God, not because of your circumstances, but in spite of them?

Those are the questions with which Habakkuk struggled. In his message to God, he made it clear that he did not like what was going on in his life. And he really did not like God's plan to deal with the stuff going on in his life. We are a lot like Habakkuk, aren't we? We have expectations as to what should and shouldn't happen . . . how God should and shouldn't work. But in his conversation with God, Habakkuk came to the sober and worshipful conclusion that we read in today's passage.

Can I rejoice in the midst of unmet expectations? Can I be joyful carrying around unfulfilled dreams? Can I sing the Doxology when my job is eliminated? Can I quote praise passages when the sickness lingers? Can I delight in God when yet another burden is piled on my heavy heart? Habakkuk teaches me that true joy in "God my Savior" is independent of my current issues. I can praise God even when I stand before fruitless trees, failed crops and empty stalls.

Father, it is not easy to thank you, let alone praise you, when the trees of my life are fruitless, when the crops of my life have failed and when the stalls of my life are empty. But help me come to Habakkuk's conclusion. Help me experience true joy that comes from you, despite my circumstances. In Jesus' name. Amen.

reflection

_____

_____

_____

_____

_____

further suggested reading:

Habakkuk 1-3

He Is There

September 21

Zephaniah 3:17

> The LORD your God is with you, he is mighty to save. He will take great delight in you; in his love he will no longer rebuke you, but will rejoice over you with singing.

I love this verse! For years it hung in a homemade frame on the wall of our home. Let's break it down.

The LORD your God is with you. The eternal God is always with us. In our great joy or deep sorrow, he is there. He provides comfort, encouragement, instruction, correction and strength. He never leaves nor forsakes us.

He is mighty to save. There is nothing in our lives that is too big for God. He will give us all we need to do everything he calls us to do.

He will take great delight in you. God sent Jesus to die just for you! That's how much he loves you! You are a child of the living God. He takes great pleasure in you.

He will quiet you with his love. Life has a way of cranking up the anxiety level. Stuff comes into our lives that cause stress and doubt. But that's when the Holy Spirit takes over. He breathes calmness into our soul. He reminds us that he is on our side.

He will rejoice over you with singing. We know what it's like to sing songs to God. But do you realize the heavenly Father sings over us? Like a parent sings songs to his or her children, so God sings songs of joy over us. That amazes me!

Heavenly Father, thank you for never leaving me alone. Thank you for your power to save me from my sins and myself. Thank you for taking pleasure in me. Thank you for calming my anxious heart. Thank you for rejoicing over me. Thank you for being my heavenly Father. In Jesus' name. Amen.

reflection

_____

_____

_____

_____

_____

further suggested reading:

Zephaniah 1-3

Unfinished Work

September 22

Haggai 1:3-4

Then the word of the LORD came through the prophet Haggai: "Is it a time for you yourselves to be living in your paneled houses, while this house remains a ruin?"

When you drive through the neighborhoods in the rural towns of Panama, you'll see many unfinished houses. People with little means build only when the resources become available. Many houses are half finished with families crowded into the "completed" quarters. Other structures have been started and then abandoned. The neighborhoods are a picture of great intentions but unfinished work. That's what's going on in Haggai.

In 538 BC, Cyrus, the king of Persia, allowed 50,000 Jews to return to Jerusalem in order to rebuild the temple. Led by Zerubbabel, the foundation of the temple was completed in about two years. But opposition arose (surprise!?), and the Jews shut down the work. It remained on hold for the next 18 years! In 520 BC, God sent Haggai and Zechariah to arouse the people from their fear and lethargy.

Are there uncompleted spiritual structures in your life? Any great intentions but unfinished work? When God wanted the temple to be rebuilt, he was not satisfied with just the foundation. When God wants you to do great things for him, he is not satisfied with a good start but no follow-through. Get up and get to work. Finish the task God has called you to! The ball is in your court. Or should I say, the pick and shovel are in your hands.

Father, don't let us be satisfied with unfinished work. Arouse our hearts to finish everything that you have called us to do. Don't let us live with excuses. Help us complete the task for your honor and your glory. In Christ's name. Amen.

reflection

further suggested reading:

Haggai 1

Haggai 1:12-15

Then Zerubbabel son of Shealtiel, Joshua son of Jozadak, the high priest, and the whole remnant of the people obeyed the voice of the LORD their God and the message of the prophet Haggai, because the LORD their God had sent him. And the people feared the LORD. Then Haggai, the LORD's messenger, gave this message of the LORD to the people: "I am with you," declares the LORD. So the LORD stirred up the spirit of Zerubbabel son of Shealtiel, governor of Judah, and the spirit of Joshua son of Jozadak, the high priest, and the spirit of the whole remnant of the people. They came and began to work on the house of the LORD Almighty, their God, on the twenty-fourth day of the sixth month.

The temple rebuilding effort got off to a great start. The people got to work, cleared the rubble and built the foundation in two years. Of course, their success caught the attention of the neighboring countries. The opposition started. Instead of staying focused, the builders started to fear. Instead of pressing on, they gave in. They used the opposition for an excuse to quit. The great work the people had started was put on hold for 18 years! Haggai called the people back to work.

Any significant effort will draw criticism. Most people just don't like change. For many the status quo is fine. But it's not fine with God. This world is broken! Lethargy, laziness, turning a blind eye, pretending that disobedience is acceptable - ignoring the needs of others is not what God has called us to do. You may have a great spiritual foundation, but unfinished lives don't honor God.

Here's my challenge. Pray that God stirs your spirit. Pray that he moves you like he did with Zerubbabel and Joshua. Pray that his "I am with you" promise fills that spot in your heart where fear once lived. Begin today to build the lives that God has called you to build! One day you will stand before him to give an account. On that day, you'll be glad that you finished the project.

Father, give us the courage to do what you called us to do. And give us the urgency to get it done. Today, help us start or restart the work you have for us. In Jesus' name. Amen.

reflection

further suggested reading:

Haggai 2

Fine Garments

Zechariah 3:3-4

Now Joshua was dressed in filthy clothes as he stood before the angel. The angel said to those who were standing before him, "Take off his filthy clothes." Then he said to Joshua, "See, I have taken away your sin, and I will put fine garments on you."

Zechariah paints quite a picture. Joshua, the high priest, was standing before the angel of the LORD. At Joshua's right side, Satan stood to accuse him. But God was having none of Satan's allegations. "The LORD rebuke you, Satan! The LORD who has chosen Jerusalem, rebuke you!" And Satan was sent on his way.

Joshua now stood only before the angel of the LORD. As he stood next to the angel, Joshua's clothes, representing the sin in his life, were dirty. The angel gave instruction to take off the soiled garments. Joshua's sin was taken away, and he was clothed with clean expensive clothes. What a picture of salvation and restoration! Joshua's picture looks a lot like ours.

Scripture says that Satan stands before God day and night accusing us (Revelation 12:10). And his accusations are on target. Helpless, hopeless and spiritually bankrupt, we were dressed in the filthy tattered garments of a beggar. Then we met Jesus. He took away the soiled clothing and dressed us in the fine garments of his salvation. Because of Jesus, we stand before God forgiven and restored. And Satan, the accuser, is sent on his way.

Lord Jesus, thank you for removing our dirty garments of sin and clothing us with the rich robe of your righteousness! Thank you for transforming sinful beggars into children with an eternal inheritance. In your name. Amen.

reflection

_____

_____

_____

_____

_____

_____

_____

_____

further suggested reading:

Zechariah 1-4

Basket of Wickedness

Zechariah 5:6-8

I asked, "What is it?" He replied, "It is a basket." And he added, "This is the iniquity of the people throughout the land." Then the cover of lead was raised, and there in the basket sat a woman! He said, "This is wickedness," and he pushed her back into the basket and pushed its lead cover down on it.

In Zechariah's vision, a large basket was opened before him. Represented by a woman, the basket contained "the iniquity of the people throughout the land." The wickedness was pushed down into the basket, and a heavy cover was placed over it. In the vision the basket of wickedness was taken far away.

While the prophet's vision is unique, the truth it teaches occurs repeatedly throughout Scripture. Believers need to get sin out of their lives. We need to put our wickedness in a container, so to speak, and dispose of it. We cannot coddle sin and love Jesus at the same time. We need to be sorry for our sin and turn from it (in one word, repentance).

This is God's powerful promise to all believers: "If we confess our sins, he is faithful and just to forgive us our sins and purify us from all unrighteousness" (1 John 1:9). When we confess our sin, we put the heavy lid on the basket of our wickedness. God does the rest. He forgives. He purifies. And he takes the basket and "hurls all our iniquities into the depths of the sea" (Micah 7:19).

Father, thank you for taking away my sin. Thank you for throwing all my sin into the depths of the sea. Help me move from the guilt of my sin to the freedom of forgiveness. In Jesus' name. Amen.

reflection

_____

_____

_____

_____

_____

_____

_____

further suggested reading:

Zechariah 5-6

True Worship

Zechariah 7:9-10

This is what the LORD Almighty said: 'Administer true justice; show mercy and compassion to one another. Do not oppress the widow or the fatherless, the foreigner or the poor. Do not plot evil against each other.'

The people of Israel asked, "Should I mourn and fast in the fifth month as I have done for so many years?" But God said, "Time out. Let's think through this. Have your yearly religious observances really been for me? Or were you simply going through the motions to soothe your conscience and check off your 'Religious Observance' box?" Then God offered some action to demonstrate true worship.

Instead of going through the motions, God said, show true justice to others. Demonstrate mercy and love to each other. Take care of the needy widow. Take in the orphan. Accept the foreigner. Provide for the poor. Stop premeditated, hurtful actions against each other.

Without meaningful actions, worship can quickly become meaningless ritual. A powerful prayer becomes pointless by mindless repetition. A timeless creed encompassing the essentials of the faith can lose its impact with numbing recitation. A song that moved us to tears when we first heard it can wear a rut through our heart so that we are bored of the words. We can't just go through the motions. True worship is proven by actions.

Father, point out to me any area of my worship and service to you where I am simply going through the motions. Show me any area that I am doing for myself and not for you. When you show me where I need to change, help me change. In Jesus' name. Amen.

reflection

_____

_____

_____

_____

_____

further suggested reading:

Zechariah 7-8

The Coming King

Zechariah 9:9

Rejoice greatly, Daughter Zion! Shout, Daughter Jerusalem! See, your king comes to you, righteous and victorious, lowly and riding on a donkey, on a colt, the foal of a donkey.

Zechariah exhorted his audience to warmly welcome the Messiah when he came to his people. The coming king would not show up as an overbearing conqueror. He would gently demonstrate love and compassion. Righteousness would characterize his person and his reign. In the Near East, a king coming for battle rode a war stallion. One coming in peace rode on a donkey. Jesus came to provide man the ultimate peace by his death on the cross.

Five hundred years after Zechariah's prophecy, Jesus rode into Jerusalem on a donkey. Many welcomed him that Sunday shouting, "Hosanna to the Son of David! Blessed is he who comes in the name of the Lord! Hosanna in the highest!" The large crowd spread their cloaks out on the road. Others cut branches from trees and spread them before Jesus. But by the end of that week, the fickle crowd was shouting, "Crucify him!"

What turned the crowd against Jesus? They didn't get what they wanted. They wanted a powerful king to deliver them from the rule of Rome. Jesus came as a servant to deliver them from the rule of sin. They wanted a king to reign; Jesus came to die. Their attitude about Jesus changed because he wasn't who they wanted him to be. Let us never make the same mistake.

Father, may I worship you for who you are, not for who I want you to be. In Jesus' name. Amen.

reflection

_____

_____

_____

_____

_____

_____

_____

further suggested reading:

Zechariah 9-11

Real Strength

Zechariah 12:5

Then the clans of Judah will say in their hearts, 'The people of Jerusalem are strong, because the LORD Almighty is their God.'

What makes a person strong? Is it his environment - something in his family that weaved strength into his heart? Is it his background - classes in the school of hard knocks? Maybe it's in his DNA - he was born with an inner strength that developed and matured?

Or . . . maybe human strength is way overrated. It always falls short. It can't keep marriages together. It cannot keep fear away. It can't shield against illness. The strongest can never climb the heights to God. At the end of the day, the strongest in mind, emotions and body cannot conquer death.

Real strength comes from only one place. We can be strong only because the LORD Almighty is our God. His strong arm is never too short to help us. He can mend broken relationships. He provides a peace that is beyond our circumstance and understanding. He will carry us through the most difficult time. And one day, he will carry us from death to eternal life. Real strength comes from God alone.

Father, I am weak, fearful and helpless. Thank you for the strength that carries me through this life and into eternity. In Jesus' name. Amen.

reflection

_____

_____

_____

_____

_____

_____

_____

_____

_____

further suggested reading:

Zechariah 12-14

Guard Your Relationships

September 29

Malachi 2:15

Has not the one God made you? You belong to him in body and spirit. And what does the one God seek? Godly offspring. So be on your guard, and do not be unfaithful to the wife of your youth.

God's design is for a husband and wife to become one. This oneness is to be experienced in every area of the relationship. It involves the following:

Developing together as followers of Christ.
An exclusive fulfilling sexual commitment.
Commitment not to consider other relationship options.
Commitment to exclusive feelings.

God is the One who joins the husband and wife together. "You belong to him in body and spirit." And what God joins together, man should never separate. The marriage covenant must be guarded and kept. God explains his position on divorce very clearly. He hates it (Malachi 2:16).

Husbands and wives, guard your relationship! Make time for each other. Read Scripture together. Pray together. Bring the date night out of your relationship closet. Have fun together. Allow your relationship to grow and flourish. One day your children and grandchildren will thank you for keeping the marriage covenant.

Father, may we never take the marriage commitment lightly. Give us the strength to stick it out for better or worse. Help us not evaluate relationships by the standard of the world. Thank you for joining me together with my spouse. May that commitment never be broken. In Jesus' name. Amen.

reflection

_____

_____

_____

_____

_____

_____

_____

further suggested reading.

Malachi 1-2

The Power of Money

Malachi 3:8

Will a mere mortal rob God? Yet you rob me. But you ask, 'How are we robbing you?' In tithes and offerings.

Money. It's a powerful thing, isn't it? Jesus puts it on the level of a rival god. "No one can serve two masters," Jesus said. "Either you will hate the one and love the other, or you will be devoted to one and despise the other. You cannot serve both God and money" (Matthew 6:24).

God knows the power of money. That's one reason the Bible has more to say about it than any other subject. There are over 2,300 verses that make reference to the god of wealth. It has been said that the way we handle our finances says more about us and what we value than anything else.

The last book of the Old Testament asks the question, "Will a mere mortal rob God?" Will a person use all that God has given for personal possessions? Will a man refuse to give to God the "tithes and offerings" that he requires in our worship and service to him? This is an issue each of us must deal with. Jesus said that our heart follows after the things we really treasure and value. In what direction is your heart headed?

Lord, we need your help in the area of money. We all know its powerful pull. Remind us that all things come from you and are to be used to honor you. Thank you for your gracious provision of resources. Please don't let them drag our heart away from you. In Jesus' name. Amen.

reflection

_____

_____

_____

_____

_____

_____

_____

_____

further suggested reading:

Malachi 3-4

God Is with Us

Matthew 1:23

The virgin will give birth to a son, and they will call him Immanuel (which means, "God with us").

What a powerful name! What a comforting name! Immanuel - God with us. At one point in history Immanuel walked planet Earth. Now for the rest of history, he is with us and lives in us. The God who never changes is the constant in our lives of constant change. The Spirit of the living God indwells each believer.

- When December 31 of the old year becomes January 1 of the New Year . . . *God is with us.*

- When we have another birthday - even "The Big One" . . . *God is with us.*

- When the job changes . . . *God is with us.*

- When our location changes . . . *God moves with us.*

- When illness alters our life . . . *God is there with us.*

- When dread fills our heart . . . *God is with us.*

- When joy overflows . . . *God is with us.*

- When our dream dies . . . *God is with us.*

- When we breathe our last breath . . . *God is with us.*

I have no idea what tomorrow will bring. I know that the next phone call could change my life. But whatever happens in the uncertainty of life, this one thing I am certain of - God is always with me. He is Immanuel, and he will be with me to the end.

Father, remind me that I am never alone. Fill my heart with the assurance of Immanuel. Thank you for always being with me. In Jesus' name. Amen.

reflection

further suggested reading:

Matthew 1-4

280

Treasure

Matthew 6:21

For where your treasure is, there your heart will be also.

I have always thought "For where your treasure is, there your heart will be also" should have read "For where your *heart* is, there your *treasure* will be also." Don't we always follow our heart? Jesus knew exactly what the word placement should be. He well understood that man's heart always follows his stuff.

It's hard for us to get a good assessment of our heart. I have seen the most "rational" people rationalize the most ridiculous things. I have seen many "spiritual" people spiritualize the most earthly things. I have seen "godly" people go down a God-forsaken path. The Old Testament prophet Jeremiah hit the nail on the head when he said, "The heart is deceitful above all things and beyond cure. Who can understand it?" (Jeremiah 17:9). We need to evaluate the tangible things in our life to determine where our heart is.

- Check your checkbook. Where is the money going? *That's where your heart is.*
- Check your calendar. How do you spend your time? *That's where your heart is.*
- Check your entertainment. How do you amuse yourself? *That's where your heart is.*
- Check your Internet history. *That's where your heart is.*
- Journal your thoughts. What are the reoccurring themes? Those "echoes" - *that's where your heart is.*
- Replay your conversations. How do you use words? *That's what's in your heart.*

My "treasure" is the best tool to evaluate my "heart." Convicting, isn't it?

Father, I want my heart to beat for you. Help me slow down long enough to assess where my heart is by evaluating where I put my money, time and energy. Where I am off base, give me the desire to repent and the courage to change. In Jesus' name. Amen.

reflection

_____

_____

_____

_____

further suggested reading:

Matthew 5-7

Lighten the Load

Matthew 11:28-30

Come to me, all you who are weary and burdened, and I will give you rest. Take my yoke upon you and learn from me, for I am gentle and humble in heart, and you will find rest for your souls. For my yoke is easy and my burden is light.

Life can get heavy. When it comes to things that can weigh us down, the list is long. Worry and anxiety weigh down our souls. Burdens consume our thinking. Trials can suck the energy out of our bodies. Life's loads bring weariness - spiritually, physically and emotionally.

But Jesus invites us to lighten the load. He asks all who are weighed down to find relief in him. He promises to bring peace and calmness to our souls. When we partner with him on the journey, he takes the heavy burden and makes it light. He is a gentle and humble teacher. Through life's inevitable challenges, we can learn from him when we are yoked with him.

Why are you trying to do it all on your own? Why have you settled for a life of stumbling under the load? Isn't it time you began the journey with Jesus? Isn't it time you gave your worry and anxiety to him? Aren't you ready to see what God has to teach you? It's time to come to Jesus and find rest for your soul.

Lord Jesus, I have carried this burden far too long. My present sin is disabling my heart. My past guilt has paralyzed my future obedience. Anxiety over things I can't control has taken siege over my soul. I am worn out. I cannot continue on my own. Right now, I come to you. I am taking you at your word. I am seeking to partner with you and have you take my load. I am ready for my burden to be lightened. I am ready for some real rest. I am counting on you. In your name. Amen.

reflection

_____

_____

_____

_____

_____

_____

_____

further suggested reading:

Matthew 8-11

Fine Pearls

Matthew 13:45-46

Again, the kingdom of heaven is like a merchant looking for fine pearls. When he found one of great value, he went away and sold everything he had and bought it.

All his life he searched for something to fill the hole in his heart. Everything fell short. As you'd expect, pleasure was . . . pleasurable. But it's funny (sad, really) that so much "fun" the night before can feel so empty the day after. The next purchase was always something to look forward to. But every time he sat behind the wheel or held what he had to have in his hands, a voice inside said, "This isn't it. There's still something bigger, better, faster that you need." The adrenaline rush of success was addictive. But even the socially accepted addictions lauded by our culture have haunting dark sides. Do you know this person?

The person in today's passage was looking for fine pearls . . . those things that would satisfy. He followed every lead to find that "one" he was looking for. No doubt, some of his efforts led to dead ends. But one day he found it . . . a costly pearl . . . one of great value. It meant more to him than anything else. In fact, he "went away and sold everything he had" just to buy it. Jesus said that's what having a relationship with him is like. It is of great value . . . eternal value! It requires giving up everything else and bowing before Jesus alone as Savior and Lord.

How about you? Are you wearing yourself out with the futile search to fill the emptiness inside? Are you learning the hard way that the things this life offers can't meet your greatest need? Jesus offers you a personal relationship with him. Are you ready to turn from the stuff you've been chasing and accept his free gift of eternal life?

Father, I pray for the people exhausted by their efforts to find something . . . anything . . . to fill the emptiness they are feeling. Send a friend to tell them that what they are looking for is you. In Jesus' name. Amen.

reflection

---

further suggested reading:

Matthew 12-15

Everything . . . and Nothing

Matthew 19:16-22

Now a man came up to Jesus and asked, "Teacher, what good thing must I do to get eternal life?" "Why do you ask me about what is good?" Jesus replied. "There is only One who is good. If you want to enter life, obey the commandments." "Which ones?" he inquired. Jesus replied, "You shall not murder, you shall not commit adultery, you shall not steal, you shall not give false testimony, honor your father and mother, and love your neighbor as yourself." "All these I have kept," the young man said. "What do I still lack?" Jesus answered, "If you want to be perfect, go, sell your possessions and give to the poor, and you will have treasure in heaven. Then come, follow me." When the young man heard this, he went away sad, because he had great wealth.

The young man began with the right question: How can I have eternal life? Inherent in his query was a desire for the eternal. He longed to live beyond himself and sought the right person for counsel. It's hard to find fault with his credentials. Murder, adultery, theft and lying were appropriately absent in his resume. He had treated his parents with respect and honor. He had reached out to his neighbors. If I'm Jesus, I'm saying, "Let's ditch the fishermen, tax collector and zealot. Follow me. Let's go change the world!" But Jesus, always able to peer deep into the messy heart, saw a clogged spiritual artery - a little problem with the god of money. When Jesus pinpointed the issue, the rich young man dropped his head and walked away from the Giver of eternal life.

I wonder what happened to that young man. If he continued on the journey away from Jesus, by all human accounts he lived a rich full life. I am sure he and his beautiful wife lived in the big house on prime property barely visible from the road. He gave his kids everything they wanted, including the best education available. He traveled to exotic places, stayed in extravagant hotels and ate exquisite foods. The cars he drove were the envy of many. He continued to make money. It seemed everything that he touched turned to gold. Financial advisors drooled to have him as a client. He retired in luxury to a beautiful island swinging on a hammock, fanned by servants and fed grapes the size of tangerines. Yet people wondered why there was such sadness in his eyes.

He had everything . . . and nothing . . . at the same time. And then one day, the sad old man died. They said he experienced a rich full life . . . as he experienced an empty hellish eternity. He gained the world and lost his soul.

Father, help us not make the same mistake as the rich young ruler. May we be willing to give up anything . . . everything . . . for you. In Jesus' name. Amen.

further suggested reading:

Matthew 16-19

Free Gift of Grace

Matthew 20:14-16

Take your pay and go. I want to give the one who was hired last the same as I gave you. Don't I have the right to do what I want with my own money? Or are you envious because I am generous? So the last will be first, and the first will be last.

The law abiding citizen "deserves" forgiveness. But what about the murderer? The faithful husband "deserves" a home in heaven. But what about the adulterer? A person who leaves the comforts of home and serves for forty years in a foreign land "deserves" salvation. But what about a person who rejected God all her life and then trusted him on her deathbed? Is God's grace fair?

Today's passage is the conclusion of a story Jesus told about a man who hired some workers. Some went out early in the morning to start working in his vineyard. About 9:00 a.m., he hired some others to join them. He hired additional workers at noon, some more at 3:00 p.m. and then a final group at 5:00 p.m. - an hour before quitting time. When the workers lined up for their pay, everyone was given the same amount of money. The men who had started early in the morning were none too pleased to learn that those who had worked less received the same amount. But the landowner said, "Friend, I am not unfair to you. Didn't you agree to work for a denarius? Take your pay and go."

The point of Jesus' story is not about a vineyard, workers and frustration in wages. Jesus told the story to teach us about his free gift of grace. Those of us who have been believers for some time can start to feel like we deserve what God gives us. We have been at it hard and long. How dare he show grace to "sinners"? That's when he sternly reminds us that grace is a free gift and can never be earned. The "Good Citizen" and the murderer, the faithful wife and the adulterous husband, the missionary who gave his life in service or the person who turns to Christ with his last breath - grace is available for all. Thank God that grace is never fair.

Father, thank you for your grace. May those of us who have followed you for many years never begin to feel deserving. In Jesus' name. Amen.

reflection

_____

_____

_____

further suggested reading:

Matthew 20-21

Vertical and Horizontal

Matthew 22:34-40

Hearing that Jesus had silenced the Sadducees, the Pharisees got together. One of them, an expert in the law, tested him with this question: "Teacher, which is the greatest commandment in the Law?" Jesus replied: "Love the Lord your God with all your heart and with all your soul and with all your mind. This is the first and greatest commandment. And the second is like it: 'Love your neighbor as yourself'. All the Law and the Prophets hang on these two commandments."

Loving God with all your heart, soul and mind is a pretty tall order, isn't it? It means that we are to be devoted to the heavenly Father with our emotions and desires (heart), our inner person (soul) and our thought life (mind) that drives our actions. We are to love God with our whole heart and whole self. That's the first and greatest commandment. And there is a close second command that practically demonstrates how we are doing on the first. We are to love our neighbors (those whom God places in our lives) as we love and care for ourselves. The tall order just got taller.

In this passage, Jesus explains that our relationship with God is both vertical and horizontal. It reaches up to him by the work of his Son and reaches out to others by the empowering work of the Holy Spirit. It calls for nothing less than all we are and all we have. This wholehearted love starts with those closest to us and spreads out from there. This love shows itself to your wife and to the person at the hardware store who asks you to fill out five pages of information when all you need to do is exchange a 7/8 inch rubber washer for a 3/4 inch rubber washer. Loving others as ourselves can be painfully practical.

Here's the thing. Jesus said, "All the Law and the Prophets hang on these two commandments." I am always amazed at how Jesus brings clarity and focus. He makes the confusing clear and the complex simple. He sums up the entire Old Testament with these two commands. Now all that's left is the application. Hmm . . . that's always the hard part, isn't it?

Father, may I love you today with everything I am and everything I have. May I demonstrate that love in practical ways to others. May others know that I love you by the way I treat them. In Jesus' name. Amen.

reflection

further suggested reading:

Matthew 22-23

Significant Service

Matthew 25:40

The King will reply, "Truly I tell you, whatever you did for one of the least of these brothers and sisters of mine, you did for me."

It was time for the King's people to enjoy their reward. The King told them how much he appreciated their service. There were times, he explained, that he was hungry and thirsty, a stranger and in need of clothes, sick and in prison. Each time his people met his need.

The people were thankful but a little confused. When had they ever seen the King hungry and provided food or thirsty and provided water? When did they ever provide clothes to the King? They never remembered a time when they looked after the King when he was sick or visited him when he was imprisoned. When did they ever do these things? Then the King explained, "Whatever you did for one of the least of these brothers and sisters of mine, you did for me."

Significant service to God is seldom high and mighty; rather, it is low and humbling. God honors giving money, providing food and serving meals at the homeless shelter. God smiles when we clean out our packed closets and give good clothes to the poor. He smiles even broader when we buy only the clothes we need and use the money for those in need. Tending to a sick friend is not wasted time in God's sight. And visiting those in prison . . . those who need a message of forgiveness and grace . . . are times of weighty service. Let us remember that every act of service is significant to God.

Father, it's easy to think that our service is worthwhile only when it is from the "stage" seen by others. Give us your heart for service. Remind us often that when we serve others we are really serving you. In Jesus' name. Amen.

reflection

_____
_____
_____
_____
_____
_____
_____

further suggested reading:

Matthew 24-25

The Great Commission

Matthew 28:19-20

Therefore go and make disciples of all nations, baptizing them in the name of the Father and of the Son and of the Holy Spirit, and teaching them to obey everything I have commanded you. And surely I am with you always, to the very end of the age.

It's called the Great Commission. It does not offer suggestions but four distinct commands. Jesus was clear that those who follow him must follow hard after him. We have work to do. Life is short and eternity is long. We are called to "make hay while the sun shines" (as my mom was fond of saying).

Let's check out these four commands.

- **GO!** Jesus calls us to action. Life with Jesus is more than simply reading another theological book or attending a Christian conference. Those things are needed for refueling, but Christians don't live at the "gas station." It's time to get on the road and go!

- **MAKE DISCIPLES OF ALL NATIONS!** Disciplemaking includes leading a person to Christ, but it doesn't stop there. Jesus does not call us to mass produce nominal Christians. We are commanded to help people throughout the world become rooted in the foundations of the faith.

- **BAPTIZE!** Baptism is a public demonstration of what Jesus has done inside. It is driving a spiritual stake in the ground. In essence, baptism is the ordinance that says, "I'm all in!"

- **TEACH!** We must accurately explain God's inerrant authoritative Word with practical application. Bible knowledge is not for making our heads bigger but is for making our hearts stronger. Knowing what the Bible says is the starting line; doing what the Bible says is participating in the race.

And check this out. Wherever we go, we are never alone. Jesus is always with us . . . even to the end. That great promise is the exclamation to the Great Commission.

Lord Jesus, give us courage to go, urgency to make disciples, commitment to baptize and passion to teach. Thank you for always being with us. Amen.

reflection

further suggested reading:

Matthew 26-28

Saving Faith

Mark 2:5

When Jesus saw their faith, he said to the paralyzed man, "Son, your sins are forgiven."

The room was packed like sardines. The crowd was spilling out the door. But that didn't stop them. The determined men found the staircase that led to the roof, dug a hole through the thick clay and lowered their paralyzed friend right in front of Jesus. Impressed by their faith, Jesus, interestingly, responded by forgiving the man's sins. This, of course, caused quite a stir among the Jewish teachers who accused Jesus of blasphemy. They asked, "Who can forgive sins but God alone?"

Jesus used the opportunity to drive home a spiritual point.

> *"What is easier to say?" he asked. " 'Your sins are forgiven,' or to say, 'Get up, take your mat and walk'? But that you may know that the Son of Man has authority on earth to forgive sins" He said to the paralytic, "I tell you, get up, take your mat and go home." He got up, took his mat and walked out in full view of them all (Mark 2:8-12).*

Practical faith is demonstrated by our actions. Certainly, the paralyzed man and his friends demonstrated practical faith. Every believer demonstrates this same kind of faith when we depend on Jesus to provide all we need to do all he has called us to do. But it is important to understand that practical faith follows saving faith. Saving faith is trusting in Jesus as the only one who can forgive our sins and place us into an eternal relationship with the living God. Jesus healed the man's heart; then he healed his body. First saving faith, then practical faith. That's the order we have to get right.

Father, thank you for working from the inside out. Thank you for taking care of our greatest need, our eternal need, before dealing with the temporal needs of our life. In Jesus' name. Amen.

reflection

---

further suggested reading:

Mark 1-3

Fear of Faith

Mark 4:40

He said to his disciples, "Why are you so afraid? Do you still have no faith?"

The storm raged. The winds were so strong and the waves so furious that the seasoned fishermen were sure that the boat was going down. But as the water pounded the boat, Jesus slept. Knowing the whole story that makes me chuckle. But the disciples didn't know the whole story, and they were not humored by Jesus napping. Finally, the panicked disciples woke him up and asked, "Don't you care if we drown?"

"Jesus, don't you care?" That's often our "storm" question as well. "Don't you care that I just lost my job?" "Don't you care that my marriage is on the rocks?" "Don't you care that I'm single?" "Don't you care that I'm sick?" "Why did he have to die so young, don't you care?" But Jesus always gets to the heart of the matter. The Master Teacher answers our question with a question, "Why are you so afraid? Don't you trust me?" Jesus knows that a heart absent of faith is full of fear.

Believers, in the midst of our storms we have two options. We can fill our hearts full of fear convincing ourselves that Jesus doesn't care. Or we can trust him to calm the storm or calm us. I know it's easier said than done, but those are our choices - fear or faith. It's an easy answer; it's a hard application. Let's pray for his help.

Lord Jesus, storms are frightening. Like the disciples, we panic and question your care. We know you died for our sins. But we are weak and in constant need of your help. It's easy to talk about faith but live in fear. Please, speak calmness to our hearts just like you did to the wind and the waves. Thank you for the promise that you will always be with us. In your name we pray. Amen.

reflection

---

further suggested reading:

Mark 4-7

True Service

Mark 10:35-45

Then James and John, the sons of Zebedee, came to him. "Teacher," they said, "we want you to do for us whatever we ask." "What do you want me to do for you?" he asked. They replied, "Let one of us sit at your right and the other at your left in your glory." "You don't know what you are asking," Jesus said . . . "For even the Son of Man did not come to be served, but to serve, and to give his life as a ransom for many."

The introduction to the request was bold enough: *We want you to do for us whatever we ask.* But the request itself took the prize: *Let one of us sit at your right and the other at your left in your glory.* The other disciples were outraged at such an over-the-top request. Can't blame them. But Jesus used the entreaty for a teachable moment.

The ways of the world are built around power and control - people lording it over others. The golden rule of the world is - he who has the gold, rules. Power is used to make others stoop. Jesus, however, turned the tables. For those who follow him, true greatness is measured by service. In his model, if you want to be first in line, you must go to the back of the line. Jesus showed us how that works. He did not come to earth to sit on a throne. He left his throne in heaven to hang on a cross. He did not come to be served but to serve and give his life a ransom for many. In his death, he demonstrated the ultimate act of service.

Following hard after Jesus is not about positions of honor or power. Following hard after Jesus is more "backstage" than "front stage." The rewards are given to those willing to serve wherever and whenever they are needed. Many times that will mean no one ever sees - no one, that is, except Jesus. He looks deeply into the heart and sees our motives and intentions. And when he sees a true servant, he smiles.

Lord Jesus, thank you for teaching us about service and for showing us how to serve. May we follow hard after you as our Savior and follow your example of true service. In your name we pray. Amen.

reflection

---

further suggested reading:

Mark 8-10

Learned Discipline

Mark 11:22-24

"Have faith in God," Jesus answered. "Truly I tell you, if anyone says to this mountain, 'Go, throw yourself into the sea,' and does not doubt in their heart but believes that what they say will happen, it will be done for them. Therefore I tell you, whatever you ask for in prayer, believe that you have received it, and it will be yours."

In his amazing life of faith, George Mueller watched God supply the needs of his orphan ministry time and time again. He simply prayed and believed that God would provide all that was needed. And God did. Mueller said that his faith was the same kind of faith that all Christians have. His faith, however, had "been a little more developed by exercise." Here is Mueller's instruction on how a Christian can develop his or her faith.

> *Now, my beloved brothers and sisters, begin in a little way. At first I was able to trust the Lord for ten dollars, then for a hundred dollars, then for a thousand dollars, then for one hundred thousand dollars, and now, with the greatest of ease, I could trust him for millions of dollars if there were occasion for it. But first, I should quietly, carefully, deliberately examine and see whether what I was trusting for, was something in accordance with his promises in his written Word. If I found it was, the amount of difficulties would be no hindrance to my trust . . . God has never failed me! Trust him for yourselves and find how true to his Word he is.*

Mueller reminds us of two important truths about faith. First, we must trust God for things that are in line with his will. Mueller says to trust God for the things that are "in accordance with his promises in his written Word." Second, faith is a learned discipline. Start by trusting God for smaller things. "Begin in a little way." For Mueller, it was trusting for ten dollars, then for a hundred dollars. Like lifting weights builds muscle so God's answered prayer builds faith. Here is Mueller's challenge to each of us: "Trust him for yourselves and find how true to his Word he is." Like Mueller, we will find that God never fails!

Father, we have so much to learn about trusting you. Help us take the baby steps we need to take in order to walk and live in faith. Help us to find out for ourselves that you are always true to your Word. In Jesus' name. Amen.

reflection

further suggested reading:

Mark 11

Daily Dependence

October 14

Mark 12:41-44

Jesus sat down opposite the place where the offerings were put and watched the crowd putting their money into the temple treasury. Many rich people threw in large amounts. But a poor widow came and put in two very small copper coins, worth only a few cents. Calling his disciples to him, Jesus said, "Truly I tell you, this poor widow has put more into the treasury than all the others. They all gave out of their wealth; but she, out of her poverty, put in everything - all she had to live on."

Jesus and his disciples sat in a very strategic spot that day. From their vantage point they could see people putting money into the temple treasury. Some rich people were in the crowd and threw in large amounts. Notice that they threw the money in its place. It takes a lot of effort to throw in large amounts of money, and just imagine the sound all those coins made. In contrast to the rich people and their clanging coins, a poor widow came. She "put in" a couple of small coins worth only a few cents. In response to her action, Jesus made this astounding claim, "this poor widow has put more into the treasury than all the others." How is that even possible?

In this story, Jesus teaches us this important lesson: Giving is not about amounts; it is about our attitude. The rich people gave out of their wealth. Honestly, they never missed what they gave. There was no sacrifice to their offering. They gave a lot but they had a lot left over. On the other hand, the poor widow "put in everything." She had no husband who provided for her, no company pension, no life insurance and no retirement plan. She gave "all she had to live on." She worshiped God not only by her sacrificial giving but also by her daily dependence.

Here are some questions to assess your giving. Do you give only out of your wealth? Do you give only what's left over? Do you give sacrificially? Do you give as an act of worship? Do you give as an act of daily dependence? Remember, giving is not about the amount we give; it is about the attitude with which we give it.

Father, check our hearts in this area, and then show our heart to us. Forgive us for trying to impress you with amounts. You don't need our money. You want our hearts. Help us give as an act of worship and dependence. In Jesus' name. Amen.

reflection

---

further suggested reading:

Mark 12-13

Extravagant Worshipers

Mark 14:3

While he was in Bethany, reclining at the table in the home of Simon the Leper, a woman came with an alabaster jar of very expensive perfume, made of pure nard. She broke the jar and poured the perfume on his head.

On Wednesday, before going to the cross, Jesus told his disciples that he was going to be crucified. The religious leaders made plans to seize him, and Judas made plans to betray him. And on that Wednesday, as Jesus ate at the home of Simon the Leper, a woman poured a jar of expensive perfume on the head of our Lord.

Picture the scene. While the disciples were worried about the waste, a woman, very quietly and tenderly, demonstrated deep love and devotion for Jesus. She took perfume worth a year's wages and prepared Jesus for burial. Here was a woman who understood that worship was more than an hour on the weekend. Her worship was extravagant. Jesus said, "I tell you the truth, wherever the gospel is preached throughout the world, what she has done will also be told, in memory of her." Jesus loves extravagant worshipers.

That night as Jesus lay on his bed, he alone knew it would be his last time to sleep until he closed his eyes in the painful death of the cross. But on that night, as he closed his eyes, he smelled the fragrance of the perfume sacrificially given to show love and honor to him alone.

Father, may our worship demonstrate such a deep devotion and love for you that it gives off a fragrant aroma to all around us. In Jesus' name. Amen.

reflection

_____

_____

_____

_____

_____

_____

_____

_____

further suggested reading:

Mark 14-16

The Gift of Jesus

October 16

Luke 2:1-7

In those days Caesar Augustus issued a decree that a census should be taken of the entire Roman world. (This was the first census that took place while Quirinius was governor of Syria.) And everyone went to their own town to register. So Joseph also went up from the town of Nazareth in Galilee to Judea, to Bethlehem the town of David, because he belonged to the house and line of David. He went there to register with Mary, who was pledged to be married to him and was expecting a child. While they were there, the time came for the baby to be born, and she gave birth to her firstborn, a son. She wrapped him in cloths and placed him in a manger, because there was no room available for them in the inn.

No breaks. The decree could not have come at a worse time. Mary was in the last days of her pregnancy. The seventy mile trip from Nazareth to Bethlehem over rough terrain was challenging to say the least. They arrived just in time.

No room. Joseph and Mary were not the only ones who made the trip to register. The city was swarming with people. Every possible place to sleep was taken. They settled for a barn.

No advantages. Jesus was born in a little village to an unwed mother from a backwoods town and placed in a feeding bin. The word was out that he was an illegitimate child. Not quite the start you'd expect for a king.

God tiptoed quietly into humanity. The Creator in a cradle. The Wonderful Counselor wrapped in cloths. The Mighty God placed in a manger. The Everlasting Father in flesh. The Prince of Peace in a world of sin. But Jesus came as the Lamb of God to take away the sin of the world. On the cross he paid sin's penalty. He bought us back from sin's slavery. He freed us from sin's prison.

Have you trusted in Jesus Christ alone as the Lamb of God who paid the penalty for your sin? Have you trusted in Jesus as the only one who can place you into an eternal relationship with God? You can't save yourself. Only Jesus can save you. Trust him completely to take you through this life and one day carry you home.

Father, thank you for the gift of Jesus! Today I trust in him alone as the only way to have a relationship with you. Please forgive my sins and accept me as your child. I desire to be a follower of Jesus. In his name I pray. Amen.

further suggested reading:

Luke 1-2

Mercy

Luke 6:32-36

If you love those who love you, what credit is that to you? Even sinners love those who love them. And if you do good to those who are good to you, what credit is that to you? Even sinners do that. And if you lend to those from whom you expect repayment, what credit is that to you? Even sinners lend to sinners, expecting to be repaid in full.   But love your enemies, do good to them, and lend to them without expecting to get anything back. Then your reward will be great, and you will be children of the Most High, because he is kind to the ungrateful and wicked.   Be merciful, just as your Father is merciful.

Loving those who love you back . . . you scratch my back; I'll scratch yours . . . the expectation of a favor returned . . . that's the world we live in. And, be honest, it makes sense. We expect a return on our investment. I'll pay for this one; you catch the next one. We get irritated at the person who never pulls his weight. But that thing called "mercy" takes worldly sense and turns it upside down.

You love those who love you? No big deal, Jesus says. Even sinners - the ungrateful and wicked - do that. Most people are willing to give when they know the rebound is coming their way. But how about giving to those who have no intention of repaying you? Jesus said that's the kind of character that produces great rewards.

This is a tough one, isn't it? But the basis for this godly action is in the character of God himself. He showed mercy to us by sending his Son to die on the cross for our sins. He paid a debt that we could never repay. Knowing that we had nothing to give in return, he gave everything. He gave everything, knowing we had nothing to give in return. When we show a no-strings-attached-mercy, in a small but powerful way, we reflect the character of God.

Father, I don't want to love my enemies. It is totally against my nature. Once again, I stand with my sinful nature doing battle with your Word. I ask that you align my heart with yours. Help me reject the fastfood rewards and live for those that you will hand out in heaven. In Christ's name. Amen.

reflection

_____

_____

_____

_____

further suggested reading:

Luke 3-6

Great Faith

Luke 7:9

When Jesus heard this, he was amazed at him, and turning to the crowd following him, he said, "I tell you, I have not found such great faith even in Israel."

The man was no wimp. He had risen in the ranks by hard work, skill and valor. More than once, he had risked his life in the heat of battle. His character and leadership had been observed and rewarded. He was a commander of one hundred Roman soldiers in the world's most powerful army. But now the strong leader was helpless. A loved and valued servant was sick and about to die. The man who could overpower countries couldn't save his friend. In his time of trial, he turned to Jesus.

Before Jesus reached his house, the commander sent friends to tell him, "Lord, don't trouble yourself, for I do not deserve to have you come under my roof." The man understood what it meant to trust others in battle; now he transfers that trust to Jesus. "Say the word," he told Jesus, "and my servant will be healed." Jesus was amazed at the man's trust. He said, "I tell you, I have not found such great faith even in Israel."

Some people conclude that either you have faith or you don't. That is simply not true. Trusting God is something we develop throughout our life. George Mueller, the great man of faith, said, "We must allow [God] to educate us through trials . . . It is through trials that faith is exercised and developed more and more." Mueller said that he would gladly pass through the trials of faith, "if [God] might be glorified, and his church and the world benefited." Here's the question: When the trial comes, what will you do? Will you give way to fear or hold on to faith? Are you willing to pass through the trial of faith in order to glorify God?

Father, I believe. Help my unbelief. Drive fear from my heart and replace it with faith. In Jesus' name. Amen.

reflection

_____

_____

_____

_____

_____

_____

further suggested reading:

Luke 7-9

Pray Boldly

Luke 11:5-8

Then Jesus said to them, "Suppose you have a friend, and you go to him at midnight and say, 'Friend, lend me three loaves of bread, a friend of mine on a journey has come to me, and I have no food to offer him.' And suppose the one inside answers, 'Don't bother me. The door is already locked, and my children and I are in bed. I can't get up and give you anything.' I tell you, though he will not get up and give you the bread because of friendship, yet because of your boldness he will surely get up and give you as much as you need."

Look again at today's passage. Why did the man finally get up and give his friend three loaves of bread? He gave the persistent friend the bread because of the man's boldness. Throughout the prayers of Scripture, it comes up over and over again - boldness before God. Here are some examples.

Abraham prayed boldly when he asked God to spare the righteous in Sodom.

> *Far be it from you to do such a thing - to kill the righteous with the wicked, treating the righteous and the wicked alike. Far be it from you! Will not the Judge of all the earth do right?* Genesis 18:25

Moses prayed boldly after the Golden Calf incident.

> *O LORD, why should your anger burn against your people, whom you brought out of Egypt with great power and a mighty hand? Why should the Egyptians say, 'It was with evil intent that he brought them out, to kill them in the mountains and to wipe them off the face of the earth'? Turn from your fierce anger; relent and do not bring disaster on your people.* Exodus 15:11-12

Jesus instructed us to pray boldly. In today's passage, he teaches us to pray with persistence. Ask God to do great things. He gives good gifts to his children and always exactly what we need.

This is not instruction for presumptuous prayer. After all, God knows the beginning from the end. We only know what just happened. But Jesus tells us to pray bold, persistent and confident prayers. Ask and he promises to answer you. Seek and he promises you will find exactly what you need. Knock and he promises the right doors will open. **Pray boldly!**

Father, teach us to pray. We never want to be presumptuous. You teach us to be persistent. Teach us to pray reverently, humbly and boldly. In Jesus' name. Amen.

further suggested reading:

Luke 10-12

298

Life of a Prodigal

October 20

Luke 15:11-13

Jesus continued: "There was a man who had two sons. The younger one said to his father, 'Father, give me my share of the estate.' So he divided his property between them. Not long after that, the younger son got together all he had, set off for a distant country and there squandered his wealth in wild living."

This well-known parable tells the story about a lost son and a loving father. Today let's focus on the prodigal; tomorrow we'll see the great love of the father.

Rebellious. Disrespectful. Demanding. I am sure you could think of a few more words to describe the son. Unwilling to wait for his inheritance, he told his father in essence, "I wish you were dead" and demanded his share of the estate. The father complied. And the boy wasted no time in getting "out of Dodge." He wanted to get as far from home as he could.

Money is a magnet for "friends," and his "friends" stayed as long as the money lasted. He was having too much fun to think about his family, let alone miss them. He was immersed in wine, women and song . . . heavy on the women. But it wasn't long before he had squandered all his inheritance. The friends left, the women couldn't be bought and "he began to be in need." He took a job feeding pigs. After a while his hunger made the pig slop look appetizing. Finally, (I love this part) "he came to his senses" and decided to go back home, not to be reinstated as a son, but simply to work as a servant.

I don't know where you are today. Maybe your rebellious life has led you to a distant country far from the Father. Maybe you know all about the life of a prodigal. I am praying today that you come to your senses. I am praying that you get up from the pig slop of sin and head back home. I can promise that the Father is waiting. His arms are open wide. He is ready to forgive and restore. But you have to come back home. It's time, isn't it?

Father, I pray today for that person who has left and traveled to a distant land far from you and far from the support of those who love them. I pray that you will help him or her come to his or her senses, admit his or her sin, desire to change and come back home. Father, help him or her to see you waiting with open arms. Help him or her run to your embrace. In Jesus' name. Amen.

reflection

---

further suggested reading:

Luke 13-14

The Road That Led Home

Luke 15:20

But while he was still a long way off, his father saw him and was filled with compassion for him; he ran to his son, threw his arms around him and kissed him.

This well-known parable tells the story about a lost son and a loving father. Yesterday we focused on the prodigal; today we'll see the great love of the father.

His son's words were cutting; his calculated actions were cold. He left with a bag full of money and a heart full of bitterness. He didn't say goodbye. The father's heart was broken as the door slammed shut and his son headed to a distant country. He knew that the money he had worked all his life to earn would soon be gone. He knew that the son he loved might not ever return. But he waited.

Every day, the dad watched the road that led home. Every day he prayed to see his son return. Each day he watched and waited . . . then the next day he watched and waited again. Finally, it happened! He saw his son! And while the son was a long way off, the father broke out into a full sprint and ran to his son. He met him, threw his arms around him, lifted him in the air and twirled around, kissing him all the while. When the son began his repentant plea to become a servant, the father gently put his hand to the boy's mouth to stop such talk. He forgave him on the spot, reinstated him as his son and restored him to full privileges.

And that is exactly what our loving Father does for us. He waits with open arms for all repentant sinners to come home. His heart is filled with compassion as he welcomes us back with wide open arms of grace. Today the gracious and loving Father is waiting for you. It's time to come home.

Father, thank you for loving the unlovely. Thank you for grace to the undeserving. Thank you for open arms of forgiveness. Thank you for restoration. Thank you for bringing us back home. In Jesus' name. Amen.

reflection

further suggested reading:

Luke 15

Childlike Faith

Luke 18:15-17

People were also bringing babies to Jesus for him to place his hands on them. When the disciples saw this, they rebuked them. But Jesus called the children to him and said, "Let the little children come to me, and do not hinder them, for the kingdom of God belongs to such as these. Truly I tell you, anyone who will not receive the kingdom of God like a little child will never enter it."

I wonder why the disciples tried to stop parents from bringing their children to Jesus. Maybe it had to do with the value of children in that day. Maybe the disciples were trying to guard the Lord's busy schedule. Maybe only the people who could "make a difference" were given the disciples' approval. Whatever the reason, Jesus didn't agree. He called the children to himself. In fact, he said that the kingdom of God has to be received like a little child. What does that mean? I believe childlike faith has these five characteristics.

1. **Children come without pride.** They have nothing to prove. They come as they are.

2. **Children demonstrate dependence.** They can't make it on their own. They have to depend on their parents.

3. **Children demonstrate trust.** They will jump off a ledge into their parent's outstretched arms. They are certain their dad will catch them.

4. **Children are open and frank.** They haven't learned to hide behind masks yet.

5. **Children are sincere.** Yes, they are sinners at birth. Yes, they will learn the art of manipulation soon enough. But the requests of children are straightforward and genuine.

The faith of a child. It's not just refreshing; it's required. It's sad when people get too big for Jesus, isn't it?

Father, please keep our hearts childlike before you. When it comes to faith, don't let us grow up. In Jesus' name. Amen.

reflection

_____

_____

further suggested reading:

Luke 16-18

Full of Forgiveness

Luke 19:5

When Jesus reached the spot, he looked up and said to him, "Zacchaeus, come down immediately. I must stay at your house today."

How many of you can't hear the name "Zacchaeus" without breaking into song? "Zacchaeus was a wee little man and a wee little man was he." Okay, I am forcing myself to stop. This is not a story of a wee little man but a story of a big God with a big heart full of forgiveness.

Zacchaeus, a chief tax collector, had risen to the top of a despised profession. He was a Jew who worked for the Romans. That was bad enough, but tax collectors were notorious for figuring inflated amounts and pocketing the surplus. Zacchaeus was wealthy, which means what he lacked in height, he made up in shrewdness. But on this day, Zacchaeus wanted to see the man named Jesus. Little did he know that day Jesus had an appointment with him. The Lord called Zacchaeus down from his vantage point and invited himself for lunch, in spite of the muttering from the crowd that he was going to eat with a "sinner." Before the salads were served, Zacchaeus was already repenting. As a tangible sign of a changed heart, he promised to give half of his money to the poor and return four times the amount to anyone whom he had cheated. Then came the best news. Jesus said, "Today salvation has come to this house."

Most of the people in the crowd that day had written Zacchaeus off when it came to anything spiritual. He was a crook and a cheat. Then he met Jesus. As I read this story, I wonder how many people I have written off. Why do I so often forget that Jesus "came to seek and to save what was lost?" Zacchaeus reminds me to turn my judgment to prayer.

Father, forgive me for my judgment on the "sinners" around me. Forgive me for forgetting where I was before you found me and or where I would be without your grace. Remind me why you came to this earth. Give me a new commitment to share your forgiveness with those you've placed in my life. In Jesus' name. Amen.

reflection

_____

_____

_____

_____

further suggested reading:

Luke 19-21

The Blood of the Lamb

October 24

Luke 22:7

Then came the day of Unleavened Bread on which the Passover lamb had to be sacrificed.

The day came when the Passover lamb had to be sacrificed. What a statement Luke makes! In this sixteen word sentence, he takes us all the way back to Exodus and then brings us back . . . to the cross.

In Exodus 12, the nation of Israel was getting ready to move out of Egypt after 400 years of slavery. The last meal before they left was to be a lamb prepared according to God's specific instructions. They were to take the blood of the slaughtered lamb and paint it on their doorposts. The Angel of Death would be coming to strike down the firstborn sons in Egypt. But the Angel would pass over all the homes where the blood was applied and spare the life of the firstborn. The Israelites never forgot that night. They never forgot the saving power of the blood of the lamb.

But now, as Luke ends his gospel, it was time for the blood of another lamb to be applied. The Passover lamb was a great reminder; the Passover Lamb was the Great Redeemer. When John the Baptist introduced Jesus as "the Lamb of God," he was not referring to his meekness. He was getting us ready for the saving work of Jesus. When we trust in Jesus - his death to pay the penalty of our sins - his blood is applied to us. Our sins are forgiven. We are declared righteous before God. Because Jesus rose again, his resurrection is applied to us as well. We pass from death to eternal life. Thank God for the Passover Lamb!

Heavenly Father, thank you for sending Jesus - our Passover Lamb - to die in our place and pay the penalty for our sins. Words cannot express our eternal gratitude. We desire to thank you with our lives. In Jesus' name. Amen.

reflection

_____

_____

_____

_____

_____

further suggested reading:

Luke 22-24

The Word Became Flesh

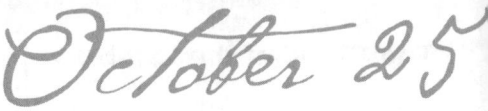

John 1:14-18

The Word became flesh and made his dwelling among us. We have seen his glory, the glory of the one and only, who came from the Father, full of grace and truth. (John testified concerning him. He cries out, saying, "This, 'He who comes after me has surpassed me because he was before me.'") From the fullness of his grace we have all received one blessing after another.   For the law was given through Moses; grace and truth came through Jesus Christ. No one has ever seen God, but the one and only son, who is himself God and is in closest relationship with the Father, has made him known.

Tiny hands waving about uncontrollably. A shrill cry piercing the damp air of a borrowed cave. A mother's peaceful smile. A mysterious smile on the face of her husband who helped deliver a miracle. The Word became flesh: God confined to an infant.

Growing hands pointing to ancient scrolls. An adolescent voice asking and answering questions. The teachers amazed. A mother who "treasured all these things in her heart." A Father smiling with favor. The Word became flesh: God growing in stature.

Gentle hands touching blind eyes, deaf ears and withered limbs. Powerful hands turning water into wine, feeding multitudes with a single meal and touching life into lifeless bodies. Thankful faces without words to express their gratitude. The Word became flesh: The Father glorified through the Son.

Constricted hands, the result of spikes driven through his wrists. Arms outstretched, fastened to a wooden beam. A mother stands below feeling every painful throb as her own. The just Father turns his back on his Son. The Word became flesh: Our sins on Jesus.

Scarred hands in resurrected glory. A chariot of clouds lifting him to the Father. A joyful mother watching her Son ascend. A promise from the lips of the risen Savior: Just as I go, I will return again. The Word became flesh: Resurrection Assurance.

Open hands inviting every sinner. Accepting all who come to him in faith. Blind eyes see; prison doors are opened. The prince or pauper; none are turned away. Eternal life to all who believe. The Word became flesh: Sinful man in communion with the Holy God!

Heavenly Father, thank you for the Word - Jesus Christ. Thank you for his life, death and glorious resurrection. Thank you that through Jesus we can have an eternal relationship with you. In Jesus' name. Amen.

further suggested reading:

John 1-2

Do You Want To Get Well?

John 5:2-6

Now there is in Jerusalem near the Sheep Gate a pool, which in Aramaic is called Bethesda and which is surrounded by five covered colonnades. Here a great number of disabled people used to lie - the blind, the lame, the paralyzed. One who was there had been an invalid for thirty-eight years. When Jesus saw him lying there and learned that he had been in this condition for a long time, he asked him, "Do you want to get well?"

"Do you want to get well?" That seems like an odd question, doesn't it? The man had been sick for almost four decades. The man was lying next to what many believed to be a healing pool. And yet Jesus asks the question, "Do you want to get well?" The man does not respond with a "Yes" or "No." He simply gives the reason why he can't get well. Someone, the man explained, always beat him to the healing waters.

Now move with me from the physical to the spiritual . . . from physical disabilities to spiritual ones. Is it possible that some people are satisfied with their spiritual disabilities - at least not dissatisfied enough to do anything about them? Many people too quickly excuse their spiritual weaknesses, perhaps even blaming someone else. Let's be honest; sometimes weakness is more comfortable. The expectations are lower and the responsibilities less. It is often easier to explain why you can't do the right thing than it is to get the right thing done. A person with an addiction is satisfied to continue in it because, quite honestly, getting clean is much harder than finding another fix at the bottom of a bottle or at the end of a needle or clicking to the sick sites of cyberspace. Certainly it is harder to bite your tongue and squelch a rumor than it is to open wide and freely spread it.

The man in John 5 had been sick for 38 years. Thirty-eight years! It would seem that just one time, somehow, he could have made it into the waters. Thus, Jesus asks, "Do you want to get well?" Spiritually speaking to all who have been lying on a mat of spiritual weakness for some time, are you getting too comfortable there? Do you want to get well? If you do, the Healer stands before you. Hear his instruction - stand up and walk in obedience. He desperately wants you to get up off the spiritual mat and follow hard after him. Do you want to?

Lord Jesus, forgive us for becoming comfortable with our sin. Forgive us for staying down on the spiritual mat. Give us the desire to get up and walk away from our sin. Thank you for the power you promise to forgive us, cleanse us and give us the strength to follow hard after you. In your name. Amen.

further suggested reading:

John 3-5

Great Things

John 6:10-12

Jesus said, "Have the people sit down." There was plenty of grass in that place, and they sat down (About five thousand men were there.) Jesus then took the loaves, gave thanks, and distributed to those who were seated as much as they wanted. He did the same with the fish.   When they had all had enough to eat, he said to his disciples, "Gather the pieces that are left over. Let nothing be wasted."

The feeding of the 5,000 is one of the most well-known events in the New Testament. Feeding a great number from such a small portion, with leftovers, grabs our attention. It reminded those in the crowd that day of the time in Israel's history when God provided manna. Now, they thought, another had come to provide daily food, and the people were ready to crown him their king. But Jesus had different reasons for the miracle. Let me offer two fresh observations from this well-worn story.

1. When Jesus asked Philip how food could be provided for such a large crowd, it was not a question but a test. Jesus "already had in mind what he was going to do." He still does. And he still tests us, not to trick us but to show us what's in our hearts. Jesus' questions drill down on our faith: "Will you follow me?" "Will you look to me or keep the focus on your impossible circumstances?"

2. I am always intrigued by the little boy. He thought ahead, or at least his mother did. He packed a lunch. He was as hungry as everybody else. Yet he gave up all he had. His willingness to sacrifice a little gave Jesus the resources to satisfy many. What a great reminder! Jesus can take my gifts (spiritual and monetary) and make them grow. Jesus does big things with small gifts and willing hearts.

The two questions we have to ask ourselves are these: Can we trust Jesus even when the circumstances seem impossible? Will we give to him all we have so that he can do big things in our lives? When you demonstrate your willingness to trust him and not hold back . . . get ready . . . he is going to do some great things in your life!

Father, there are times I feel that what I have is so small. There are times I feel paralyzed by my problems. Remind me often that you are more than capable of taking the little I have and accomplishing big things. Help me trust you with all I am and all I have. In Jesus' name. Amen.

reflection

further suggested reading:

John 6

Even His Own Brothers

John 7:1-5

After this, Jesus went around in Galilee. He did not want to go about in Judea because the Jewish leaders there were looking for a way to kill him. But when the Jewish Festival of Tabernacles was near, Jesus' brothers said to him, "Leave Galilee and go to Judea, so that your disciples there may see the works you do. No one who wants to become a public figure acts in secret. Since you are doing these things, show yourself to the world." For even his own brothers did not believe in him.

For even his own brothers did not believe in him. That statement astounds me. Can you imagine growing up with Jesus and not believing in him? Listen to his brothers' sarcasm: "Go to the big city to do your big works. A public figure as popular as you doesn't lay low. If you are who you say you are, make yourself known."

For even his own brothers did not believe in him. Let me write specifically to those who have unbelieving family. Some of you have or are beating yourself up over the fact that your husband or wife, sister or brother, son or daughter, or friend has not come to Christ. You reason that demonstrating the presence and power of Christ should cause them to believe. You feel that you are doing or saying something wrong. You ask yourself, "Why isn't my life attracting them to Jesus?" I appreciate your passion for seeing loved ones and friends come to Christ. I know you want that desperately. But . . . please . . . stop beating yourself up.

For even his own brothers did not believe in him. Come to grips with the fact that you cannot cause a person's heart to change. Jesus said, "No one can come to me unless the Father who sent me draws him" (John 6:44). Honor God with your life, keep sharing the gospel and pray for God to do his work in the life of your loved one. The Father must do the "drawing." Leave his work to him.

Father, we desperately want to see family and friends trust in Jesus and live a life that pleases him. We are willing instruments to be used by you in the process. We confess that no one will come to Jesus unless you draw them. We ask that you do your work in their lives. In Jesus' name. Amen.

reflection

_____

_____

_____

_____

further suggested reading:

John 7-8

The Whole Story

John 11:1-4

Now a man named Lazarus was sick. He was from Bethany, the village of Mary and her sister Martha. (This Mary, whose brother Lazarus now lay sick, was the same one who poured perfume on the Lord and wiped his feet with her hair.) So the sisters sent word to Jesus, "Lord, the one you love is sick." When he heard this, Jesus said, "This sickness will not end in death. No, it is for God's glory so that God's Son may be glorified through it."

It all makes sense when you know the whole story, doesn't it? Lazarus was sick. Jesus took his time in going to see him. Lazarus died. Jesus raised him from the dead. What would have been a miraculous healing turned out to be a magnificent resurrection. With this miracle, Jesus proved that he held power over that last enemy - death itself. Jesus is the Resurrection and the Life. But in order to prove that, he had to wait until Lazarus died. It all makes sense when you know the whole story.

I readily admit that I don't understand why people are born with deformities, why babies die, why moms and dads get cancer. I do not understand why people who are closely walking with the Lord are not healed while people who seem to have a casual relationship with Christ claim, "The doctor couldn't explain why the tumor was gone." I don't understand why children from great solid Christian homes jettison the faith. I don't understand why a missionary whom I met in Spain will have to bring his Parkinson's-tortured body back home and put to death his dream while some godless pagan will live in great health submerged in materialism.

But I know this: *It will all make sense when we have the whole story.*

Just remember whatever you're going through is not the final chapter. The Author has not yet put the finishing touches on his grand finale. On the last page of our lives, God erases "The End" and writes "The Beginning"! We don't understand it all now. But when we have the whole story it will all make sense.

Father, we know that you are working all things out for our good. We also know that living without the whole story is hard. Give us the courage to do what you are calling us to do. We are trusting that it is all for your glory. In Jesus' name. Amen.

reflection

further suggested reading:

John 9-12

Great Joy

John 16:21-22

A woman giving birth to a child has pain because her time has come; but when her baby is born she forgets the anguish because of her joy that a child is born into the world. So with you: Now is your time of grief, but I will see you again and you will rejoice, and no one will take away your joy.

During the birth of our four children, I had two jobs: Keep a cool cloth on Lori's forehead and keep spooning ice into her mouth. I started out as the "Breathing Coach." But my "hee, hee, hee's" were not well received for some reason, and I got fired early in the first labor. I liked the title "Breathing Coach" much better than "Cool Cloth Boy" and "Ice Boy" but such is life. Labor is . . . well . . . labor, and keeping the cool cloths and ice coming was not easy work. And I'm sure it wasn't easy for Lori either. But when that baby was born and the doctor said, "It's a girl!" "It's a boy!" "It's a girl!" "It's a girl!" our hearts melted in pure joy at God's blessing and miracle.

Jesus knew that his disciples were getting ready to go through a tough stretch. He likened the emotions that his disciples were going to experience something similar to a woman giving birth. His time on earth was drawing to a close. The dreaded cross was days away. The disciples would see him go through the most excruciating death (in fact the word "excruciate" means "out of the cross"). They would experience pain. Their Master would appear helpless. It would seem that God had taken away the power of the One who ruled over nature, sickness and death. All his promises would turn to questions in the minds of the disciples. Was he really who he said he was? Did they follow an imposter? Had they followed a pipedream? But then . . . on the third day . . . he rose from the dead. New Life! Great joy replaced great anguish. He was exactly who he said he was! And his words were true, "I will see you again and you will rejoice, and no one will take away your joy."

Today that same promise is yours. You may be experiencing a difficult time, a time of pain and grief. But whatever this life brings, listen to the great promise of our Lord: "I will see you again and you will rejoice, and no one will take away your joy." The fact of the resurrection finally drives out all pain, sorrow, loss and tears. The resurrection replaces our present anguish with great joy.

Father, thank you for the present and eternal joy that comes because you raised your Son from the dead. Because you raised Jesus, we know you can and will raise us as well, and we will spend eternity with you. Give resurrection confidence to the person going through a rough time. Remind him or her that joy is coming . . . a joy that no one can take away. In Jesus' name. Amen.

further suggested reading:

John 13-17

Where You Are

John 19:25-27

Near the cross of Jesus stood his mother . . . When Jesus saw his mother there, and the disciple whom he loved standing nearby, he said to her, "Woman, here is your son," and to the disciple, "Here is your mother."

It was a long way from Nazareth to that Bethlehem stable . . . especially long for a woman in the last days of her pregnancy. No doubt she felt every bit of the rough terrain on the seventy mile trip. And then they arrived to find every room occupied. They could only find a cave where animals were kept. It was not the best place to birth a child, but by that point Mary was not picky. It was warm and dry, and the baby was on the way. What emotions did she feel that night? She was a young girl holding her firstborn. Surely there were tears of joy and wonder as she reflected on the visit from the angel. She was a virgin holding her baby! She felt the little heart beating against her chest and a mysterious wonder beating in her heart.

It was a long way from that Bethlehem stable to the cross. Most mothers could not bear watching their son crucified, but Mary could not leave. She longed to hold him. She longed to wipe the blood from his beaten face. She longed to give him a drink. She longed to comfort him, but he was beyond her reach. She cried tears of agony. Her son was on a cross. She watched his chest expand as he labored to breathe. She felt a crushing pain in her heart. Finally, mercifully, the end came.

It was a long way from heaven to the cross. But there hung God in the flesh. Beaten. Spit upon. Mocked. Flogged. Stripped. Crucified. A "kingly crown" of thorns mockingly thrust onto his head. God loved us so much that he sent his only Son to go through that awful death in order to pay sin's penalty. But death could not keep him there. And now the resurrected Lord brings his cross work to meet you wherever you are. Rich . . . and empty. Poor . . . and needy. Successful . . . and searching. Fallen . . . and struggling to get up. Jesus meets you where you are with his once-for-all sacrifice and carries you all the way to eternity.

If you have not trusted in the completed work of Jesus, please pray this prayer:

Lord Jesus, I cannot imagine the pain of the cross. But I know you died there for me. Thank you for paying the penalty for my sins. I am sorry for them. I seek your forgiveness. I want to stand clean before you. I trust in you as the Risen Savior. Thank you for accepting me as your child. In your name I pray. Amen.

further suggested reading:

John 18-21

Get Moving

Acts 1:8

> But you will receive power when the Holy Spirit comes on you; and you will be my witnesses in Jerusalem, and in all Judea and Samaria, and to the ends of the earth.

Today's passage is the passionate command that Jesus left his followers just before he ascended into heaven. This powerful passage contains these four important parts.

The Promise: Power through the Holy Spirit
Jesus will always provide us with the strength that we need to do whatever he calls us to do. The Holy Spirit lives in each believer. He encourages and empowers!

The Command: You will be my witnesses
Jesus said that our assignment is to tell others about him. Empowered by the Spirit, we are to share the message of Jesus.

The Scope: Your world and The World
"Jerusalem" describes your immediate area. This includes your home, neighborhood and community. "Judea and Samaria" broadens your scope of influence. This includes the city in which you live and the place where you work and interact with people. The "ends of the earth" describes the world. We are to take and support the taking of the gospel to every part of the globe.

The Motivation: Love for Jesus
In 2 Corinthians 5:14, Paul writes, "For Christ's love compels us because we are convinced that one died for all." Man is a sinner separated from God. Jesus paid the penalty of man's sins. Our love for Jesus and our love for others compels us to share that message of eternity.

As a result, you have a couple of choices. You can sit, soak and sour. Or you can put passion to action and follow the command of Jesus. You know what you need to do . . . what you must do. What are you waiting for?

Father, give us the courage not only to hear your Word but also actually to get up, get out and get moving. For Jesus' sake, Amen.

reflection

_____

_____

_____

further suggested reading:

Acts 1-4

311

Let Your Light Shine

Acts 7:55-56

But Stephen, full of the Holy Spirit, looked up to heaven and saw the glory of God, and Jesus standing at the right hand of God. "Look," he said, "I see heaven open and the Son of Man standing at the right hand of God."

Stephen was a man known for his great faith. He demonstrated God's grace and power. He did "great wonders and miraculous signs among the people." That's why the religious leaders of the day decided to bring him to court. There they produced false witnesses to charge Stephen with blasphemy. Stephen gave a stirring speech condemning the leaders' rejection of Jesus. They dragged him out of the city and stoned him.

Stephen was the first Christian martyr but not the last. Juvenal, a Roman poet, said that Christians belonged in the sewage. Suetonius, a Roman historian, said that Christians were "a race of men given to novel and baneful superstition." The Roman historian, Tacitus, described the horrid deaths of the early Christians. He wrote the following:

> Consequently, to get rid of the report, Nero fastened the guilt and inflicted the most exquisite tortures on a class hated for their abominations, called Christians by the populace. Mockery of every sort was added to their deaths. Covered with the skins of beasts, they were torn by dogs and perished, or were nailed to crosses, or were doomed to the flames and burnt, to serve as a nightly illumination, when daylight had expired.

While we may not be called to die for Christ, each one of us is called to live for him. And we are called to live for him in a way that demonstrates his power in our lives. Jesus said, "Let your light shine before men, that they may see your good deeds and praise your Father in heaven." Today, let's let our light shine!

Father, thank you for the many examples of men and women who have gone to their deaths for you. We pray for those throughout the world who are being persecuted today. Father, give us the courage to live for you and to demonstrate your power in our lives. And if you should ever call us to die for you, give us the same courage and resolve that you gave Stephen. In Jesus' name. Amen.

reflection

further suggested reading:

Acts 5-7

Get Ready

Acts 8:26-27

Now an angel of the Lord said to Philip, "Go south to the road - the desert road - that goes down from Jerusalem to Gaza." So he started out, and on his way he met an Ethiopian eunuch, an important official in charge of all the treasury of the Kandake (which means "queen of the Ethiopians").

In Acts 6, when the Apostles were looking for some men to help them out, they sought those who were "known to be full of the Spirit and wisdom." Philip fit the bill. Then Philip hit the road. Driven from Jerusalem by persecution, he went to Samaria to proclaim Christ. God honored his efforts. In fact, so many people were trusting in Christ that Peter and John went to Samaria to help out.

But during the awakening in Samaria, God told Philip to leave the area. What? God was demonstrating his power. People were coming to Christ. Philip was right in the middle of the action, and God gave him a new assignment. From the spiritual activity of Samaria, God sent Philip to a desert road. It was on the road that Philip met a man in charge of the treasury of Candace, the Ethiopian queen. Philip shared the gospel. The man trusted in Jesus and was baptized. And, no doubt, the important official shared the message back in Ethiopia.

Do you feel like God has taken you out of the action? Do you feel like he has placed you on a desert road? Remember, God never wastes our time. Whether you are in the hubbub of spiritual activity or alone on your "desert road," God is working his plan. Stay on the journey . . . keep looking up . . . get ready. There, just around the bend, God has an eternally important assignment just for you.

Father, whether we are right in the midst of tremendous spiritual activity or in a dry deserted place, help us keep our eyes on you. Wherever we are in our spiritual journey help us see your next assignment. We don't want to miss it! In Jesus' name. Amen.

reflection

---

further suggested reading:

Acts 8

A Light from Heaven

Acts 9:3-4

As he neared Damascus on his journey, suddenly a light from heaven flashed around him. He fell to the ground and heard a voice say to him, "Saul, Saul, why do you persecute me?"

Bang! Just like that! A light from heaven and Saul fell to the ground.

Saul was intent on destroying the church, "breathing out murderous threats against the Lord's disciples." Dragging men and women off to prison, he made house calls on Christians. He approvingly supervised the stoning of Stephen. And he was on his way to Damascus to level some more damage when God stopped him in his tracks. You know the rest of the story. Saul trusted in Christ, God changed his name to Paul, and the last of the Apostles took the message of Jesus throughout the world. And . . . he wrote thirteen of the twenty-seven books in the New Testament.

We call a change like Paul's a "Damascus Road Conversion." A person is blatantly opposed to everything Christian. They have nothing to do with Jesus. They breathe hatred to all who follow Christ. Then suddenly God gets their attention. They become a follower of Jesus.

Whom do you know who is blatantly opposed to Christianity? Think of a person that needs a "Damascus Road" experience. Our job is not to hate or damn them. Jesus said that our job is to love and pray for them (Matthew 5:44). Write the person's name down. Put him on your prayer list. I know what you're saying, "This person will never come to Christ!" That's the same thing people said about Paul.

Father, help us obey the command of Jesus to love our enemies and pray for them. We do that right now. I ask that you bring _____ to yourself. Cause _____ to trust in you. Give _____ a Damascus Road experience. In Jesus' name. Amen.

reflection

_____

_____

_____

_____

further suggested reading:

Acts 9

314

I Trust You!

Acts 12:7

Suddenly an angel of the Lord appeared and a light shone in the cell. He struck Peter on the side and woke him up. "Quick, get up!" he said, and the chains fell off Peter's wrists.

King Herod enjoyed pleasing people. Nothing pleased his people more than watching Christians lose their heads. As a result, the king had Peter arrested. The night before his trial, Peter slept between two soldiers with his hands and feet in chains. Suddenly an angel appeared, the chains fell off and Peter was freed from the prison. He headed for a home where he knew believers had gathered to pray for him. There was, no doubt, a great celebration when he walked through the door.

But Peter was not the only disciple arrested. Days prior, Herod arrested James and had him beheaded. Wait a second! How did that happen? Did the church forget to pray for James? Did they not pray long enough or hard enough? Certainly, there was no great celebration when this news reached the friends of James.

Why did Peter lose his chains and James lose his head? Why do some people "just miss" a tragic car accident, and others are killed in a crash? Why does disease ravage one person's body while another goes into remission? We don't know. We may never know. But this we do know. God is perfect and all his ways are perfect. He doesn't make mistakes. He never acts arbitrarily but uses all things for his eternal purposes. Somehow he works all things out for good for those who love him. Sometimes the only thing we can do is trust him even when we don't understand his ways. Can you do that? Can you trust him . . . even standing in the whirlwind of your questions?

Father, I admit that I don't understand your ways. I don't understand why (mention something that has happened or not happened that you are questioning in your life). But today I proclaim - I trust you! Even as I stand in the middle of my pain and questions - I trust you! Even though my finite mind does not allow me to understand, I know that you are working all things for my good. I trust you . . . I trust you. In Jesus' name. Amen.

reflection

---

further suggested reading:

Acts 10-12

Human Like You

Acts 14:11-13

When the crowd saw what Paul had done, they shouted in the Lycaonian language, "The gods have come down to us in human form!" Barnabas they called Zeus, and Paul they called Hermes because he was the chief speaker. The priest of Zeus, whose temple was just outside the city, brought bulls and wreaths to the city gates because he and the crowd wanted to offer sacrifices to them.

It was impressive. Paul looked directly at a man crippled from birth and called out, "Stand up on your feet!" The man who had never taken a step "jumped up and began to walk." When the people saw this they shouted, "The gods have come down to us in human form!" Pretty heady stuff for Paul and Barnabas.

When I read this passage, I thought of the Christian celebrity market. From conferences to cruises; from book signings to blockbuster seminars; from the pulpit to podcasts; from twitter to YouTube; from church attendance to church budgets . . . Christian leaders, in their desire to minister, can get some unhealthy attention. But listen to the apostles' response when the people were getting ready to offer sacrifices to them:

> *Men, why are you doing this? We too are only men, human like*
> *you. We are bringing you good news, telling you to turn from*
> *these worthless things to the living God, who made heaven*
> *and earth and sea and everything in them. (Acts 14:15).*

There is no biblical market for Christian celebrities. Don't place leaders on pedestals. The higher you place them, the farther they will eventually fall. Each one is human . . . disgustingly so. Together let's work to turn people from worthless things to the living God. Together let's direct people to the one who made the heaven and earth and sea and everything in them. There is only one name above every name. There is only one to whom we all bow.

Father, keep us from worshiping humans. Keep us from a celebrity mindset. Help us never desire a pedestal, and help us never place a person there. Our allegiance is to you and you only. Make that more than a statement. Make that the reality of our life. In Jesus' name. Amen.

reflection

_____

_____

_____

further suggested reading:

Acts 13-15

Sing in the Darkness

Acts 16:25

About midnight Paul and Silas were praying and singing hymns to God, and the other prisoners were listening to them.

By all accounts, it was a really bad day. Paul and Silas had been attacked by an angry crowd. The city official had them stripped and beaten. Then they were "severely flogged" and thrown into the inner cell with stocks - used for security and torture - locked to their feet. The godliest saint would have been calling it an unfortunate day but not these two. Around midnight, they started a prayer and praise service.

Don't forget their condition. They had been severely flogged, but they prayed through their pain. They were in stocks, yet they sang. These men, needing rest, raised their voices in praise. Then . . . God delivered them.

No doubt some of you read these words today with a heavy heart. Circumstances have beaten you down. You feel imprisoned by things beyond your control. Another person has delivered an emotional blow, and you feel your hands are tied. It's not easy to sing in the darkness of your inner cell. But I encourage you to try. Pray through the pain that holds down your heart. Sing in spite of the chains that are holding you back. I can't promise deliverance from your situation, but I can promise freedom within your situation. God will work in his way and in his time. But for now, pour out your heart in prayer, and sing a hymn of praise to the God who is always worthy.

Pray with me.
Father, I feel defeated. I feel pain and hurt because of (name the situation). I don't feel like praying, and I certainly don't feel like singing. But right now I am going to pour out my heart to you (let God know all that is on your heart). And I am going to sing my favorite song of praise (sing from the bottom of your heart). I wait for you and for your timing. In Jesus' name. Amen.

reflection

_____

_____

_____

_____

_____

further suggested reading:

Acts 16-18

Finishing Strong

Acts 20:23-24

I only know that in every city the Holy Spirit warns me that prison and hardships are facing me. However, I consider my life worth nothing to me; my only aim is to finish the race and complete the task the Lord Jesus has given me - the task of testifying to the good news of God's grace.

It was pure art. She ran effortlessly. Her legs glided down the track. Her arms were pumping in what looked like three-quarter speed. Yet she distanced herself from the rest of the runners. As the 100 meter first place timer, my eyes were on her. She, no doubt, was the winner. But then . . . with about twenty meters to go, she committed the cardinal sin of sprinting. She looked back to check out the runners behind her. The motion disrupted her stride and caused her to stumble. She fell hard, her body skidding on the track. In great pain, she crawled over the finish line . . . in third place.

I will never forget that moment and the lesson that God taught me. Stumbling can occur even when you are ahead and almost finished. It's great to start well. It's important to run hard. But you have to finish strong. That is Paul's desire in this passage. He knows the race will not be easy. His future days include prison and hardship. But he is committed to finish the race and complete the task that Christ has given him. Nothing else matters.

What about you? Are you on target to finish the race and complete the task that God has given you? Are your eyes fixed on him? Is your focus so intense that nothing else matters? What is the Spirit compelling you to do? Life is too short to be running the wrong race. The race is too important to run without determination and focus. Run hard! And finish strong!

Father, you have given us a great race to run. Help us look forward, push ahead, keep our focus. Help us run hard and finish strong. In Jesus' name. Amen.

reflection

further suggested reading:

Acts 19-20

318

Take Courage!

Acts 23:11

The following night the Lord stood near Paul and said, "Take courage! As you have testified about me in Jerusalem, so you must also testify in Rome."

Today's passage took place in Jerusalem, where Paul was arrested and put on trial. After he was given the opportunity to share Christ, those listening shouted, "Rid the earth of him! He's not fit to live!" In other words, when Paul gave the invitation, no one came forward. Not quite the response he wanted.

When we share Christ, we will not always receive the response that we want from friends and family. We probably won't hear, "Rid the earth of him! He's not fit to live!" but that may well be the impression that is left. Then again, we might get the tepid, dismissive answer of relativism, "Well, I'm glad that works for you, but it doesn't work for me." Often we don't get the desired response.

But God's encouragement to Paul rings true for us too. His loud whisper fills our heart, "Take courage! We are not finished. Just as you have shared here, I have many other places. Just as you told that person about me, I have many other people who need to hear." At the end of the day the words, "Take courage!" from the heavenly Father is the only response we need.

Father, thank you for your encouragement. Thank you for lifting us when we are low, for holding us when we are shaky, for steadying our trembling voice and for speaking courage into our fearful hearts. In Jesus' name. Amen.

reflection

_____
_____
_____
_____
_____
_____
_____
_____
_____

further suggested reading:

Acts 21-23

Repentance

Acts 26:20

First to those in Damascus, then to those in Jerusalem and in all Judea, and then to the Gentiles, I preached that they should repent and turn to God and demonstrate their repentance by their deeds.

Repentance. We don't hear that word much today, do we? We talk a lot about "trusting in Jesus," "having your sins forgiven" and "having a personal relationship with God," but the repentance thing kind of gets left out. What does repentance mean, and why did Paul preach that people should repent?

The word "repent" means "to feel remorse." It means "to change one's mind and direction." I am living life and living large. I am headed my own way doing my own thing. But then, God gets my attention . . . maybe through a conversation with a friend, through the birth of a child, through the emptiness of success or through the dark night of failure. God stops me in my tracks, and I repent. Instead of walking away from him, I turn to him. My repentance is shown to be real by my deeds. I am a new creation. The old is gone; the new has come.

Let's get personal about repentance. Have you turned from your old way of life to the new? Have you moved your residence from "darkness" to "light"? Was there a time when you made the decision to stop walking away from God and walk toward him? Has anyone around you noticed a change - in behavior, words, and/or attitude - since you have trusted in Christ? Being a Christian is not about future life insurance; it's walking with Christ today. When you follow Jesus, repentance will be demonstrated by your deeds.

Jesus, there was a day when I said a prayer, but honestly there has been no change in my life. Right now I repent. I am sorry for my sin. I am sorry for walking away from you. I am sorry for living a life that I know displeases you. Please change me from the inside out. I want to demonstrate my true repentance by my actions. In Jesus' name. Amen.

reflection

further suggested reading:

Acts 24-26

He Has Come

Acts 26:22-23

But God has helped me to this very day; so I stand here and testify to small and great alike. I am saying nothing beyond what the prophets and Moses said would happen - that the Messiah would suffer and, as the first to rise from the dead, would bring the message of light to his own people and to the Gentiles.

The good news about Jesus is not a New Testament phenomenon. His story didn't start after the Old Testament ended. To those in Paul's day who claimed that Paul was promoting a new religion, he made it clear that he was saying "nothing beyond what the prophets and Moses said would happen." Let's take a quick review of the prophet Isaiah's words 700 years before Jesus came.

- **The Messiah would suffer . . .**

    But he was pierced for our transgressions, he was crushed for our iniquities; the punishment that brought us peace was on him, and by his wounds we are healed.

    Isaiah 53:5

- **First to rise from the dead . . .**

    After he has suffered, he will see the light of life and be satisfied . . .

    Isaiah 53:11

- **Message of light . . .**

    And now the LORD says . . . "It is too small a thing for you to be my servant to restore the tribes of Jacob and bring back those of Israel I have kept. I will also make you a light for the Gentiles, that my salvation may reach to the ends of the earth"

    Isaiah 49:5-6

Remember the conversation that Jesus had with the two men on the road to Emmaus after his resurrection? They didn't recognize Jesus and were lamenting his death. Jesus said, "Did not the Christ have to suffer these things to enter into his glory?" Then "beginning with Moses and all the Prophets, he explained to them what was said in all the Scriptures concerning himself" (Luke 24:26-27). The entire Old Testament shouts, "Jesus is coming!" And the New Testament celebrates and proclaims the fact that he has come.

Father, thank you for making it clear from the beginning of Scripture that Jesus was coming. Now that he has come and his work is completed, help us worship him every day of our lives. In Jesus' name. Amen.

further suggested reading:

Acts 24-26

Without Hindrance!

Acts 28:30-31

For two whole years Paul stayed there in his own rented house and welcomed all who came to see him. He proclaimed the kingdom of God and taught about the Lord Jesus Christ - with all boldness and without hindrance!

Fittingly, the book of Acts ends with an exclamation mark! The good news of Jesus is being spread throughout the known world; communities of believers are worshipping together and taking care of each other; doctrine is being established as the Apostles' teaching is recorded and followed. It all ends with an exclamation mark . . . even as Paul lives under arrest.

The book of Acts ends with Paul in a room under house arrest. Later, he would be put to death under the order of Nero. But for now, he is in a rented house with guards at the door. All who want to come see him are welcomed. And there, under arrest in that rented house, Paul proclaims Jesus "with all boldness and without hindrance!"

Do you feel restrained or restricted today? Maybe a past failure bores a hole of paralyzing pain in your soul. Maybe an illness has robbed you of health and restricted you to your home. Maybe discouragement has taken away your drive. Maybe life's circumstances have left you feeling like you're under arrest. Could it be that God has you right where you are for a reason? Could it be that he is getting ready to demonstrate his strength through your weakness? Could it be that God is getting ready to bring some people to you who need to hear about Jesus? There you are . . . like Paul . . . limited . . . and yet there God is bringing people to you. Are you ready to proclaim Christ boldly and without hindrance right from your present situation? Only God can put a triumphant exclamation mark on our restraints and restrictions.

Father, from right where we are today . . . use us. Right from today's circumstances, let us boldly proclaim Jesus. Help us see beyond ourselves. Give us opportunities to speak out boldly for you. In spite of our circumstances, help us to live with an exclamation mark! In Jesus' name. Amen.

reflection

further suggested reading:

Acts 27-28

Salvation

Romans 1:16-17

For I am not ashamed of the gospel, because it is the power of God that brings salvation to everyone who believes: first to the Jew, then to the Gentile. For in the gospel the righteousness of God is revealed - a righteousness that is by faith from first to last, just as it is written: "The righteous will live by faith."

The gospel is the power of God for salvation. In the Gospel is God's enabling power to save us and keep us saved. But let's stop right there. What is "salvation" anyway? What does it mean when we say that a person is "saved"?

There are three critical parts to salvation, each described by a rich theological word. When we trust in Jesus alone as the only way to have a relationship with the living God, these three things happen. Ready?

1. **Justification: An instantaneous act of God in which he sees our sins forgiven and Christ's righteousness belonging to us. He declares us "Not Guilty!" and "Righteous!"(right before God).**

2. **Sanctification: The progressive work of God in our lives. As we partner with God to allow the Spirit's control, we grow in our Christian walk.**

3. **Glorification: The final work of God in salvation when he delivers us home to heaven - resurrected bodies built for eternity.**

We could say it like this:
We were saved: Justification
We are being saved: Sanctification
We will be saved for eternity: Glorification

Salvation declares me not guilty; it produces spiritual growth; it delivers me home. That's why Paul can say, and that's why we can say, "I am not ashamed of the Gospel!"

Father, thank you for the Gospel - the news of victory. Thank you for declaring me, "not guilty," for producing spiritual growth and for the promise that one day you will deliver me safely home. Thank you for my salvation! In Jesus' name. Amen.

Do you know what salvation means? Have you trusted in Christ for salvation? Email me at rmoore@biblechapel.org. Visit http://ronmoore.org/good-news-bad-news/ for a resource that will explain how you can place your faith in Jesus.

further suggested reading:

Romans 1-3

Trust in Jesus

Romans 5:8

But God demonstrates his own love for us in this: While we were still sinners, Christ died for us.

God loves us.
That's an amazing truth, isn't it? The eternal God has deep affection and affinity for us. He wants us to be his children. He longs to know us and have a relationship with us. He desires to bless us and show us his great love. But there is a problem.

Man is a sinner.
We are not sinners because we sin; we sin because we are sinners. We are a sinner by nature. And our sin separates us from God. There is a great chasm between us and God that cannot be crossed by our own efforts (good works). All of us have sinned and fall short of God's holy standard. Trying to get to God on our own would be like trying to jump across the Grand Canyon. You might jump farther than me, or I might jump farther than you, but the rescue workers are not going to be measuring the distance when they pick up our bodies off the rocks. A confirmation class, CCD class, baptism, first communion, church attendance or generous giving cannot propel us to God. Since we couldn't get to God, God came to us.

Christ died for us.
God loved us so much that he did something about our predicament. He sent his Son to do for us what we could not do for ourselves. Jesus came to pay the penalty for our sin on the cross. Jesus was fully God and fully man. Being God, he was sinless, so he didn't have to die for his sins. He went to the cross as a sinless sacrifice. Being man, he died in our place. He died as our substitute.

Being a Christian is simply this: I come to the point where I realize that I am a sinner and cannot have a relationship with God on my own. I know that God loved me so much that he sent his Son to die for me. And I trust in Jesus as the One who died on my behalf. I trust in Jesus as the only way to have a relationship with God, experience his new life now and live with him forever. Would you like to have a relationship with the heavenly Father who loves you with that kind of love? Then use the following prayer as your guide to trust in Jesus.

Dear heavenly Father, I admit that I am a sinner and cannot earn my way to you. I thank you for loving me so much that you sent Jesus to die on the cross for my sin. I thank you for raising him back to life. Today, I trust in Jesus alone as the One who paid the penalty for my sin on the cross. I trust in Jesus as the only way to have a relationship with you. In Jesus' name, Amen.

further suggested reading:

Romans 4-5

I Am His Forever

Romans 8:38-39

For I am convinced that neither death nor life, neither angels nor demons, neither the present nor the future, nor any powers, neither height nor depth, nor anything else in all creation, will be able to separate us from the love of God that is in Christ Jesus our Lord.

I grew up believing that I could lose my relationship with God. I thought that you could be a Christian in the morning, sin at lunch and be headed for hell in the afternoon. All sins were disqualifiers, but there were some "big ones" that carried a more serious threat, like dancing, drinking, swearing and smoking. Later, I came to understand that smoking will not send you to hell, but it will make you smell like you've already been there. (Like that one? Here's another - no one really smokes, it's the cigarette that does the smoking; they're the suckers.) Movies were also on the list of things that ended one's salvation. Anytime I wanted to see a movie with my friends, the standard line was, what if Jesus comes back while you are in the theatre! No one could possibly be raptured from the Perry Theatre. Actually, that argument made some sense because the floor of the theatre was very sticky. It would have been possible to get "stuck" in there even during the Rapture! That's how I grew up. Sometimes certain of heaven, other times, following an act of sin, believing I was headed to hell.

Then one day, studying Scripture, I learned that nothing can separate me from the love of God found in Christ alone. It was as if a burden had been lifted from my shoulders. That day, in a hot parking lot in Dallas, Texas, I learned that I was a child of God and would forever be.

Salvation, from beginning to end, is of the Lord. When I trust in Christ - when Jesus calls me to himself—I am his forever! Once I am truly saved, I will always be saved! Because Jesus paid all my debt on the cross, I am eternally secure! I can live with assurance of my salvation! Nothing can snatch me out of his hand. I will pass from death to life. Does that give me a license to sin? Absolutely not! This truth gives me freedom to respond to God's amazing grace in loving obedience. Is that the life you're living?

Father, thank you for your amazing love. Thank you that nothing can separate me from you. Thank you for the confident security that is found in Jesus. Help me respond by following hard after you. In Jesus' name. Amen.

reflection

further suggested reading:

Romans 6-8

The Magnitude of God

Romans 11:33-36

Oh, the depth of the riches of the wisdom and knowledge of God! How unsearchable his judgments, and his paths beyond tracing out! Who has known the mind of the Lord? Or who has been his counselor? Who has ever given to God, that God should repay them? For from him and through him and to him are all things. To him be the glory forever! Amen.

Paul's great doxology proclaims that the greatness of God blows the wiring of man's mind! Included in this passage are seven truths about the magnitude of God.

1. **God is beyond man's full discovery.** On our best day with our clearest thinking we will never be able to fully ascertain the "depths of the riches of the wisdom and knowledge of God."

2. **God's ways are beyond man's comprehension.** There is no way our finite minds can grasp the infinite Creator.

3. **God is beyond the need for man's counsel.** God does not need man's advice on how to run the universe.

4. **God is not indebted to man.** No man has offered anything to God that he needs to repay.

5. **God is the first cause.** He is the Source from which all things come.

6. **God is the efficient cause.** He is the Agent through which all things exist.

7. **God is the final cause.** To him all things return and wait his judgment.

Father, there is only one way to respond to your power and majesty. To you alone be the glory forever and ever! Amen.

reflection

_____

_____

_____

_____

_____

further suggested reading:

Romans 9-11

Change Our Course

November 17

Romans 12:2

Do not conform to the pattern of this world, but be transformed by the renewing of your mind. Then you will be able to test and approve what God's will is - his good, pleasing and perfect will.

I am writing this on a plane headed overseas. The pilot has announced that there are some serious storms ahead. We are going to have to alter our course and fly around them. This flight has been bumpy enough. Thankfully, the pilot is choosing not to conform to the original flight pattern. He is going to adjust our path in order to avoid the danger.

The flight pattern of the world takes us directly into danger. The world stands in opposition to the things of God. Living together before marriage is becoming the popular option. Commitment after marriage is becoming practically optional. And same-sex marriage is not just optional but acknowledged and celebrated. The world tells me what I need to buy to make me happy and feel significant. I am told that friends and good times always come when I am having cold ones at the bar or the beach. The flight pattern of the world takes me directly into sinful storms.

That's why Paul tells us to change our course. For the believer, this transformation takes place when we renew our minds by spending meaningful time in Scripture. It's God's Word that instructs and warns of sin and shows us how to avoid the turbulence. It is God's word that strips away the lies of the world. With renewed minds we can evaluate what God's "good, pleasing, and perfect will" is for us. Read God's Word and avoid the sinful storms!

Father, please give us the desire to read your Word each day. And may we not be simply readers but doers of your instruction. In Jesus' name. Amen.

reflection

further suggested reading:

Romans 12

The Clothing of Christ

Romans 13:14

Rather, clothe yourselves with the Lord Jesus Christ, and do not think about how to gratify the desires of the flesh.

In today's passage, Paul uses an interesting word picture. He instructs believers to "clothe" ourselves with the Lord Jesus Christ. What does that mean? What does this apparel of Jesus look like?

I believe the clothing of Jesus is woven together with three brilliant threads.

THE THREAD OF ACCEPTANCE: As a believer, I have been forgiven and declared "not guilty" (Romans 5:1-2). I am a child of the living God (John 1:12). I can even call God, *Abba*, Father" (Romans 8:15).

THE THREAD OF SECURITY: Because of Jesus, I am free from any condemnation (Romans 8:1). Because of Jesus' work for me on the cross there is nothing in all creation that can separate me from the love of God (Romans 8:38-39). I live with the confidence of knowing that "God's gifts and his call are irrevocable" (Romans 11:29).

THE THREAD OF SIGNIFICANCE: I am blessed to be God's work of art (Ephesians 2:10). I can always approach God's throne of grace with confidence. There I will "receive mercy and find grace to help [me] in [my] time of need" (Hebrews 4:16).

The clothing of Christ is woven with the brilliant colors of acceptance, security and significance. When you are clothed with Christ, you are never out of style.

Father, thank you for forgiving me and making me your child. Thank you for giving me security through eternity. Thank you for giving me true significance. Help me wear the clothing of Jesus well. May others see the beauty of Christ in me. In Jesus' name. Amen.

reflection

_____

_____

_____

_____

further suggested reading:

Romans 13-16

Freedom from the Chains of Sin

November 19

1 Corinthians 6:9-11

Or do you not know that the wicked will not inherit the kingdom of God? Do not be deceived: Neither the sexually immoral nor idolaters nor adulterers nor men who have sex with men nor thieves nor the greedy nor drunkards nor slanderers nor swindlers will inherit the kingdom of God. And that is what some of you were. But you were washed, you were sanctified, you were justified in the name of the Lord Jesus Christ and by the Spirit of our God.

"There but for the grace of God go I." Ever hear those words? They came from the lips of an English martyr named John Bradford, who, like the Apostle Paul, was a lawyer turned preacher. He lived during the reign of Mary Tudor, who was not fond of Protestants. A month into her reign, Bradford was arrested and confined to the Tower of London. He uttered these famous words when he saw a criminal going to execution.

Bradford's words are true for us all, aren't they? Paul is clear that without God's grace we either were or would have been wallowing in sin like a pig wallows in the mud. Some of us were saved at a young age and graciously spared a sinful lifestyle. But we know our inclinations and shudder to think where our wicked heart would have taken us if not for God's grace. Others walked far down the path of sin and have the scars to prove it. Like the prodigal son, they were brought to their senses and graciously guided home. For all of us, it is only by God's grace that we have been washed, sanctified and justified in the name of the Lord Jesus Christ and by the Spirit of our God.

As for Bradford, he continued to preach and write from prison until January 31,1555, when he was burned at the stake. He was chained to another martyr named John Leaf. After begging forgiveness of any person he might have wronged and forgiving everyone who had wronged him, he turned to Leaf and said, "Be of good comfort brother, for we shall have a merry supper with the Lord this night." Bradford knew God's grace in life and death.

Father, thank you for saving us from who we were and who we might have been without your grace. Thank you for cleansing us, setting us apart and declaring us "not guilty!" through Jesus and by the Holy Spirit. May we live as those freed from the chains of sin. In Jesus' name. Amen.

reflection

_____

_____

_____

further suggested reading:

1 Corinthians 1-6

1 Corinthians 7:17

Nevertheless, each person should live as a believer in whatever situation the Lord has assigned to them, just as God has called them. This is the rule that I lay down in all the churches.

Are you happy with where you are in life? Are you always looking for the next "BIG" adventure? Do you find yourself always wanting to be where you're not? Does tomorrow or yesterday always seem better than today? Now, granted, there are some stations in life that are not pleasant, and there are issues that we want to get over and challenges that we want to get through. But for many, maybe for you, life has become a series of daily discontentments.

Check out today's passage. Believers are to live confidently in the station of life that God has assigned. I know that it's not always easy, but in each task God will give you all that is needed to do what he has called you to do. Life with God has mountain passages that expand our lungs, valleys that demand trust, challenges that stretch us and storms that cause us to run to him for protection.

And remember, your present station is not permanent. The right job will come. Grief will finally move out of your heavy heart. There will not always be diapers to change or two kids hanging onto your knees. You'll survive the teenage years (okay, I can't promise that). Healing will come . . . in this life or when you see him face to face. Through it all, the Father is right there with you. Whatever your present station, you can experience and enjoy (yes, enjoy) the journey with him.

Father, thank you for all the assignments that you give me. There are some I don't enjoy at the time. They cause pain, fear and anxiety. And I want out of those situations. But help me trust in you today. Give me strength to stand and confidence to endure. Work in my heart to make me your man (woman). Even though my assignment today is difficult, I thank you for it. In Jesus' name. Amen.

reflection

---

further suggested reading:

1 Corinthians 7-10

The Love Chapter

1 Corinthians 13

If I speak in the tongues of men or of angels, but do not have love, I am only a resounding gong or a clanging cymbal. If I have the gift of prophecy and can fathom all mysteries and all knowledge, and if I have a faith that can move mountains, but do not have love, I am nothing. If I give all I possess to the poor and give over my body to hardship that I may boast, but do not have love, I gain nothing. Love is patient, love is kind. It does not envy, it does not boast, it is not proud. It does not dishonor others, it is not self-seeking, it is not easily angered, it keeps no record of wrongs. Love does not delight in evil but rejoices with the truth. It always protects, always trusts, always hopes, always perseveres. Love never fails. But where there are prophecies, they will cease; where there are tongues, they will be stilled; where there is knowledge, it will pass away. For we know in part and we prophesy in part, but when completeness comes, what is in part disappears. When I was a child, I talked like a child, I thought like a child, I reasoned like a child. When I became a man, I put the ways of childhood behind me. For now we see only a reflection as in a mirror; then we shall see face to face. Now I know in part; then I shall know fully, even as I am fully known. And now these three remain: faith, hope and love. But the greatest of these is love.

The Love Chapter. We find it in books of literature. We hear it read at weddings. We listen to its words put to music. This passage is beautiful in its poetic flow and powerful in its conceptual truth. But is it ever hard to apply! It would have been convicting enough if Paul just left us to deal with love in all its abstractness. But, as usual, he had to go and get practical.

Paul explains that the absence of love sucks the significance out of the most gifted speaker, paralyzes the most profound prophet and makes great faith fall flat. No love will bankrupt radical giving and quench the fire of the flaming martyr. Love shows up in everyday life. It doesn't want what others have. It doesn't boast about achievement. It doesn't fly off the handle. It is never secretly pleased when a person gets what's coming to them. True love demonstrates kindness, trust, hope and patience. It never gives up.

Can you imagine what our homes would look like and feel like if we began to apply this well-known chapter? Can you imagine how the atmosphere at our schools and workplace would change? Can you imagine the impact churches could make in their communities if the Christians in them . . . well, acted like Christians? What will you do today to begin to take "The Love Chapter" off the page and apply it in your life?

Father, give us the desire to love others and the strength to love deeply. Help us to move from simply reading your word to emphatically responding to it. In Jesus' name. Amen.

further suggested reading:

1 Corinthians 11-14

The Resurrection

1 Corinthians 15:19-20

If only for this life we have hope in Christ, we are of all people most to be pitied. But Christ has indeed been raised from the dead, the firstfruits of those who have fallen asleep.

The Resurrection is the center of Christian teaching. It's the foundation on which our faith is built. It is the glue that holds our faith together. Jesus died for our sins; he was buried and he was "raised on the third day." Then, as proof, he appeared - alive! - to Peter, the Twelve, a group of 500 people, James, all the apostles and last of all to Paul. But the Resurrection is more than a powerful doctrine or an Easter sermon. There are times in our lives when it gets very personal.

Gary Habermas is a noted theologian. He has written extensively about the proof of the Resurrection. But the truth became very real to him when his wife, Debbie, passed away in 1995. Here's how Habermas explained how the Resurrection became real to him in an interview with Lee Strobel.

> *"Losing my wife was the most painful experience I've ever had to face, but if the Resurrection could get me through that, it can get me through anything."*
>
> *Habermas locked eyes with mine. "That's not some sermon," he said quietly. "I believe that with all my heart. If there's a Resurrection, there's a heaven. If Jesus was raised, Debbie was raised. And I will be someday, too."*
>
> *"Then I'll see them both" (The Case for Christ, p. 242).*

Lord Jesus, thank you for coming to die for my sins. And thank you for your glorious resurrection from the dead! Thank you that my hope is not only in you during this short lifetime but also through all eternity. Amen.

reflection

further suggested reading:

1 Corinthians 15-16

Share His Power

2 Corinthians 1:3-4

Praise be to the God and Father of our Lord Jesus Christ, the Father of compassion and the God of all comfort, who comforts us in all our troubles, so that we can comfort those in any trouble with the comfort we ourselves receive from God.

Our God is the "Father of compassion." He knows who you are and where you are. He understands what you are going through. He sympathizes with you. He loves you deeply. And he is the "God of all comfort." He comes to us with strength. He brings peace to our pain and calm to our chaos. As the Psalmist said, "When anxiety was great within me, your consolation brought joy to my soul" (94:19).

Now check this out. He comforts us so that we can comfort others. Having experienced God's work in our lives, we have the privilege and responsibility to share that needed help with others. We are to take the comfort that we have received and use it to help those God places in our lives.

Have you ever lost a job? Find a person going through that experience now. Have you survived divorce? Who is more equipped than you to minister to a person going through divorce today? Have you lost a loved one? There is no shortage of grieving people. Did God deliver you from an addiction? All around you are people stumbling and struggling. God's work in our lives serves a twofold purpose. God powerfully worked in your life; now, it's time to share his power with someone else.

Father, today, lead us to a person who is going through what we have gone through. Just as you comforted us, help us minister that same comfort to them. In Jesus' name. Amen.

reflection

further suggested reading:

2 Corinthians 1-5

Do Not Be Yoked Together . . .

2 Corinthians 6:14

Do not be yoked together with unbelievers. For what do righteousness and wickedness have in common? Or what fellowship can light have with darkness?

All followers of Jesus need to take the transforming message of the Gospel into their world. Sin separates us from God, and it is only through Jesus that we can have a relationship with the living God. As Jesus interacted with sinners, so must we. God has given us a network of friends and family. We need to tell the people in our lives about Jesus. But today's passage addresses more than sharing the Gospel. It warns Christians about entering into a partnership - a covenant - with nonbelievers. Let's focus on one important application of this passage.

Scripture warns a Christian not to marry a non-Christian. Yes, I know there are great stories where the husband or wife comes to Christ after they are married. Thank God for his grace. But we are not to presume on his grace. And there are plenty of sad stories where one spouse never came to Christ. This instruction is clear and straightforward - "Do not be yoked together with unbelievers." By the way, marriage starts with dating, so the same instruction applies to that phase of your relationship.

I know, I know, it's different with you. He's the nicest guy you've ever met. She is the girl of your dreams. Unfortunately, I see too many of these relationships five or ten years later. I see moms trying to raise children in the church with no support from their husbands. And I see husbands trying to lead their family in a godly way with opposition from their wives. There are always consequences to disobedience. Consequences always show up . . . sooner or later. And one more thing, if you choose to ignore this instruction, please don't ask me to officiate the ceremony. I cannot condone your disobedience.

Father, guard our hearts from the emotions of making bad relationship decisions that will haunt us for years to come. Remind us before we sin that there are consequences to sin. You designed and ordained marriage. Give us the wisdom to follow your instructions. In Jesus' name. Amen.

reflection

further suggested reading:

2 Corinthians 6-7

Rich with Spiritual Blessings

2 Corinthians 8:9

For you know the grace of our Lord Jesus Christ, that though he was rich, yet for your sake he became poor, so that you through his poverty might become rich.

In the beginning was the Word, and the Word was with God and the Word was God! The Word - God the Son - is eternal. There was never a time when he did not exist, and there will never be a time when he does not exist. God the Son is omnipotent. He is limitless in power. God the Son is omniscient. He knows everything there is to know about everything there is to know. God the Son is omnipresent. He is everywhere at the same time in his full being. In one word . . . God the Son is . . . rich!

Yet for our sakes, the eternal Word took on flesh. The Dweller of Heaven moved into our neighborhood. The omnipresent God confined himself to a human body. The all-powerful God submitted himself to die on the cross. Jesus came to give his life as a ransom for our sin. And it was through that poverty of his submission that we have become rich.

Now, in Christ, we are rich with spiritual blessings. We have been redeemed. We stand justified - declared "not guilty!" We have been adopted as God's children. The Holy Spirit lives in us. We are free from condemnation. We can never be separated from God. We have direct access to the throne of grace. We are God's workmanship. We know that God is working through all the circumstances of our lives. We are confident that God will complete the good work he has started in us. In one word . . . we, the sons and daughters of God, are . . . rich!

Lord Jesus, thank you for becoming poor . . . all the way to the cross . . . so that we could have all the spiritual blessings of eternity! We want to thank you with our lives. Amen.

reflection

_____

_____

_____

_____

_____

_____

_____

further suggested reading:

2 Corinthians 8-9

God's Sufficient Grace

2 Corinthians 12:9

But he said to me, "My grace is sufficient for you, for my power is made perfect in weakness."

Do you have something that drags you down? Maybe it's a chronic illness that tears at your body and soul. Maybe it is a relationship that is not getting any better. Maybe you are stuck in a job that is neither satisfying nor fulfilling. Maybe you are estranged from a son or daughter. You have prayed and prayed . . . and yet no answer seems to be coming.

If you have an ongoing prayer for an ongoing need, then you can relate to the Apostle Paul. Although we don't know what Paul's "thorn in the flesh" was, we know he wanted it out of his life. In three separate times of intense prayer, he asked God to take it away. But each time God said, "No." God used the "thorn" to keep Paul dependent on him. The "thorn" was a continual reminder of God's sufficient grace. It was Paul's weakness that best demonstrated God's strength.

We don't invite thorns into our lives. And when they come, we pray for God to take them away. But sometimes he doesn't. This doesn't mean he has forgotten you, or has lost interest in you or doesn't care for you. God doesn't waste your time. He is reminding you that he is all you need, that his grace is abundant and that he shows up with great power in your weakness. Like Paul, you can say, "For when I am weak, then I am strong."

Father, thank you for the thorns. Show your awesome power through our weakness and inadequacy. In Jesus' name. Amen.

reflection

further suggested reading:

2 Corinthians 10-13

Christlikeness

November 27

Galatians 6:4

Each one should test their own actions. Then they can take pride in themselves alone, without comparing themselves to someone else.

Comparing ourselves to others. We do it all the time, don't we? From appearance to attitudes, from education to experience, from clothes to cars to career, we like to see how we are matching up with those around us. But here's the problem. The exercise leaves me at one end or the other of the pride spectrum. I feel either "better than thou" or "woe is me." Comparing myself to others is a lose - lose proposition.

The remedy is found in today's passage.

- **Each one should test his or her own actions.** At the end of the day, I will stand before God to give an accounting of what he has given me. How have I used the gifts of time, money, opportunities and spiritual gifts? Other people have been given different backgrounds, gifts, experiences and opportunities. But I won't have to answer for them. The accounting before God will be very personal.

- **Each one should take pride in his or her personal actions.** Taking pride in what I do is not a bad thing as long as I understand the source and focus of my actions. Anything I do worthwhile is empowered by the Holy Spirit with the purpose of bringing honor to God. When I submit to the Spirit's control for the purpose of honoring God, this is something for which I can be appropriately proud.

When I compare myself to others, my progress is either paralyzed or puffed up. Our goal is Christlikeness. And we all have a long way to go!

Father, please keep me from falling into the trap of comparing myself to others. May you always be the focus and standard for my thoughts, words and actions. In Jesus' name. Amen.

reflection

_____

_____

_____

_____

_____

further suggested reading:

Galatians 1-6

Serious Spiritual Stuff

Ephesians 1:15-23

For this reason, ever since I heard about your faith in the Lord Jesus and your love for all God's people, I have not stopped giving thanks for you, remembering you in my prayers. I keep asking that the God of our Lord Jesus Christ, the glorious Father, may give you the Spirit of wisdom and revelation, so that you may know him better. I pray that the eyes of your heart may be enlightened in order that you may know the hope to which he has called you, the riches of his glorious inheritance in his holy people, and his incomparably great power for us who believe. That power is the same as the mighty strength he exerted when he raised Christ from the dead and seated him at his right hand in the heavenly realms, far above all rule and authority, power and dominion, and every name that is invoked, not only in the present age but also in the one to come. And God placed all things under his feet and appointed him to be head over everything for the church, which is his body, the fullness of him who fills everything in every way.

Sometimes prayers for my children become wooden and repetitive. "And Lord, help them have a great day at school" hardly scratches the surface for the three daughters and son God has graciously given my wife, Lori, and me. However, here is a prayer that asks for some serious spiritual stuff.

Here are nine things to pray every day for our children and grandchildren.

Thanksgiving: Thank God for the gift of your children (and their spouses!) and grandchildren.

Wisdom: Ask him to give them spiritual wisdom to make godly decisions.

Know him better: Ask God to grow them deeply in their knowledge and love for Christ.

Future hope: Pray that they live today with eternity in mind.

Glorious inheritance: Thank God for the eternal inheritance he has in store for them.

Great power: Ask God to give them the power to live obediently.

Strength: Ask the Holy Spirit to provide strength to resist temptations.

Established in love: Pray that they demonstrate a 1 Corinthians 13 love.

Grasp the love of Christ: Pray that they know and live in the freedom of the unconditional love of Jesus.

Lord, to you who is more than able to do immeasurably more than I can think to ask, to you who is able to do even more than I could ever dream, Father, according to your power that is at work in me and in my children - to you be the glory for ever and ever. Amen.

further suggested reading:

Ephesians 1-6

Eternal Purposes

November 29

Philippians 1:12-18

Now I want you to know, brothers and sisters, that what has happened to me has actually served to advance the gospel. As a result, it has become clear throughout the whole palace guard and to everyone else that I am in chains for Christ. And because of my chains, most of the brothers and sisters have become confident in the Lord and dare all the more to proclaim the gospel without fear. It is true that some preach Christ out of envy and rivalry, but others out of goodwill. The latter do so love, knowing that I am put here for the defense of the gospel. The former preach Christ out of selfish ambition, not sincerely, supposing that they can stir up trouble for me while I am in chains. But what does it matter? The important thing is that in every way, whether from false motives or true, Christ is preached. And because of this I rejoice. Yes, and I will continue to rejoice.

As the Apostle Paul penned these words to the Philippians, he found himself in a problematic situation. The man called and committed to take the Good News of Jesus Christ throughout the world was confined to a Roman prison. His calling seemed stymied. But Paul lived his life with this foundational belief: He was confident that God would never waste his time. Paul knew that God would use every situation for his eternal purposes - even those situations that don't quite make sense at the time.

Do you believe that? I know it is difficult. I know it is especially hard for those living in disappointment, discouragement, loss or grief. You are wondering how in the world God is going to use your present situation for good. How can he use setbacks, failure, hurt, illness and injustice for good? You must believe God's word. For those who love him and are called to his purposes, he doesn't waste our time.

Remember this: *The heavenly Father uses earthly problems for eternal purposes.* It doesn't mean the pain is less; it simply means the hurt is used by God to grow you into his man or woman. He is not done with you. Your impact for him is just beginning. He is molding you today for the person he needs you to be tomorrow.

Father, I pray for those about ready to throw in the spiritual towel. Please encourage their hearts as only you can do. Please remind them of your love. Give them the strength that they need for today. Give them the hope of a better day tomorrow. In Jesus' name. Amen.

reflection

_____

_____

further suggested reading:

Philippians 1-4

The Great Change

November 30

Colossians 1:1-6

Paul, an apostle of Christ Jesus by the will of God, and Timothy our brother, To God's holy people in Colossae, the faithful brothers and sisters in Christ: Grace and peace to you from God our Father. We always thank God, the Father of our Lord Jesus Christ, when we pray for you, because we have heard of your faith in Christ Jesus and of the love you have for all God's people - the faith and love that spring from the hope stored up for you in heaven and about which you have already heard in the true message of the gospel that has come to you. In the same way, the gospel is bearing fruit and growing throughout the whole world - just as it has been doing among you since the day you heard it and truly understood God's grace.

There are some things you never want to hear. For instance, you never want to hear a surgeon say, "Whoops!" during surgery. With your mouth propped wide open, you never want to hear a dentist say, "Now which molar was I supposed to pull?" You never want to hear the person who set up the blind date say, "You are going to love her personality." You never want to hear the coach of a college basketball team that won one game and lost twenty-nine say, "Yeah, but the good news is that next year we have everybody back!" But here is the worst. You never want to hear a person who professes to be a Christian say, "Really, there has been no change in my life."

The Gospel of Jesus Christ is more than a truth. It is a dynamic power that changes a person from the inside out. I love the way William Wilberforce - the primary person behind the abolition of slave trade in Great Britain - described his coming to Christ. He called it the "Great Change." The Gospel changes things!

Paul says to the believers in Colossae, "We have heard of your faith in Christ Jesus and the love you have for all God's people." Paul did not hear of these things because the Colossian Christians believed their faith was "a private matter." Paul heard of their faith and love because they were demonstrating visible acts of faith and love. Their invisible inward change resulted in visible outward action. Paul wrote that all over the world the dynamic power of the Gospel was "bearing fruit!" Are you bearing spiritual fruit? Is anyone hearing about your faith and love?

Father, may we be those who demonstrate your power with our lives. May our family and friends see our faith lived out in real life. May all in our lives see a "Great Change." In Jesus' name. Amen.

reflection

further suggested reading:

Colossians 1-4

Intentional Work

December 1

1 Thessalonians 2:11-12

For you know that we dealt with each of you as a father deals with his own children, encouraging, comforting and urging you to live lives worthy of God, who calls you into his kingdom and glory.

Here is a great passage for parents! Writing to the Thessalonians, Paul likens his dealing with the believers to a father's interaction with his children. We learn from this passage that there are three things parents should be doing.

1. **Encourage.** The Greek work here is *parakaleo*. It means "to call to one's side," "to summon," "to invite." The purpose of the invitation is to build confidence and courage into the heart. Many times the word is translated "comfort." Parents, what a great reminder of what we should be doing. Let's build up our children!

2. **Comfort.** This word means "to console." It is used in John 11 when Lazarus died. Many friends came to "console" Mary and Martha. Sometimes our children don't need more instruction or a lesson on how we handled a similar situation. Sometimes we need to replace our "walking uphill both ways in the snow" stories with sympathy. Parents, let's demonstrate some compassion.

3. **Urge.** This word means "to insist" or "implore." You are the parent! There are some things that you must be adamant about. Being firm is not a fault. Being resolute is not wrong. Leaders lead . . . but don't miss the goal - "to live lives worthy of God." We're not talking about batting averages here. We are talking about deliberately building into our children the framework of spiritual urgency that will allow them to make an impact with their lives in their world.

Parenting is intentional work. Let's pray that God gives us the strength and courage to lead our children well.

Father, give us a passion to be the fathers you desire us to be. May we encourage, comfort and urge our children on to be those who have a burning desire to follow hard after you. In Christ's name. Amen.

reflection

further suggested reading:

1 Thessalonians 1-2

Sinful Static

1 Thessalonians 4:3-7

It is God's will that you should be sanctified: that you should avoid sexual immorality; that each of you should learn to control his own body in a way that is holy and honorable, not in passionate lust like the pagans, who do not know God; and that in this matter no one should wrong his brother or take advantage of a brother or sister. The Lord will punish all those who commit such sins, as we told you and warned you. For God did not call us to be impure, but to live a holy life.

When I was young, I listened to the St. Louis Cardinal baseball games on my little transistor radio. The Yankees were my favorite team (Mickey Mantle and Bobby Mercer were both from Oklahoma), but there was no way I could pick up the New York games. I listened to the Cardinals . . . at least I tried to. The static and interference always presented a challenge. I usually lost the broadcast in the bottom of the ninth, two runners on, the score tied and Orlando Cepeda at the plate. Then I had to wait until the next day to read the *Perry Daily Journal* to see whether or not Cepeda delivered. Static can play havoc on a transistor radio broadcast, and static can play havoc in your life.

One of the things that can get in the way of clearly hearing God's voice is sinful static. God lays before us a clear message of what he expects - his revealed will (It is God's will that you should be sanctified or set apart). But when we do not follow God's revealed will, the "sinful static" keeps us from hearing his specific will for our lives. For instance, if a single person prays, "God, I really want to know what you want me to do with my life" but is sexually involved, there is "sinful static" that interrupts the reception. In essence, God says, "Why do you want to know my specific will when you are unwilling to follow my revealed will?"

Discovering God's will is not just looking to the future; it is taking stock of the present. Do you need to get rid of some sinful static so you can clearly hear God's voice?

Father, I want to know exactly what you want me to do. I do not want to live this one and only life and miss your will. Show me my sinful static. Help me confess it and deal with it. Please rid the static so that I can hear you loudly and clearly. In Jesus' name. Amen.

reflection

---

1 Thessalonians 3-5

Spiritual Transformation

December 3

2 Thessalonians 1:3

We ought always to thank God for you, brothers and sisters, and rightly so, because your faith is growing more and more, and the love all of you have for one another is increasing.

For too many people, being a Christian is kind of like buying life insurance - it amounts to a one-time decision that gets cashed in when you die. Now, granted, you might think about your life insurance every once in a while. You might even increase it when another child arrives. "Life Insurance Christians" do the same. They periodically think about the decision they made and re-up their "convictions" during certain periods of their life. But having life insurance is not life changing. And neither is being a "Life Insurance Christian."

A true Christian is a follower of Jesus. Trusting in him alone for salvation opens the door to a new life. A true Christian lives a life of transformation. Like the Christians in Thessalonica, our faith should be a growing expression of trust and dependence in Christ. And our love for one another is constantly demonstrated as we serve each other. The Christian life is not a one-and-done event. It is a lifelong process of spiritual transformation.

Take some time to think about and honestly answer these five important questions.

1. Is my past decision to trust in Jesus making a difference in my life today?
2. Do I consider being a Christian an event (e.g. confirmation, baptism, church membership) or a daily interaction with Jesus?
3. Am I following Jesus more closely this month than last? This year than last?
4. Can I honestly say that my "faith is growing more and more"?
5. Can I honestly say that my love for others is being demonstrated?

Being real with God and ourselves is the first step in a life of spiritual transformation.

Father, I ask that you examine my heart. Please give me the insight to answer these questions truthfully. Then give me the courage to move from where I am to where you want me to be. In Jesus' name. Amen.

reflection

_____

_____

_____

further suggested reading:

2 Thessalonians 1-3

1 Timothy 4:12

Don't let anyone look down on you because you are young, but set an example for the believers in speech, in conduct, in love, in faith and in purity.

I have had the privilege of taking two mission trips to Panama with 80 high school students and youth leaders from our church. We have shared the Gospel to elementary, junior high and high school students. We have spent afternoons with orphans, shared Christ at hospitals, ministered in local churches and have gotten our hands dirty with some good ole manual labor.

Along with the ministry and work, there were nightly meetings to sing, debrief and pray. I have been extremely impressed with these teenagers. Many of these students had their spiritual act together much earlier than I ever did. I was impressed that these students were willing to take the time out of their summer to share the message of Christ in another country and culture. I was impressed by the depth of commitment that many of the students possessed. They truly set an example of what it means to follow hard after God.

Howard Hendricks, one of my seminary professors used to say, "We train teenagers to fly multimillion dollar jets, but we won't let them take up offering in the church!" We can do better than that, can't we? We must never look down on our youth. They are tomorrow's church. Preparation for the future always begins today. Take the time to get to know some of the teens in your church. But I have to warn you: When it comes to following hard after Christ, some of you may need to run to catch up to their pace.

Father, protect our teens and keep them following hard after you. For those straying, bring them back to the fold. For those questioning, turn their natural queries into rock solid belief. For those living a lukewarm faith, light a fire in their hearts. Lord, may we never look down on our youth. In Christ's name. Amen.

reflection

_____

_____

_____

_____

_____

further suggested reading:

1 Timothy 1-6

2 Timothy 2:1-2

You then, my son, be strong in the grace that is in Christ Jesus. And the things you have heard me say in the presence of many witnesses entrust to reliable people who will also be qualified to teach others.

Our oldest daughter calls it the "Death Box." It's a metal box that contains our passports, birth certificates, important papers and our will. We have told Brittany, "If anything ever happens to us, be sure to go through the box." Every once in a while she'll ask, "Where are you keeping the Death Box these days?" Believe me, when we go, we aren't leaving much behind. But we want to give over some of the things that remain to our children. However, the most important things we can entrust to them don't fit in the box.

In this passage, Paul gives Timothy the instruction of legacy. Paul passed on the things that he received so that the recipients could continue the "passing on" process. Timothy, Paul's spiritual son, had heard the truth from Paul's lips and watched it being worked out in his life. Now it was Timothy's turn to entrust the truth to faithful and reliable people who in turn would do the same. The future of the Gospel depends on this process of entrustment.

Parents, how are you doing? What are you passing on to your children? Your good looks? Your sense of humor? A nice little inheritance? All that is fine, but it's temporal stuff. Our job is to pass on the eternal. Don't you want your children and grandchildren and great-grandchildren to have more than the family business and the vacation home?

Lord Jesus, drill deeply into our souls the conviction of what is eternally important. Help us pass on everything that is; help us squelch anything that isn't. In your name. Amen.

reflection

further suggested reading:

2 Timothy 1-4

Titus 2:2

Teach the older men to be temperate, worthy of respect, self-controlled, and sound in faith, in love and in endurance.

"Spiritual maturity" and "chronological age" are not synonymous. Many believers, with the benefit of years, have not used them for spiritual advancement. There are those who have moved into their 50s, 60s, 70s and 80s without moving farther along in their walk with Christ. Paul tells Titus to do some teaching.

The characteristics and qualities listed in today's passage are not for older men only. But those blessed with years in the church need to demonstrate these qualities to the younger men who are watching. Yes, we are to respect our elders . . . and . . . our elders should be "worthy of respect" by demonstrating temperance and standing firm "in faith, in love and in endurance."

There is no such thing as sliding for home in the Christian life. Nowhere in Scripture do we find instruction for when we can retire from the Christian life. We are told to press on, not sit it out. The Church desperately needs older men willing to empty themselves into the lives of another generation. The future depends on it. Older men, it's time to sign up for significant leadership! Impacting the future begins today.

Father, fill the church with older men who have the experience of the past, obedience in the present and a vision for the future. In Jesus' name. Amen.

reflection

_____

_____

_____

_____

_____

_____

_____

_____

_____

further suggested reading:

Titus 1-3

Grace Givers

Philemon 1:1-3

Paul, a prisoner of Christ Jesus, and Timothy our brother, To Philemon our dear friend and fellow worker, to Apphia our sister Archippus our fellow soldier and to the church that meets in your home: Grace and peace to you from God our Father and the Lord Jesus Christ.

Grace receivers should be grace givers. Those who have been given much should be generous in giving back. Those whose thirst is quenched should offer a drink. Those whose stomachs are full should share a bit of food. Those whose barns are overflowing should be more than generous with the overflow. But it's not always the case, is it?

Paul writes this very tactful letter to a believer named Philemon with a specific purpose in mind. Philemon's slave, a man named Onesimus, had stolen from Philemon and run away. In Paul's day, this act was punishable by death. But in God's sovereign plan, the fugitive slave met Paul and trusted in Christ. As a follower of Jesus, Onesimus was willing to return and make amends even if it meant death. Paul wrote this personal appeal to ask Philemon to show grace and accept Onesimus as a Christian brother. Paul's appeal is based on grace. Grace receivers should be grace givers.

Some of you are reading this with some outstanding relational issues. You are estranged from your mom, dad, sister or brother. You are distanced from a son or daughter. You are separated from a friend. There is a wedge between you and your spouse. Sure there are reasons. Sure you got hurt. And yes, maybe it was mostly their fault. But anything people have done to us, we have done to God . . . in spades. And he extends his grace and forgiveness. If he is willing to forgive us, we must be willing to forgive others. Grace receivers must be grace givers. That's a foundational truth for a follower of Jesus. Pick up the phone. Write the note. Send the email. You are a grace receiver. Be a grace giver.

Lord, please give me the grace right now to extend grace to
_____. I do this because I follow the greatest grace giver of time and eternity. In Jesus' name. Amen.

reflection

further suggested reading:

Philemon

Hebrews 1:1-3

In the past God spoke to our ancestors through the prophets at many times and in various ways, but in these last days he has spoken to us by his Son, whom he appointed heir of all things, and through whom also he made the universe. The Son is the radiance of God's glory and the exact representation of his being, sustaining all things by his powerful word. After he had provided purification for sins, he sat down at the right hand of the Majesty in heaven.

A great teacher uses different methods to drive home the point. That's what God did in the Old Testament. He put forth his message in a variety of ways. Sometimes he used visions, dreams and supernatural interventions. Other times he wrote the Law on tablets of stone and delivered it to the people by his servant Moses. Sending warning and encouragement there were times when God spoke through the prophets. While the delivery systems varied, the point was clear: God desired to speak to man. In the New Testament, the Word became flesh.

Jesus became the human mouthpiece of God. He clearly revealed the person of God and vividly explained the promises of God. Jesus not only explained how a person could know God; he made that relationship possible by his voluntary, sacrificial death on the cross. Then Jesus was raised to life to show God's power over death itself, and "sat down at the right hand of the Majesty in heaven."

Think of it this way. The Old Testament believers held a package. It was wrapped with the law and sacrificial system. They knew the Gift was inside, and they placed their faith in the promised Gift. On this side of the cross, the Gift is unwrapped, and the Person of Jesus is revealed. We see Jesus - the "radiance of God's glory and the exact representation of his being." And every day we thank God for the work of his Son!

Dear Father, thank you for revealing yourself in Jesus. Lord Jesus, thank you for coming to earth and loving us all the way to the cross. May we respond with a life of love and worship. In Jesus' name. Amen.

reflection

_____

_____

_____

_____

further suggested reading:

Hebrews 1

The Rescuer

Hebrews 2:3

How shall we escape if we ignore so great a salvation?

Moving from room to room like a wild animal on the run, the fire swept throughout the home.For those trapped inside the inferno, it seemed there was no escape. But then the firemen arrived and bolted into action. One brave rescuer pushed through the front door. He made his way through the falling structure to those imprisoned by the flames. He knocked a hole in the wall where the family huddled and yelled, "Follow me!" The opening provided a way of escape, and, without hesitation, the mom, dad and two children followed the rescuer to safety.

But what if those caught in the fire refused to follow? What if the trapped family decided a hole knocked in another wall would have been better? What if those awaiting certain death argued that the hole should have been bigger? What if those imprisoned criticized the narrow-mindedness of the rescuer for only providing one way out? What if the entombed ignored the fireman? The answer is an obvious one. If the people in the inferno had ignored the rescuer and the escape route, they would have died a foolish and needless death.

Caught in the grip of sin, we were helpless and hopeless. There was no way out. But then the Rescuer came. Jesus died on the cross for our sin. He provided the way out of our past prison and the way into a relationship with the Father. This is the great salvation that the Rescuer provides. If we ignore it, there is no way of escape. I invite you to follow the Rescuer today.

Dear Father, work in the hearts of all reading this today. Help them see where they are - trapped in sin's prison. Help them see what Jesus came to do. Help them today put their trust in the Great Rescuer who leads them through this life and into life eternal. In Jesus' name. Amen.

reflection

further suggested reading:

Hebrews 2

Sin's Total Force

Hebrews 4:14-16

Therefore, since we have a great high priest who has ascended into heaven, Jesus the Son of God, let us hold firmly to the faith we profess. For we do not have a high priest who is unable to empathize with our weaknesses, but we have one who has been tempted in every way, just as we are - yet he did not sin. Let us then approach the throne of grace with confidence, so that we may receive mercy and find grace to help us in our time of need.

Our confidence as believers is anchored in the fact that Jesus knows what it is like to live in human flesh. He can sympathize with our weaknesses. He knows the spirit is willing, but the flesh is weak. He understands my temptation because he has endured it to the fullest extent.

Suppose, for a moment, that you are standing behind one of those big diesel-powered tractors. You are holding a rope attached to the back of the gigantic machine. And your job is to keep the monster tractor from moving. That's right, as the engine revs and the smoke bellows from the stack and as the gears engage, your job - in this man-against-machine moment - is to stand strong and keep the tractor from moving forward. Think you can do it? Yeah, I know it's a foolish question. In one nanosecond, you will be pulled along behind the tractor. You will feel a fraction of the power before you go down. Now suppose that you could actually keep the tractor from moving. As the tractor engages all its power, you hold your ground. If you could actually keep the tractor from moving, you would feel the full power of the machine.

Here's my point. Regarding sin, Jesus felt all of its entire power. He was tempted but never gave in. He experienced sin's total force. He was tempted to the max, yet never once lost his footing. Jesus has experienced temptation. This is the One we approach with confidence. And he, who was tempted fully, without sin, will give us all the mercy and grace we need to resist sin as well.

Lord Jesus, thank you for the promise of grace and mercy to help in my times of need. There are many times when the waves of temptation seem to bowl me over. Help me stand strong in your strength. Amen.

reflection

_____

_____

_____

_____

further suggested reading:

Hebrews 3-4

Source of Eternal Salvation

December 11

Hebrews 5:7-9

During the days of Jesus' life on earth, he offered up prayers and petitions with fervent cries and tears to the one who could save him from death, and he was heard because of his reverent submission. Son though he was, he learned obedience from what he suffered and, once made perfect, he became the source of eternal salvation for all who obey him.

What comes to your mind when you picture Jesus? Stoic expression? Unflappable focus? Amazingly, he was able to resist Satan's temptation after prolonged fasting. Eyes set on the cross, only pausing long enough to do some needed teaching and gracious healings, he walked through life. Then I read this passage.

This passage tells us of our Lord's great emotion. His prayers and petitions were made "with loud cries and tears" to the only One who could save him from the cross. Even within the tears and requests, there was a "reverent submission." And through it all he "learned obedience." At the point of perfect submission he became the "source of eternal salvation."

But here's the question: Is Jesus your personal "source of eternal salvation"? By your own efforts, you cannot have a relationship with God no matter how hard and how long you try. Your baptism and religious classes do not save you. You cannot work your way to the Father. It is by grace through faith that we place our confident trust in Jesus. I plead with you to trust in the work that he has done for you.

Lord Jesus, I confess that I am a sinner. Try as I might I cannot save myself. Right now, I trust in your work on the cross. I trust that you died in my place on the cross. Today I trust in you alone to forgive my sins and place me into an eternal relationship with the Father. Amen.

reflection

further suggested reading:

Hebrews 5-7

Certain Truth

Hebrews 10:23

Let us hold unswervingly to the hope we profess, for he who promised is faithful.

She told me to make a fist. I did. She attached a tight bandage on my upper left arm. I let her. She swabbed my arm with brownish liquid. I watched. She was wearing a blue nurse-like jacket and nurse-like rubber gloves and a name badge that looked pretty official to me. I was there to give blood; she was there to take it. She said, "This is going to pinch and burn" as she inserted the needle into a vein. She was right. Why wouldn't I believe her? She had done this hundreds of times (I hoped) before.

Why wouldn't I believe him? He has been there from eternity past. He is the Creator of all and put this whole world into motion. He breathed into man the breath of life. He chose a people and then, like the loving Father that he is, jealously cared for, protected and disciplined his children. Through his people, he sent his Son. Jesus loved us all the way to the cross and paid the penalty for our sin. Demonstrating his approval and showing us our future, God raised his Son from the dead. Then he sent his Spirit to reside in us.

I will not always understand what happens in this life. Some things will shake my world. But who else is there to cling to? Where else is there to run? What else is there to trust? When my world is shaking, I can hold on for dear life to the certain truth he proclaims and I profess. Even amidst my fears, doubts, and questions, he will always keep his promises

Father, thank you for your faithfulness. Help me always to trust you and trust in you. In Jesus' name. Amen.

reflection

_____

_____

_____

_____

_____

_____

_____

_____

further suggested reading:

Hebrews 8-10

Developed by Exercise

Hebrews 11:1

Now faith is being sure of what we hope for and certain of what we do not see.

George Mueller was a man of great faith. During his life, which spanned most of the 19th century, Mueller pastored the same church for sixty-six years, read the Bible from cover to cover over 200 times and was influential in the ministries of D. L. Moody, C. H. Spurgeon and Hudson Taylor. While his accomplishments were significant, he was most known for his ministry to orphans. He built five large orphan houses and cared for 10,024 abandoned children during his lifetime.

Mueller said, "The orphan houses exist to display that God can be trusted and encourage believers to take him at his word." Mueller was grieved that "so many believers . . . were harassed and distressed in mind, or brought guilt on their consciences, on account of not trusting the Lord." Mueller said that the supreme passion of his life was to "display with open proofs that God could be trusted with the practical affairs of life."

Mueller made it a point never to ask people for money to support the orphanages; he only asked God. While this is certainly not the only way funds can be raised in a biblical manner, it is estimated that over $40 million, by today's standards, were given to the orphanages. Mueller said, "My faith is the same kind of faith that all God's children have had . . . though there may be more of it because my faith has been a little more developed by exercise."

Father, help us exercise our faith. Help us put our faith into action. Drive out the fear that causes spiritual retreat, and help us step out with confidence that you will provide everything that we need to do all that you have called us to do. In Jesus' name. Amen.

reflection

_____
_____
_____
_____
_____
_____
_____
_____

further suggested reading:

Hebrews 11-13

Temptation

James 1:13-14

When tempted, no one should say, "God is tempting me." For God cannot be tempted by evil, nor does he tempt anyone; but each person is tempted when they are dragged away by their own evil desire and enticed.

James was clear that temptation does not come from God. God "cannot be tempted by evil, nor does he tempt anyone." What is the source of temptation that shows itself so strongly in our lives?

1. **World.** The world around us is at odds with God. It presents a culture that puts man in charge and God at the back of the line. It hits us with wanting what we don't have and having what we don't need.

2. **Flesh.** We are tempted to blame temptation on the tempter or on someone else. But sometimes the mirror reflects the source. As believers, the penalty of our sin is gone, but the propensity to sin will remain until the day we die. We are tempted by our "own evil desires." When we give in, we are "dragged away and enticed."

3. **Satan.** Finding Jesus at a weakened physical state, the "tempter" showed up to test Jesus in the desert. Like a hungry lion seeking to devour us, the same tempter comes roaring after us. He works to drive a wedge of disobedience between us and the Father. Satan desires to destroy our witness before others.

Here's the hard truth. Whether the source is the world, the flesh or the devil, at the end of the day we own our disobedience. God will always provide a way out of temptation (1 Corinthians 10:13). Here's the hard question. Are you willing to take the escape routes?

Father, by your grace and your strength may the answer to that question always be "Yes!" In Jesus' name. Amen.

reflection

_____

_____

_____

_____

_____

_____

further suggested reading:

James 1-5

Great Examples  *December 15*

1 Peter 4:19

So then, those who suffer according to God's will should commit themselves to their faithful Creator and continue to do good.

One by one they died. James, the brother of John, was beheaded. Thomas was killed in India. Simon was crucified in Egypt. Mark, the first Bishop of Alexandria, was burned and buried in Egypt as well. Bartholomew was beaten, crucified and beheaded. Andrew, Peter's brother, was crucified in Rome. Matthew was killed with a spear. Phillip was stoned and hung on a cross. James, the brother of Jesus, was beaten to death after it was learned that his being thrown from the temple didn't kill him.

Two years after writing his first letter, Peter was put to death in Rome. The records of the early church indicate that he was crucified. Eusebius, the "Father of Church History," cites the testimony of an eyewitness named Clement who said that before Peter was crucified, he was forced to watch the crucifixion of his own wife. As he watched her being led to death, Peter called his wife's name and said, "Remember the Lord." When it was his turn, he pleaded to be crucified upside down because he wasn't worthy to die as Jesus. He was nailed to the cross head-downward.

The Apostles followed hard after Jesus during their lives and in their deaths. They committed "themselves to their faithful Creator." They are not only great teachers; they are great examples of suffering according to God's will.

Father, give us the courage to die for you if need be. For only when we are willing to die for you can we truly live for you. In Jesus' name. Amen.

reflection

_____

_____

_____

_____

_____

_____

_____

_____

further suggested reading:

1 Peter 1-4

A Needed Promise

1 Peter 5:6-7

Humble yourselves, therefore, under God's mighty hand, that he may lift you up in due time. Cast all your anxiety on him because he cares for you.

It was a particularly hot day in Dallas, and I was driving around the city looking for an apartment. Since I had just graduated from seminary, Lori and I needed to move from the condo we had rented for four years. I had resumes scattered throughout the country but was getting no response; rather, I was getting a response - "No." We thought that we would be looking for a place to live and minister in another part of the country. But, for the time being, we were staying in Dallas. It was a discouraging stretch of my journey.

These were the days before God blessed us with children, but for some reason there was a *Psalty the Songbook* cassette in our car, left after a visit from Lori's sisters or my nieces. The Psalty series was a children's Christian "musical." I inserted the tape and heard Psalty sing, "I cast all my cares upon you. I lay all of my burdens down at your feet. And anytime I don't know what to do, I will cast all my cares upon you." With tears in my eyes, I played that song, based on today's passage, over and over again. I had just finished four years of Greek, Hebrew, Bible and theology courses, but it was a child's song that delivered a needed promise of Scripture right to my heart.

I will never forget that day. God cared enough for me to orchestrate someone to leave a tape behind in order tenderly to teach me that I could throw all my frustration, fear and anxiety on him. If you are on a discouraging stretch of the journey, you have to know what I was reminded of that day - God really does care for you . . . he really does.

Father, thank you for reminding me of your care that hot day in Dallas. Remind those reading this devotional of your care as well. In Jesus' name. Amen.

reflection

_____

_____

_____

_____

_____

_____

further suggested reading:

1 Peter 5

356

Effective and Productive

2 Peter 1:5-9

For this very reason, make every effort to add to your faith goodness; and to goodness, knowledge; and to knowledge, self-control; and to self-control, perseverance; and to perseverance, godliness; and to godliness, mutual affection; and to mutual affection, love. For if you possess these qualities in increasing measure, they will keep you from being ineffective and unproductive in your knowledge of our Lord Jesus Christ. But whoever does not have them is nearsighted and blind, forgetting that they have been cleansed from their past sins.

Recently, I officiated a memorial service for Lois, a believer who lived her days following hard after Christ. One word that described her entire life was "service." Not long before this dear saint's passing, her daughter-in-law took several of Lois' great-grandchildren to visit her in a care facility. They became worried when she was not in her room and began searching for her. Finally, they found Lois at the end of a hall in her wheelchair. She was reading to a person who was unable to see.

In today's passage, the Apostle listed several qualities that the believer needs to possess. The qualities of goodness, knowledge, self-control, perseverance, godliness, brotherly kindness and love should be added to our faith. Then he reminds us that these qualities need to be used and developed so that we will be effective and productive believers. When we do not develop these qualities, Peter says that we are "nearsighted and blind." We live as if we have forgotten that God has "cleansed [us] from [our] past sins."

I was so encouraged to hear Lois' family describe her life. She was effective and productive. She encountered many challenges in life and used them to become stronger. She didn't use the aging process as an excuse to slide for home. She used what she had to demonstrate love and kindness to others. She didn't waste a day of her 85 years. May Lois serve as an example for us all.

Father, until you call us home, may we use every day to develop the qualities that make us productive and effective servants. Help us not waste a minute of our days on this earth. In Jesus' name. Amen.

reflection

---

further suggested reading:

2 Peter 1-3

Jesus Loves Me

1 John 5:11-12

And this is the testimony: God has given us eternal life, and this life is in his Son. He who has the Son has life; whoever does not have the Son of God does not have life.

I am sitting in my church office. Bookshelves - from floor to ceiling - line one entire wall. Another large floor-to-ceiling case takes up space on an adjacent wall. Four large boxes of books sit on the floor behind me. Some remodeling has been done, and I have to figure out where these books will go. Many more books are in my office at home, not to mention all the theological information stored digitally on my Bible study software. More information is only one Google search away. In short, I am sitting in a virtual ocean of information about God. But all of the content in the volumes that surround me and that are stored on my computer can be summed up in today's passage!

Dr. Karl Barth was a brilliant, if not sometimes controversial, theologian. Among his writings is a twelve volume work on life and doctrine. A reporter once asked Dr. Barth if he could summarize the message of the Bible. Dr. Barth thought for a moment and then said, "Jesus loves me, this I know, for the Bible tells me so."

We are sinners and our sin separates us from God. The penalty of our sin is death. But driven by perfect love, the just God became the Justifier. Being fully God, Jesus was the only one who could provide a sinless sacrifice. Being fully man, Jesus was the only one who could die on our behalf. Life - now and forever - is found in Jesus alone. There is really only one question and one answer: Do you have the Son?

Father, thank you for keeping the questions of life and eternity simple. Help us not to make them confusing. Confirm in our hearts that we have Jesus. Give us courage to tell others. And help us keep the message clear with our lips and lives. In Jesus' name. Amen.

reflection

_____

_____

_____

_____

_____

further suggested reading:

1 John 1-5

Back to the Basics

December 19

2 John 1:4-6

It has given me great joy to find some of your children walking in the truth, just as the Father commanded us. And now, dear lady, I am not writing you a new command but one we have had from the beginning. I ask that we love one another. And this is love: that we walk in obedience to his commands. As you have heard from the beginning, his command is that you walk in love.

Vince Lombardi, the legendary coach of the Green Bay Packers, was a leader who knew the value of fundamentals. In preparing to play a game against the then lowly Chicago Bears he preached, "The basics, men, remember the basics. Don't forget!" They forgot. The mighty Packers were taken down by the Bears. When the team arrived back in Green Bay, Lombardi ordered the team to get dressed and meet him on the practice field. Without question, the men got ready and waited on the field for Lombardi. Finally, he appeared and stood in front of them. He reminded them that they had forgotten the fundamentals, and they were going to start from the beginning. Standing before the professional players, he held up a ball and said, "Men, this is a football!"

Sometimes we forget the basics of the Christian faith. Enamored by new messages and methods, we forget the foundational truths upon which our faith stands. When we ignore, change or alter the foundational truths in any way, our faith falls. Second John is a call back to the fundamentals. John reminds us to go back to the basics.

First, John calls the believers to live "in the truth, just as the Father commanded us." John reminds the readers this is not some new teaching but a command "we have had from the beginning." Second, foundational to the Christian faith is this: "Love one another." We are to love each other just as Christ loved us. Third, we are to "walk in obedience." Jesus said, "If you love me, you will keep my commandments." Truth. Love. Obedience. Foundational stuff . . . that we often forget.

Father, may we never forget the basics. May we be discerning enough to see beyond the book cover, the fancy website, the cool marketing schemes, the new can't-miss programs, and make sure that everything we do is anchored in bedrock fundamentals. In Christ's name. Amen.

reflection

---

further suggested reading:

2 John

Walking in the Truth

December 20

3 John 1:1-4

The elder, To my dear friend Gaius, whom I love in the truth. Dear friend, I pray that you may enjoy good health and that all may go well with you, even as your soul is getting along well. It gave me great joy when some believers came and testified about your faithfulness to the truth, telling how you continue to walk in it. I have no greater joy than to hear that my children are walking in the truth.

In John's second letter, he addressed the problem of people showing hospitality to those whom they shouldn't. In this, his third letter, the problem was with people not showing hospitality to those whom they should. Diotrephes, the church's dictatorial leader, was excommunicating those who housed John's messengers. But John had a friend named Gaius who was faithful to the truth, even in the face of persecution. Gaius walked in the truth.

"Walking in the truth" . . . what a great description of a true believer! Here the word "walking" is a metaphor for "living." Gaius was a man of integrity. When he spoke, his words were accurate. He neither exaggerated the facts nor conveniently left out important information. In business his actions were honest. He did not cut corners or promise things that could never be delivered. At home he was genuine. His character didn't change when he walked in the door. He was a faithful and loving husband.

"Walking in the truth" . . . what a great description of a true believer! Does it describe you? Are you walking in the truth? It gives God no greater joy than to hear that his children are walking in the truth.

Father, may we be those who live according to your word, not according to the world. May we be faithful to the truth in every area of our lives. May we walk in the truth. For Christ's sake. Amen.

reflection

further suggested reading:

3 John

The Same Mercy

Jude 1:22

Be merciful to those who doubt.

Is doubting a sin? Is wavering a sign of weakness? Does spiritual confusion call into question one's spiritual commitment? Do we write off a person who has questions? Is there room for doubters in the church? Is the church a safe place to ask questions?

Thomas followed Jesus for three years. He heard his sermons, watched his miracles and walked beside him on dusty roads. He heard Jesus predict his death and promise his resurrection. But Thomas had a hard time getting over the cross. Even when the other disciples said that Jesus was alive, Thomas stuck by his skeptical guns. He said, "Unless I see the nail marks in his hands and put my finger where the nails were, and put my hand into his side, I will not believe it." Thomas lived with his doubt until Jesus appeared to the disciples a week later. Jesus sought out the doubter and said, "Put your finger here; see my hands. Reach out your hand and put it into my side. Stop doubting and believe." Instead of scolding him for his doubt, Jesus mercifully showed him the truth.

Be merciful to those who doubt. That's the instruction of Jude and the example of Jesus. Find the doubters. Seek out those wavering. Discover those who are confused. Show them the truth with the same mercy that Jesus showed to you.

Father, may we be strong, passionate, vibrant followers of Jesus - tempered with mercy. Put doubters in our path. Help us mercifully point them to the truth. Give us patience when it takes more than half an hour. In Jesus' name. Amen.

reflection

further suggested reading:

Jude

Revelation 1:4-5a

Grace and peace to you from him who is, and who was, and who is to come, and from the seven spirits before his throne, and from Jesus Christ who is the faithful witness, the firstborn from the dead, and the ruler of the kings of the earth.

The Revelation ("unveiling" or "disclosure") explains how things on earth are going to end, and how things in heaven are going to begin. But more important than the "how" is the "Who." This is the Revelation of Jesus Christ. He will guide all things to their appropriate ending and then establish the new heavens and earth. Notice how the writer, John, describes our Lord.

Jesus is the faithful witness.

If you want to know what God looks like, then take a close look at Jesus. No one has ever seen God, but Jesus "has made him known" (John 1:18). Jesus is the one who testifies on the Father's behalf. The Greek word translated "witness" is "martus." We get the word "martyr" from it. For Christians who have gone or are going through persecution, Jesus is the model of how to stand firm and never compromise the truth even in the face of death.

Jesus is the firstborn from the dead.

Christ died for our sins according to the Scripture. He was buried. The third day he rose again, according to the Scripture. That's good news! And it gets even better. All who have trusted in Christ will pass from death to life.

Jesus is the ruler of the kings of the world.

Human history tells the stories of empires that rise and fall. Nations clash in war and one is named the victor (not always the noblest nation). "But behind the chaotic events of history, the believer recognizes that Jesus Christ, who chose the way of obedience and humiliation, has in fact been exalted to God's right hand where he sits as Lord, ruling over the rulers of the earth. His second coming, from one point of view, is to be understood as making manifest to the world the sovereignty which is already his" (George Ladd, *Revelation*, p. 25).

Lord Jesus, many events are going on in the world that seem out of control. There are times when we are fearful and afraid of the way things are turning. But today we are reminded in your Word that you are in complete control. You are the ruler of the kings of the world. Our trust and confidence is in you alone. Amen.

reflection

suggested reading.

Revelation 1

The Action
of Jesus

Revelation 1:5b-6

To him who loves us and freed us from our sins by his blood, and has made us to be a kingdom and priests to serve his God and Father - to him be glory and power for ever and ever! Amen.

In yesterday's devotion, John explained who Jesus is. In today's passage, the writer declares what Jesus does. Consider the action of Jesus on our behalf.

Jesus loves us.
Christ loved us all the way to the cross. But his love didn't stop there. The word *agape* is in the present tense, meaning that it keeps on happening. His love for the believer is a permanent abiding fact. Think of it! The "ruler of the kings of the earth" loves us.

Jesus freed us from our sins by his blood.
Jesus did for us what we could not do for ourselves. On the cross he paid the penalty of our sins. By his blood, he set us free. Indicating that the work of Jesus is complete, the word "freed" is in the aorist tense. We can add nothing to what Christ has done.

Jesus made us to be a kingdom and priests.
"Kingdom" refers to the body of Christ made up of believers spread throughout the world. He also made us to be individual priests. The priest in the Old Testament was the only one who had direct access to God. But Jesus changed all that. Now every believer has direct access to the eternal God and freedom to enjoy fellowship with him.

These truths about Jesus' work on our behalf lead John and us to a proclamation of praise: To him be glory and power for ever and ever! Amen.

Father, may we bring glory to you through every aspect of our lives. May your power be demonstrated in our lives as we share the Good News. All glory and power belong to you forever! In your Son's name we pray. Amen.

reflection

_____

_____

_____

further suggested reading:

Revelation 2-3

Heaven's Door  December 24

Revelation 4:1

After this I looked, and there before me was a door standing open in heaven. And the voice I had first heard speaking to me like a trumpet said, "Come up here, and I will show you what must take place after this."

In Revelation 4, as John begins to describe heaven, notice the first thing he sees. John said, "before me was a door standing open." Remember, in the first book of the Bible, sin closed the door to God's presence. But God loved us so much that he sent his Son to open the door wide. By Christ's work on the cross, we have open access to the eternal God.

The picture of heaven's door standing open vividly describes God's great grace. We don't have to wait in line. We don't have to learn a "secret" knock. We don't have to spend our time searching for the key. Heaven's door stands open and we are invited to the celebration. We are summoned to come and enjoy heaven forever. The Father desires that we know him and enjoy his presence.

The door of heaven is open for all who trust in Jesus Christ. When we trust in Jesus as the only way to have a relationship with the living God, we enter into a new life that brings intimate fellowship with our Savior during this life. Then we get to enjoy him forever in heaven. Would you like to have this new life in Christ? The following prayer is for you.

Dear Father, I know that I am far from you. I know my sin has separated me from your presence. I know there is nothing I can do to earn my way to you. Right now I am trusting in the work of Jesus Christ on the cross. I believe he died for my sins. I trust in him alone as the One who paid sin's penalty for me. I desire to enter into the new life that Jesus provides. I pray in Jesus' name. Amen.

reflection

further suggested reading:

Revelation 4-6

No Reason To Cry *December 25*

Revelation 7:17

For the Lamb at the center of the throne will be their shepherd; he will lead them to springs of living water. And God will wipe every tear from their eyes.

The Revelation describes the many things that will be in heaven and the beauty that will surround us. But I know one thing that won't be there - tears. The Lamb will wipe every tear from our eyes. In heaven there will be no reason to cry.

There will be no more death.
In heaven, there will be no more disease. No more surgery. No more car accidents. No more drunk drivers. No more murders. No more suicides. Everything that summons our last breath will cease to exist. The last enemy will be finally and forever defeated.

There will be no more mourning.
In heaven, there will be no more calls in the middle of the night to announce a tragedy. No more moms and dads gathered around their dying child. No more children walking away from their parent's grave. No more goodbyes. No more waves of grief washing over an exhausted soul.

There will be no more crying or pain.
In heaven, there will be no need for crying. The tearful emotion brought about by pain will be a thing of the past. No one will ever hurt you again. You will be protected in the presence of God, who has destroyed the author of evil.

Hold on! One day there will be no reason for your tears!

Lord Jesus, thank you for being the Lamb, dying on our behalf. Thank you for being our Shepherd, leading us to springs of living water. Thank you for the promise of no more tears and for a place specifically prepared to enjoy you forever. Amen.

Merry Christmas! Have a great celebration of our Savior's birth!

reflection

_____

_____

_____

further suggested reading:

Revelation 7-9

Jesus Wins!

Revelation 13:1

The dragon stood on the shore of the sea. And I saw a beast coming out of the sea. It had ten horns and seven heads, with ten crowns on its horns, and on each head a blasphemous name.

Revelation 13 describes the Antichrist, the person who will rise up to oppose Christ and his followers in the last days. While we do not know who this person will be or when he will appear on the world scene, John describes three characteristics of this great enemy.

He will be a powerful political leader.

In Scripture, the sea often represents the Gentile nations. Many believe the Antichrist will be a leader of a European country who will form a confederacy of ten nations and bring a time of peace to the Middle East (See Revelation 17). John describes him as a "leopard," which was a symbol of the powerful Greek Empire under Alexander the Great.

He will be a "Christlike" figure.

The Antichrist will imitate the death and resurrection of Jesus. John writes that he "seemed to have a fatal wound, but the fatal wound had been healed" (Revelation. 13:3; see also 13:12, 14).

He will accept and expect worship.

The Antichrist will utter "proud words and blasphemies" that denigrate and defame the living God. While he tries to tear God down, he will build himself up. People will bow before the Antichrist and worship him.

Through history, many have thought a particular leader was the Antichrist. And one day he will arrive on the scene. But all those who know Christ do not have to worry. We do not have to become anxious over the events of the last days. Regardless of when and how history winds down, we belong to Jesus. And this we know for sure: Jesus wins!

Father, may we place the future in your hands. We know that when you are for us, nothing can stand against us. We live in confidence knowing that we belong to you. In Jesus' name. Amen.

reflection

_____

_____

_____

further suggested reading:

Revelation 10-13

The Song of the Lamb

Revelation 15:3b-4

Great and marvelous are your deeds, Lord God Almighty. Just and true are your ways, King of the nations. Who will not fear you, Lord? For you alone are holy. All nations will come and worship before you, for your righteous acts have been revealed.

As another year winds down, we take the time to reflect on the past months. For some, this past year has been your greatest yet. You are praising God for his many blessings. Some of you can sum up this past year in one word, "stalled." You honestly conclude that other than being a year older, not much happened in your spiritual journey. For some of you much has happened but not all good. You would use words like "devastated," "storm," "sorrow" and "hurt" to explain the emotions of this past year.

Today's passage is "the song of Moses, the servant of God and the song of the Lamb." The title reminds us that the song is for us. Like Moses, we experience great miracles and trying desert experiences, great highs and devastating lows. But it also reminds us that this is a song about the Lamb. Regardless of where we are on our spiritual journey, the "Lamb" is right there with us. He never abandons us. He never disowns us.

Here is what I would ask you to do. Pray today's passage to God. Through your excitement or through your tears, proclaim that his deeds are "great and marvelous." Regardless of your circumstances, tell him that his ways are "just and true." Bow before him in a posture of worship and say, "Father, you alone are holy." He is the "King of the ages." Acknowledge him as your King. And remember, our King invites us to call him Father, even Daddy. He is the omnipotent Creator who comes to meet us right where we are. I pray that you take time to meet with him. I know he will meet with you.

Dear God, you are the Lord God Almighty! And you are my Father. Today I acknowledge you as my King, and I readily admit that I need to feel the warmth of a Father's presence. Thank you for meeting with me wherever I am and whatever I'm going through. Keep me close to you as this year winds down and another begins. I desire to walk close to you. In Jesus' name. Amen.

reflection

_____

_____

_____

further suggested reading:

Revelation 14-16

Judge with Justice

Revelation 19:11-16

I saw heaven standing open and there before me was a white horse, whose rider is called Faithful and True. With justice he judges and wages war. His eyes are like blazing fire, and on his head are many crowns. He has a name written on him that no one knows but he himself. He is dressed in a robe dipped in blood, and his name is the Word of God. The armies of heaven were following him, riding on white horses and dressed in fine linen, white and clean. Coming out of his mouth is a sharp sword with which to strike down the nations. "He will rule them with an iron scepter." He treads the winepress of the fury of the wrath of God Almighty. On his robe and on his thigh he has this name written: KING OF KINGS AND LORD OF LORDS.

It started with the manger - Jesus a helpless baby. It moved to the cross - Jesus a sacrificial Lamb. But on that final day, he will come to judge with justice.

John saw heaven open with power. The One called Faithful and True, the One called the Word of God, the One dressed in a robe dipped in blood was riding a white horse. His eyes were ablaze! And many crowns adorned his head. The armies of heaven followed his lead, and he came to make final restitution. Just in case his identity is unclear, written on his flowing robe is the name: KING OF KINGS AND LORD OF LORDS.

No longer contained in the body of a baby, no longer attached to a cross, on that day he will come with the "fury of the wrath of God Almighty." All who follow him know his strength and love. But that day when he comes riding the white horse . . . that day when he comes with his eyes ablaze . . . that day when he comes with a sharp sword . . . that day . . . you'll be glad that you're on his side!

Lord Jesus, thank you that there is no judgment or condemnation for those who know you. Thank you for your work on the cross that covers us on the day of your judgment. In your name we pray. Amen.

reflection

_____

_____

_____

_____

_____

_____

further suggested reading:

Revelation 17-19

A God of Fresh Starts

December 29

Revelation 21:5

He who was seated on the throne said, "I am making everything new!" Then he said, "Write this down, for these words are trustworthy and true."

God is a God of fresh starts.

- In the beginning, he spoke a new world into existence.

- He gave Adam and Eve everything that they needed and could ever want.

- After their sin, he personally provided skins from animals giving them a fresh start.

- The sacrificial system would provide for the fresh start of cleansing and forgiveness for the Old Testament worshipper year after year.

- At the right time, the one-time-for-all-time Perfect Sacrifice made a fresh start possible for all by his death, burial and resurrection.

- In Christ, we have new life by his initial forgiveness and the fresh start of ongoing forgiveness as we confess our sins to him.

- By his resurrection, Jesus gives us a fresh start as we pass from death to life.

- And one day, he will make "everything new!"

This year is winding down. But with Jesus, every day is a day of fresh starts. Whatever this past year has held, remember, our hope is in God . . . the God of fresh starts.

Father, thank you for being a God who allows us clean, fresh starts. Thank you for the newness that you provide in this life and for eternity! In Jesus' name. Amen.

reflection

_____

_____

_____

further suggested reading:

Revelation 20

It All Begins and Ends with Jesus

December 30

Revelation 21:6

He said to me: "It is done. I am the Alpha and the Omega, the Beginning and the End. To the thirsty I will give water without cost from the spring of the water of life."

It all begins and ends with Jesus. He is the eternal God. He was with the Father at Creation, but not as a passive bystander. Jesus was the Agent of Creation. "Through him all things were made and without him nothing was made that has been made" (John 1:3). Paul adds, "For by him all things were created: things in heaven and on earth, visible and invisible, whether thrones or powers or rulers or authorities; all things were created by him and for him. He is before all things and in him all things hold together" (Colossians 1:16-17).

It all begins and ends with Jesus. G. K. Chesterton said, "It has never been quite enough to say that God is in his heaven and all is right with the world; since the rumor is that God had left his heavens to set it right." More than a rumor, Jesus left heaven itself to enter the human race. As the poet George Herbert put it, "The God of power, as he did ride in his majestic robes of glory resolved to light; and so one day he did descend, undressing all the way." Jesus removed his majestic robes and entered the lake of humanity as a helpless baby dependent on his young mother.

It all begins and ends with Jesus. Our Lord was first introduced as the Lamb of God who came to take away the sin of the world. Jesus came to give his life a ransom for many. He came to pay sin's penalty on our behalf. He died so that we may live. He rose again so that we will follow him from death to eternal life. And all this is by grace. Sin has left our soul thirsty. But Jesus offers "drink without cost." Your thirsty soul can finally and forever be satisfied by Jesus.

Lord Jesus, you are the Alpha and Omega. Everything begins and ends with you. Thank you for leaving heaven to die on the cross for my sins. Someone reading this today comes with a dry and thirsty soul. I pray that person will come to you for living water. In your name. Amen.

reflection

_____

_____

_____

_____

further suggested reading:

Revelation 21

Citizens of Heaven December 31

Revelation 22:1-4

Then the angel showed me the river of the water of life, as clear as crystal, flowing from the throne of God and of the Lamb down the middle of the great street of the city. On each side of the river stood the tree of life. . . . No longer will there be any curse. The throne of God and of the Lamb will be in the city, and his servants will serve him. They will see his face.

Over the past years, I have had the opportunity to travel and minister in many places throughout the world. The sights, sounds and smells are different. The language is strange to me. I have been schooled on what to eat and what not to eat. I am told by my hosts that there are things I should always do and things I should never do. When I am in a different country, I stand out as a foreigner in a foreign land. While I love to travel, the best part of every trip is the moment I hear the tires touching down on the runway at Pittsburgh International Airport. And the absolute favorite part of every trip is when I am reunited with Lori and the kids back at home.

Christians are citizens of heaven. Our life is simply a journey as foreigners in a foreign land. The sights, sounds and smells of the world are not the things our hearts beat for. The language around us is strange at times. The customs are often in opposition to God's word. Disease strips away strength. Death brings unimaginable pain. Divorce leaves shattered souls with a broken heart. We know that this is not the way it's supposed to be. We yearn for something different. We yearn for home.

When Christ comes again or when we make that last journey from death to life, we will finally be home. When we arrive, we "will see his face." We will be with God, and he will wipe every tear from our eyes. Death will be a thing of the past. Mourning will be no more. Crying will not be a part of our resurrected emotions. And pain will never be experienced again. Life in the "old country" will be over. We will be home, at last, in the indescribable place that Jesus has prepared just for us. C. S. Lewis wrote, "There have been times when I think we do not desire heaven, but more often I find myself wondering whether, in our heart of hearts, we have ever desired anything else."

Father, thank you for the certain hope and reality of heaven. We look forward to the day when you welcome us home and wipe every tear from our eyes. Then we will know that in our heart of hearts, we have never desired anything else. In Jesus' name. Amen.

reflection

further suggested reading:

Revelation 22

Journey
through the
BIBLE